AF506124

Civil Society in Japan

Civil Society in Japan

The Growing Role of NGOs in Tokyo's Aid and Development Policy

Keiko Hirata

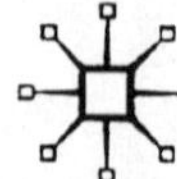

CIVIL SOCIETY IN JAPAN
© Keiko Hirata, 2002

First published 2002 by
PALGRAVE MACMILLAN™
175 Fifth Avenue, New York, N.Y. 10010 and
Houndmills, Basingstoke, Hampshire RG21 6XS
Companies and representatives throughout the world

PALGRAVE MACMILLAN is the global academic imprint of the Palgrave Macmillan division of St. Martin's Press, LLC and of Palgrave Macmillan Ltd. Macmillan® is a registered trademark in the United States, United Kingdom and other countries. Palgrave is a registered trademark in the European Union and other countries.

ISBN 0–312–23936–X

Library of Congress Cataloging-in-Publication Data

Hirata, Keiko.
    Civil Society in Japan: the growing influence of NGOs over Tokyo's
    aid and development policy/Keiko Hirata.
        p. cm.
    Includes bibliographical references and index.
    ISBN 0–312–23936–X (cloth)
        1. Civil society—Japan. 2. Non-governmental organizations—Japan.
3. Nonprofit organizations—Japan. 4. Japan—Politics and government—1989—
I. Title.

JQ1681.H575 2002
338.91'52—dc21   2002023881

A catalogue record for this book is available from the British Library.

Design by Newgen Imaging Systems (P) Ltd., Chennai, India.

First edition: August, 2002
10 9 8 7 6 5 4 3 2 1

Printed in the United States of America.

CONTENTS

LIST OF TABLES

LIST OF FIGURES

<h1 style="text-align:center">LIST OF ACRONYMS</h1>

AAR	Association to Aid Refugees
ADB	Asian Development Bank
AHI	Asian Health Institute
AIJ	Amnesty International Japan
AMDA	Association of Medical Doctors of Asia
ASEAN	Association of South East Asian Nations
BHN	basic human needs
CARE	Cooperative for Assistance and Relief Everywhere
CCC	Cooperation Committee for Cambodia
CCWA	Christian Child Welfare Association International Sponsorship Program
CMAC	Cambodian Mine Action Center
CPP	Cambodian People's Party
DAC	Development Assistance Committee
E/N	exchange of notes
EBRD	European Bank for Reconstruction and Development
ECFA	Engineering Consulting Firms Association
EPA	Economic Planning Agency
Ex–Im Bank	Export–Import Bank
FASID	Foundation for Advanced Studies on International Development
FILP	Fiscal Investment and Loan Program
FTC	Fair Trade Commission
FY	fiscal year
G-7	Group of Seven Industrialized Countries
GDP	gross domestic products
GII	global issues initiative

GNP	gross national products
HIPC	heavily indebted poor countries
IBRD	International Bank for Reconstruction and Development
ICBL	International Campaign to Ban Landmines
IDA	International Development Association
IDACA	Institute for the Development of Agricultural Cooperation in Asia
IFI	international financial institution
IGO	intergovernmental organization
IMF	International Monetary Fund
JANAN	Japan Association of NGOs and NPOs
JANIC	Japanese NGO Center for International Cooperation
JATAN	Japan Tropical Network
JBIC	Japan Bank for International Cooperation
JCBL	Japan Campaign to Ban Landmines
JICA	Japan International Cooperation Agency
JIFH	Japan International Food for the Hungry
JOCS	Japan Overseas Christian Medical Cooperative Service
JOCV	Japan Overseas Cooperation Volunteers
JOICEF	Japanese Organization for International Cooperation in Family Planning
JPC	Japan Productivity Center
JRCS	Japan Red Cross Society
JSDP	Japan Socialist Democratic Party
JSF	Japan Special Fund
JSID	Japan Society for International Development
JSRC	Japan Sotoshu Relief Committee (= Shanti Volunteer Association [SVA])
JSV	Japan Silver Volunteers
JVC	Japan International Volunteer Center
LARA	Licensed Agencies for Relief in Asia
LDP	Liberal Democratic Party
LIC	low-income countries
LLDC	least less-developed country, or least among less developed countries
LMIC	lower-middle-income countries
MAFF	Ministry of Agriculture, Forestry, and Fisheries
MDB	multilateral development bank
MIA	missing in action
MITI	Ministry of International Trade and Industry
MOC	Ministry of Construction

MOF	Ministry of Finance
MOFA	Ministry of Foreign Affairs
MOHW	Ministry of Health and Welfare
MOPT	Ministry of Posts and Telecommunications
MOT	Ministry of Transport
MSFF	Médecins sans Frontières, France
MSFJ	Médecins sans Frontières, Japan
MsLA	Kanagawa Women's Space
NFUAJ	National Federation of UNESCO Association in Japan
NGO	nongovernmental organization
NPO	nonprofit organization
ODA	official development assistance
OECD	Organization for Economic Cooperation and Development
OECF	Overseas Economic Cooperation Fund
OISCA	Organization for Industrial, Spiritual and Cultural Associations
OOF	other official flow
OPEC	Organization of Petroleum Exporting Countries
OTCA	Overseas Technical Cooperation Agency
PARC	Pacific Asia Resource Center
PARinAC	Partnership in Action
PIJ	Plan International Japan
PKO	peace-keeping operations
POW	prisoner of war
PRK	People's Republic of Kampuchea
PVO	private voluntary organization
REAL	Reconsider Aid Citizens' League
SAL	structural adjustment loan
SCJ	Save the Children, Japan
SDF	Self-Defense Forces
SHAR	Services for Health in Asian and African Regions
SVA	Shanti Volunteer Association (=Japan Sotoshu Relief Committee [JSRC])
TICAD	Tokyo International Conference on African Development
UNCED	United Nations Conference on the Environment and Development
UNDP	United Nations Development Program
UNESCO	United Nations Educational, Scientific, and Cultural Organization
UNHCR	United Nations High Commissioner for Refugees

UNTAC	United Nations Transitional Authority in Cambodia
USAID	United States Agency for International Development
WID	women in development
WVJ	World Vision Japan
WWF	World Wildlife Fund

ACKNOWLEDGMENTS

I am indebted to many people who helped me complete this research. I am especially grateful to Michael Haas, who not only gave me valuable comments on my research but also introduced me to the politics of Nongovernmental Organizations (NGOs) in Southeast Asia, particularly in Cambodia, an introduction that opened my eyes to the role of citizens' groups from all over the world. I took his course on Cambodian politics at the University of Hawai'i at Manoa in 1993. In this course I learned in detail about the tragedy of Pol Pot's "killing fields" and the senseless Cold War politics of the 1980s that aggravated the misery of the Cambodian people. I searched for answers as to how the international community could alleviate the Cambodian people's suffering and learned that an increasing number of transnational actors—intergovernmental organizations as well as NGOs—had begun to help Cambodia recover from war damages. Subsequently, I found out about Japanese NGOs providing assistance to Cambodians and became interested in learning more about their volunteerism. This eventually led to my dissertation on Japanese NGOs in Southeast Asia, research that eventually led to this book.

I also am very grateful to Charles Morrison, who was extremely helpful throughout the process of my research, providing invaluable advice and insightful comments on Japanese politics, NGOs, and issues of development. His criticisms of my analysis were always on target and thought-provoking. I also owe a debt of gratitude to Bruce Koppel, who helped me with my initial research in the mid-1990s and continued to give me valuable comments despite his serious illness. Many others have given me valuable comments and support, including Yasumasa Kuroda, Lonny Carlile, George Kent, Kate Zhou, Haruhiro Fukui, M. J. Peterson, Mark Petracca, Seki Tomoda, Ryokichi Hirono, Hideki Imaoka, Shigeru Ishikawa, Phan Huy Le, Doan Thien Thuat, Vu Duong Ninh,

Tran Van Tho, Kao Kim Hourn, Kiyoshi Aihara, Michio Okamoto, T. J. Pempel, Susan Pharr, Ellis Krauss, Satoko Mori, and Mihoko Shono.

Special gratitude is owed to the numerous NGOs, research institutions, foundations, and corporations that granted interviews and allowed me to take part in their activities during my visits to Japan in 1995, 1997, 1999, 2000, and 2001; Cambodia in 1995 and 1997; Vietnam in 1997; and Indonesia in 1997 and 2001. I also am grateful to the many government and intergovernmental officials who granted interviews and provided information. These include people in the Japanese Ministry of Foreign Affairs, the Japan International Cooperation Agency, the (former) Overseas Economic Cooperation Fund in Japan, the Japan International Volunteer Center, the United States Agency for International Development, the Australian Agency for International Development, the World Bank, the Asian Development Bank, the Council for Development of Cambodia, the Cambodia Development Resource Institute, the Vietnamese Ministries of Foreign Affairs and Planning and Investment, and the Japan Society for the Promotion of Science Research Station Cairo.

I am also grateful for financial support received during my fieldwork in Asia from the following institutions: the University of Hawai'i College of Languages, Linguistics, and Literature; the University of Hawai'i Political Science Department; the University of Tsukuba; and Matsushita International Foundation. I also greatly acknowledge the support I received from the following host institutions where I conducted research: the University of Tsukuba; Hanoi National University; the United Nations High Commissioner for Refugees in Egypt; the University of California, San Diego; and the University of California, Irvine.

Most important, I have appreciated the patience and support of my husband, Mark Warschauer. He offered me not only personal support and encouragement but also valuable comments on my work. Without his support, this research would not have been completed.

Finally, I acknowledge other places where some of this research has been previously published or reported. Parts of Chapter 4 and 5 derive from my paper, "New Challenges to Japan's Aid: An Analysis of Aid Policy-Making," which was presented at the Association of South East Asian Nations Inter-University Seminar on Social Development in 1997 and published in *Pacific Affairs* (Vol. 71, No. 3) in 1998. Parts of Chapter 6 were reported on in a paper delivered at the American Political Science Association annual meeting in 1998. The summary of this study was reported at the International Studies Association annual meeting in 2000.

Although many people provided generous assistance and valuable advice, all faults and errors in this study are mine and mine alone.

INTRODUCTION

One of the most important political issues in the world today is the rise of civil society and its influence on state policy. Nongovernmental organizations (NGOs) are one such source of citizens' power. As Rosenau (1997) and others point out, the expansion of NGOs is a global phenomenon. An "associational revolution" (Salamon, 1994, p. 109) has spread throughout the world, reflecting the decentralization and fragmentation of power once dominated by state actors.

Japan has recently witnessed a surge of civil society activism, especially by transnational NGOs working on international development and foreign aid issues. There has been an explosion of such groups in the last two decades in Japan, as seen in their rapid growth in number and size and their increased interaction with and influence over state policy. Although the expansion of NGOs has occurred relatively late compared to Western and some developing societies, the NGO growth in Japan has important implications for world politics. Japan is a highly developed country, integrated into the global economy, but it is neither geographically nor culturally part of the "West." Japan experienced dramatic economic development in the 1950s–1970s, transforming from a devastated, wartorn nation into the world's second largest economy. However, Tokyo's mighty economy began to disintegrate in the early 1990s, and, it is precisely since then that NGOs have increasingly become prominent on the Japanese political scene. Thus, Japan represents an extremely interesting case of the intersection of non–Western culture, rapid industrialization, subsequent economic recession, and the rise of civil society.

This growing NGO movement reflects changing relations between the state and civil society in Japan. As the authority of the Japanese developmental state has begun to crumble, the relationship between the state and the populace has changed. Japanese citizens are no longer inhibited from protesting state policies or demanding social justice. They are forming and joining NGOs to press their demands, and the state in turn has started paying more attention to the views of NGOs. The dual phenomena of the erosion of the developmental state and the rise of civil society mark the beginning of a new era of a more horizontal relationship between the state and civil society in Japan.

The developmental state has been directed by Japan's bureaucratic elite, especially during the 1950s–1970s era of rapid economic growth. Although my use of the term, "developmental state," is not identical to Johnson's (1982) "capitalist developmental state," I borrow some of his key concepts.[1] As Johnson argues, the Japanese developmental state played a pivotal role in promoting a unique pattern of industrialization during the developmental era of the 1950s–1970s, combining free enterprise and state-led development. In this system, the state, in particular the bureaucracy, actively intervened in the economy, determining the nation's strategic industries, providing these industries with subsidies and administrative guidance to enhance their international competitiveness, controlling foreign exchange and trade, and limiting foreign imports to protect domestic industries. The developmental state depended on the nationalist objectives of the bureaucracy, which included mercantilistic export-led industrialization (through effective state guidance and planning) and rapid economic development. These features are correctly pointed to by Johnson (1982) as the key ingredients of Japan's rapid economic growth.

In the developmental state system, the bureaucracy maintained an alliance with business and the ruling party (the Liberal Democratic Party or LDP). The bureaucracy maintained extremely close relations with the private sector through supervision, guidance, and assistance, as well as through a system called *amakudari* (descent from heaven) in which retired bureaucrats from the bureaucracy obtained top management positions in the private sector. The bureaucracy also was able to maintain close ties to the LDP, the permanent ruling party, as many bureaucrats became LDP politicians after retirement. In this system, business, the bureaucracy, and the LDP formed an alliance, often referred to as the "iron triangle," to protect and further each other's interests.

Civil society was excluded from this iron triangle. During the developmental era, rapid economic growth became the central goal of the alliance, while things viewed as unrelated or detrimental to economic growth, such as workers' rights, social justice, and human rights, were downplayed. The majority of citizens, though excluded from the developmental alliance, accepted the role of the iron triangle in economic development, believing that the trilateral arrangement produced sound economic policy and growth.

However, public sentiment toward the developmental alliance has changed greatly since the late 1980s. Due to political, economic, and cultural crises taking place domestically and globally, state authority has crumbled. Societal dissatisfaction with the state has reached an unprecedented level. Accordingly, the once subordinate civil society has become defiant, challenging state authority. NGO activists, once marginalized in Japanese society as political radicals, have increased their profile on the political scene. At the same time, civil society–state relations have evolved from mere confrontation to a combination of confrontation and cooperation. Civil society actors have found shared goals with state officials and have begun to cooperate with the state, when necessary, on equal terms.

Japan's Official Development Assistance (ODA) policy reflects most clearly the demise of the developmental state and the changing relations between the state and NGOs. Unlike the United States—where foreign aid is a peripheral political issue—in Japan, ODA is the central foreign policy issue facing the government and the public. Since 1991, Japan has been the largest single aid donor in the entire world, in spite of having an economy only 60 percent as large as that of the United States. With no military bases abroad and without having sent soldiers to war since 1945, Japan has used overseas aid as its principal mechanism for gaining economic and political influence around the world.

ODA is an important policy arena not only for the state but also for Japanese NGOs, many of which provide financial and technical assistance to the developing world. Japanese NGOs also work to change state ODA policies to respond to the needs of the poor in aid recipient countries, as well as to educate the Japanese people, through community activities and educational programs, or the interconnectedness between Japan and the developing world. Japanese NGOs are more involved in ODA policy issues than in any other foreign policy issue in Japan.

This study focuses on Japanese NGOs involved in ODA reform efforts, to examine how political, economic, and cultural change has led to increased influence of NGOs, fragmentation of power, and changed state–civil society relations in Japan. Specifically, the study address the following questions:

1. What are the political, economic, and cultural or social factors—both within Japan and globally—that have contributed to the demise of the developmental state and the rise of NGOs?

2. How do NGOs exercise their influence, in contention and cooperation with the state, on foreign aid and international development issues?
3. How have state–NGO relations been changing? What are the implications of NGO involvement for understanding the nature of state–civil society relations in Japan? How has this changing relationship been exemplified in Japan's ODA policy?
4. What do the two concurrent phenomena—increased NGO involvement and the decline of the developmental state—mean for Japanese politics? Do NGOs contribute to or hamper the consolidation of Japanese democracy?
5. What are the implications of the demise of the Japanese developmental state for Japan and the world, especially East Asia?

The changing state–civil society relations in Japan reflects economic, political, and sociocultural changes brought about by globalization and industrialization. Both phenomena have dramatically influenced every aspect of Japan's political economy. The impact of globalization is ubiquitous in Japan's political, economic, and cultural spheres, and in each of these spheres the fundamental crisis of the Japanese developmental state is visible. The Japanese economy has become more integrated into the global economy, a process that has weakened the developmental alliance of the bureaucracy, the business, and the LDP. As Japanese firms have become more global, they no longer need state protection. Politically, the end of the Cold War has weakened the power of the LDP, forcing the party out of power in 1993–1995. And, through increased global contact, Japanese NGOs have been influenced by international movements for human rights and sustainable development and have developed new organizational and political skills. Globalization has thus provided political space to citizens' groups that were previously marginalized from the developmental state system.

Meanwhile, on the domestic front, Japan's rapid industrialization similarly brought about dramatic social changes. On the one hand, improved living standards led the Japanese to think not only of their daily survival but also about the welfare of the disadvantaged within Japan and throughout the world. On the other hand, overly close ties between the state and private sector eventually resulted in corruption and economic downturn. Public frustration over these problems prompted citizens to organize against the dominance of the political and economic elite in policymaking processes. The legitimacy of the developmental state—which had primarily rested on economic growth and accumulation of national wealth—crumbled.

This book analyzes the nature of state–civil society relations in Japan as exemplified by the cooperation and contention between NGOs and the bureaucracy, especially the Ministry of Foreign Affairs (MOFA), the key ministry in charge of ODA and the main contact agency for NGOs interested in ODA. In the book, I challenge the Western scholarly and journalistic focus on the oppositional role of NGOs against a resistant state. By demonstrating both the cooperation and contention between the state and NGOs, in the context of broader international factors and forces, I attempt to convey a more nuanced understanding of how the role and authority of the state has evolved in the global era.

The growing influence of NGOs in Japanese policy making can be analyzed in the framework of pluralization. Pluralism is not a new concept for describing Japanese politics, but I use the term more broadly than others do. Since the 1980s, an increasing number of scholars have pointed out growing pluralism on the Japanese political scene, refuting a once popular but outdated notion of Japan as a unitary state, that is, the notion that Japan is exclusively ruled by the bureaucratic elite in close collaboration with the allegedly subservient business actor. However, almost all of the attention to nonstate actors has been devoted either to businesses or "special interest groups" organized around economic interests (e.g., farmers' associations; see, for example, discussion in George, 1988; Mulgan, 2000). This book seeks to move beyond simplistic notions of Japanese politics focusing exclusively on the role of bureaucrats and businesses. By focusing specifically on the impact of NGOs and their role in policy making, I hope to contribute to a better understanding of pluralism in Japan today.

This study also attempts to unravel the myth of Asian civil society and democracy. Many influential writers such as Samuel Huntington (1993) argue that civil society is a Western phenomenon and ill-suited to Confucianist East Asia. However, as this book demonstrates, it is misleading to think that East Asians remain deferential to state authority and will not develop a vibrant civil society critical of state power. On the contrary, civil society and democracy are influenced by both globalization and industrial maturity, rather than being based on supposedly unchanging civilizational values (see Cumings, 1999). People in the region have become increasingly defiant against state authority, despite the myth of Asian cultural deference to hierarchy. Indeed, the concept of "Asian values" is conveniently used today by a few regional leaders who wish to hold on to power by discouraging citizen activism in their countries.

The erosion of the Japanese developmental state has important implications for other East Asian countries in which leaders often perceive the

Japanese model as an alternative to Western liberalism. As the first non-Western country to achieve rapid industrialization, Japan has provided a development model based on economic nationalism, strong bureaucratic leadership (see World Bank, 1993), and a subservient civil society. The success and failure of Japan's developmental state, and changing state–society relations in Japan, provide an interesting case for other East Asian countries trying to emulate the Japanese development model.

Surprisingly, the growth of NGOs in Japan has been largely ignored within the academic world. Most research on the growth of NGOs and their impact in world politics has taken place in Western contexts (see, for example, Wapner, 1994; Gordenker & Weiss, 1995; Wapner, 1996; Weiss & Gordenker, 1996; Sogge, 1996; Keck & Sikkink, 1998; O'Brien, Goetz, Scholte, & Williams, 2000). Other studies have examined the role of NGOs in the developing world (e.g., Eldridge, 1995; Potter, 1996; Clarke, 1998). Little work has yet examined the role of NGOs in Japan, the world's second-biggest economy and a country that is neither Western nor developing.[2] The absence of such work is noteworthy, especially given the international economic influence of Japan, the quantity and reach of its foreign aid (Japan is the world's largest aid donor), and the leadership role of Japan in the Asia–Pacific region. By filling this gap, this book will contribute to theoretical approaches in the field of world politics.

Scholars such as Rosenau (1990, 1997) and Castells (1996, 1997, 1998) have elaborated theories of state–society relations in the age of globalization. While they have postulated an increased role for new social movements, they fail to illustrate the precise way that social movements exercise their growing power. Castells's (1997, 1998) interesting discussion of the decline of the Japanese developmental state, for example, highlights the emergence of the extremist and isolated Aum Shinrikyo cult, but does not examine citizens' groups that are more directly influencing state power. Rosenau (1997) discusses the bifurcation between a "state-centric" world and a "multicentric" world, but fails to show how state and multicentric forces actually interact in a single system. In contrast to these, this book analyzes not only the growth of citizens' groups due to globalization but also the nature of NGO–state relations in shaping state policy. This study does not aspire to provide comprehensive coverage of citizens groups in Japan. In particular, it does not include organizations labeled as NPOs (*enupiō* or nonprofit organizations), that are engaged only in domestic issues and thus are uninvolved in ODA. For the analysis of state–civil society relations, I focus on NGOs that are involved in ODA reform efforts or anti-ODA campaigns and prominent NGOs cooperating with the state in the area of aid and development.

Chapter 1 presents the theoretical and analytical framework of this study. The chapter analyzes the concept of the developmental state, explores how the developmental state came to dominate civil society in Japan and examines the factors that have contributed to the erosion of the state and the rise of civil society. The chapter also discusses the historical development of Japanese NGOs and the main characteristics of NGO involvement in Japan's ODA.

Chapters 2 and 3 further explore the factors that have contributed to the dual phenomena of the demise of the developmental state and the rise of civil society in Japan. Chapter 2 focuses on globalization and analyzes how it has both weakened the state and strengthened civil society. Specifically, the chapter discusses the globalization of Japanese economy, the acquisition of global norms and values, and individual and collective development of skills due to global technological progress. Chapter 3 focuses on aspects of Japan's industrial maturation. Issues discussed in the chapter include postmaterial value change, side effects of developmentalism such as corruption and inefficiency, and the economic recession that began in 1990 when the bubble economy burst.

Chapter 4 looks in detail at NGO advocacy. It examines three cases of NGO campaigns, two involving NGO campaigns against Japanese ODA projects, and one involving Japanese NGOs' antilandmine efforts that resulted in increased ODA funding for landmine eradication and victim assistance. These three cases illustrate how NGOs have mobilized public opinion and influenced Japanese aid and development policy.

Chapter 5 examines how state–civil society relations have been changing in Japan. It focuses on MOFA–NGO relations in ODA reform efforts and demonstrates that MOFA and NGOs have begun to cooperate with each other since the early 1990s.

Chapter 6 explores broader issues of state–civil society relations and democratization. The chapter discusses the implication of changing relations between the state and civil society, the contribution of NGOs to democracy in Japan, and the implication of the erosion of the developmental state and the rise of civil society for other East Asian countries.

Finally, the appendix provides a background of Japan's ODA history. Japan's ODA has gone through several stages. The appendix examines how Japanese aid policy has changed and how NGOs have become incorporated into the aid program in the current stage of development.

A note on transliteration: a macron is used to indicate long vowels in ordinary Japanese words (e.g., *dangō*) but not in the names of people or places (e.g., Sudo, Tokyo).

CHAPTER ONE

Civil Society and NGOs in Japan

Japan is typically viewed as a docile society, with its people subservient to their corporations and the government. Even Makido Noda, chief program officer at the leading research institute on Japan's grassroots organization, says, "Japan didn't have a civil society until recently. And our civil society remains weak."[1]

Of course, Japan has always had some level of social activism, as witnessed for example, by the small community groups in the seventeenth through nineteenth centuries known *gonin-gumi* ("group of five families," Yamamoto, 1998), by farmers' protests (*hyakushō ikki*) during the same era, and by environmental and antiwar protest movements in the 1960s and 1970s. But almost every knowledgeable observer would agree that throughout Japanese history civil society has remained extremely weak vis-à-vis the state.

Most observers also would agree that Japanese civil society has finally emerged on the scene. Although disagreement exists as to its current size and prominence, it is widely assumed that it will continue to grow and play a more prominent role in the future.

Why civil society activism has recently spurted is puzzling to many. Japan experienced unprecedented economic growth in the 1950s–1970s and eventually became the world's second largest economy. During this period of rapid economic growth, Japanese civil society was largely reticent. Only since the 1980s, and especially since the early 1990s, have Japanese grassroots groups such as nongovernmental organizations (NGOs) emerged to play an ongoing active role in political life in Japan. Given this background, we are thus faced with several important questions.

Why has Japan had a weak civil society historically? Why did a more active civil society not emerge until the 1980s? What accounts for the recent growth of grassroots activism? How is the grassroots movement reflected in policy making, particularly in relationship to overseas aid and development policy, which is a main concentration of NGO activity? And what are the implications of changing state–civil society relations for Japan?

This chapter broadly addresses these questions of changing civil society-state relations. I analyze Japan's postwar development to argue that the changing relations have been brought about by broad economic, cultural, and political transformations of Japanese society in the age of globalization and post-industrialism. No single factor or incident can explain the changing state–Japanese civil society relations; they involve processes of complex, incremental social transformation. To understand the growth of Japanese civil society, it is necessary to take into account a variety of factors related to economic, cultural, and political changes in Japan and around the world.

This chapter first defines both civil society and NGOs; the latter term has a particular meaning in the Japanese context. Next, the chapter discusses why Japanese civil society has been traditionally weak and how it has recently grown. I identify political, economic, and cultural factors that have either hindered or helped the growth of Japanese NGOs. (This chapter, however, does not provide a detailed explanation of the reasons for the recent growth of Japanese NGOs; that appears in chapters 2 and 3.) Next, this chapter examines the history of Japanese NGOs and the evolution of Japanese ODA. The involvement of NGOs in ODA is a recent phenomenon, but it is in the area of ODA that Japanese NGOs have interacted with state officials most frequently and closely. Finally, the chapter concludes with an analysis on the Japanese NGOs and their contribution to the democratization of Japan.

Civil Society

The term civil society is used with great ambiguity. Sometimes it means a society based on private property and individual rights. For example, Marx considered civil society as the sphere of market relations. To Marx, civil society was bourgeois and deserved to be abolished (Arato, 1990). At other times, the term refers to the sum of all institutions between the family—the basic unit of social organization—and the state, including not only NGOs but also any other organizations such as political parties and armed groups (Foley & Edwards, 1996). By some, the term is used even more broadly, encompassing not only the market and the public sphere, but also the family (Cohen & Arato, 1992; Wapner, 1994, 1996).

In contrast, this study takes a much narrower definition of civil society, adopting Diamond's (1999) definition:

> Civil society is the realm of organized social life that is voluntary, self-generating, (largely) self-supporting, autonomous from the state, and bound by a legal order or set of shared rules. It is distinct from "society" in general in that it involves citizens acting collectively in a public sphere to express their interests, passions, preferences, and ideas to exchange information, to achieve collective goals, to make demands on the state, to improve the structure and functioning of the state, and to hold state officials accountable. (p. 221, italic and parenthesis original)

Since civil society is an intermediary realm between the private sphere and the state, it excludes parochial society (i.e., individual and family life and inward-looking activities such as entertainment, recreation, and religious worship)[2] and economic society (i.e., profit-making individual business firms). Both parochial society and economic society are primarily concerned with private ends, not civic life or public ends.[3] Likewise, civil society is distinguished from political society (i.e., the party system). While civil society organizations may form alliances with political parties, their primary activity is not party politics (Cohen & Arato, 1992; Diamond 1999). As Diamond (1999) asserts, "If they [civil society organizations] become captured by parties, or hegemonic within them, they move their primary locus of activity to political society and lose much of their ability to perform certain unique mediating and democracy-building functions" (p. 221).

In addition to these characteristics—being voluntary, self-generating, rule abiding, and distinct from parochial, economic, and political societies—civil society entails another important characteristic: it promotes pluralism and diversity. Thus, civil society excludes narrowly focused, intolerant, ethnic chauvinist groups, hate groups, religious fundamentalist groups, and militia groups that claim, often through violence, that they are the only legitimate representation in society (Diamond, 1999). Although it is commonly assumed that civil society is equivalent to everything that entails nonstate activities, civil society does not consist of groups that deny pluralism and diversity even though they are nonstate actors. In the context of Japan, groups such as the Aum Shinrikyo (renamed "Aleph"), the Japanese Red Army, or various extreme right-wing groups (*uyoku*) are not part of civil society, primarily because they either propagate the use of violence to achieve their goals or glorify Japan's violent military past. In 1995, it was found that the Aum Shinrikyo, for example, tried to destabilize Japanese society through chemical weapons attacks as part of the group's strategy to eventually overthrow the government. The Red Army's main goal was to bring about radical revolution throughout the world, including the destruction of the state of Israel through terrorist attack. Japanese extreme right-wing organizations promote wartime militarism and racism through propagated public campaigns. These groups are by no means part of Japanese civil society.

Despite these exclusions, civil society encompasses a great range of citizens' organizations. Diamond (1994) lists various types of civil society organizations. These are generalized categories but are also pertinent to Japanese civil society: (1) economic associations (productive and commercial organizations and networks); (2) cultural groups that promote collective rights, values, faiths, and beliefs (religious, ethnic, and communal organizations); (3) informational and educational groups that promote dissemination of information and knowledge; (4) interest groups designed to advance the mutual interests of their members (e.g., groups representing veterans, workers, pensioners, or professionals); (5) developmental organizations that pool individual resources to improve the infrastructure and quality of life of the community; (6) issue-oriented movements (e.g., environmental protection groups, women's rights organizations); (7) civic groups designed to improve in nonpartisan fashion the political system through human rights monitoring and voter education; and (8) organizations and institutions that promote autonomous, cultural and intellectual activities ("the ideological market place," Diamond, 1999, p. 223), including independent mass media and publishing houses, universities and think tanks, and artistic associations and networks such as theaters and film production groups. Japanese NGOs engaged in efforts to improve Japanese ODA belong to some of these categories, such as informational and educational groups (listed as 3), developmental groups (5), and issue-based movements (6). However, not all these types are relevant to Japanese NGOs, as the following section demonstrates.

Defining Japanese NGOs

It is important to clarify the definition of nongovernmental organization in the Japanese context and distinguish among the different categories of Japanese civil society organizations. The term *nongovernmental organization* is conceptually vague, but is used in some countries or contexts to refer to almost any not-for-profit group not directly affiliated with the government. In Japan, however, the term NGO has a much narrower definition. NGOs refer to nonprofit organizations in Japan engaged in overseas aid programs, such as development assistance and emergency relief. They are voluntary, nonprofit, self-governing, nonpolitical (i.e., whose primary goal is not promoting candidates for electoral office), and nonproselytizing organizations engaged in international affairs. By a standard Political Science definition, these groups are International NGOs (INGOs). But I use the term NGOs rather than INGOs, as the latter is rarely used in Japan.

The term nonprofit organization (NPO or *enupīō*), in contrast, usually refers only to nonprofit organizations that are engaged in domestic activities in Japan (Japan Center for International Exchange, 1996). Sometimes people use the term more broadly as an umbrella term referring to both domestic groups and NGOs doing international work. I use the term in its narrower sense. Distinguishing between NGOs and NPOs is important in this study because the former is involved in ODA while the latter is not. Of course some organizations involve themselves in *both* international and domestic affairs. This study examines organizations engaged only in overseas assistance as well as groups primarily engaged in international aid and development while secondarily involved in domestic activity.

While the distinction between NGOs and NPOs is not very difficult to make, there is still a confusing array of legal categories in Japan. Legally, Japanese NGOs consist of two distinct groups: incorporated associations (*hōjin*) and unincorporated associations (*nin'i dantai*, commonly called "civic groups," *shimin dantai*). The majority of Japanese NGOs are unincorporated associations that have no legal status and are not registered with the state. While severely hampered by a lack of legal protection and tax breaks, these organizations are free from state supervision and intervention due to their unincorporated status. The number of unincorporated associations has rapidly increased since the 1980s.

In contrast are the incorporated associations, many of which are highly regulated and supervised by the state, specifically by relevant state agencies, based on the Uniform Civil Code of 1896. Some incorporated associations were established at the state's initiative and are even staffed by retired bureaucrats through the practice of *amakudari,* whereby retiring civil servants "descend from heaven" to important posts in the incorporated associations. As Amenomori and Yamamoto (1998) argue, these organizations are "in reality part of the public sector, although legally they are in the private, nonprofit sector" (p. 15). The majority of incorporated associations do not fully meet the commonly accepted definition of an NGO as being voluntary and self-governing (Salamon & Anheier, 1996).

According to Baron (1997), approximately 20 percent of incorporated organizations in Japan were established by state agencies to carry out state-initiated activities. Many incorporated organizations not only receive state funding, but also receive corporate funding intended to be used for state-related activities.

Examples of incorporated associations strongly influenced by the state are agricultural and vocational training organizations such as the Institute for the Development of Agricultural Cooperation in Asia (IDACA) and the Japan Productivity Center (JPC, in 1994 renamed the Japan Productivity Center for Socioeconomic Development). IDACA was established in 1963 by Japanese agricultural cooperatives to train agricultural specialists and to conduct research on agricultural development. Managed by the Central Union of Agricultural Cooperatives ("Zenchu"), IDACA is supervised by the Ministry of Agriculture, Forestry, and Fisheries (MAFF) (Institute for the Development of Agricultural Cooperation in Asia, 1995). JPC, established in 1955 by Japanese business leaders to promote industrial productivity in Asia, has been supervised by the Ministry of International Trade and Industry or MITI,[4] and has maintained strong connection to business groups (Japan Productivity Center for Socioeconomic Development, 1997; see M. Haas, 1989). IDACA and JPC are both highly influenced by the state and have strong ties to business and agricultural groups. Therefore, neither these nor similar organizations will be considered in this study.

However, there are different types of incorporated associations, some of which are more independent of the state. Two specific types of incorporated associations commonly referred to and treated as NGOs by the Japanese ODA administration and the Japanese NGO community are (1) public interest corporations (*kōeki hōjin*) and (2) specified nonprofit activity associations (*tokutei hi-eiri katsudō hōjin*). Public interest corporations are private–public hybrid NGOs established under Article 34 of the Uniform Civil Code of 1896. On the one hand, they are under the supervision of government agencies that have jurisdiction in their particular area. On the other hand, a number of them are relatively autonomous from the state and are engaged in international aid at the grassroots level and are included in NGO coordinating bodies by the Japanese government. Like unincorporated associations, these public interest corporations are eligible for the government's ODA subsidies and participate in ODA implementation contracts. In many respects (e.g., in terms of financial conditions and relationship with the state), these incorporate associations are often privileged and elite organizations, as opposed to mass organizations represented by unincorporated associations, but they are nevertheless a recognized part of the NGO movement. This study therefore includes in its analysis public interest associations that (a) are normally treated as NGOs by the state and other NGOs, (b) are self-governing and relatively independent of the state, and (c) are engaged in international aid at a grassroots level or have influence over the course of Japanese ODA.

These public interest corporations mainly consist of two subgroups: incorporated foundations (*zaidan hōjin*) and incorporated associations (*shadan hōjin*). The former, for example, includes the Cooperative for Assistance and Relief Everywhere (CARE) Japan; the Organization for Industrial, Spiritual and Cultural Advancement (OISCA); the Japanese Organization for International Cooperation in Family Planning (JOICEF); and Plan International Japan. Among the latter are Save the Children Japan and Japan Overseas Christian Medical Cooperative Service (JOCS). Application for a status of public interest incorporation is complex and thus prevents many NGOs from obtaining incorporated status. To apply, NGOs are required to have an endowment of ¥300 million and an annual budget exceeding ¥30 million, an impossible amount for many small NGOs (Menju & Aoki, 1995, p. 150). In addition, public interest corporations have to be authorized by relevant agencies of the central government or local governments, which can be a lengthy and complex process taking several years. Because of the nature of NGO activities (overseas development and aid), most NGOs in this category have registered with the Ministry of Foreign Affairs (MOFA) (Japanese NGO Center for International Cooperation, 1998a), which serves to draw them closer to the ministry.

The other type of incorporated associations that are included in this analysis, specified nonprofit activity associations, are former unincorporated associations that changed their status with the enforcement of the NPO Law of 1998, an amendment to the 1896 Civil Code (see Wanner, 1998; Pekkanen, 2000). The 1998 law, formally known as the Law to Promote Specified Nonprofit Activity, enables unincorporated associations through application to gain the status of specified nonprofit activity associations, thereby helping them gain social trust and more access to public and private funding. Specified nonprofit activity associations are private organizations highly independent of the state (e.g., Japan International Volunteer Center [JVC], which became incorporated in 1999 under the new NPO law). The number of specified nonprofit activity associations is expected to grow in the future, as the process of application is less cumbersome than that for public interest corporations. According to JVC director Michiya Kumaoka, it was essential for his group to become incorporated in Japan in order to conduct overseas projects effectively. Kumaoka explains that some governments, such as that of Vietnam, allow only incorporated NGOs to implement projects in their countries and that having no legal status thus severely hampers NGO activities abroad (Nikkei Weekly, 1999d). However, though incorporated under the new law, NGOs in this category still do not receive tax exemptions or tax deductibility privileges by the central government, at least for now. This shortcoming is partially compensated by many local governments that provide tax privileges to newly incorporated NGOs under the NPO Law.

Finally, this study does not treat as NGOs the remaining types of incorporated associations: "social welfare corporations" (*shakai fukushi hōjin*), "private school corporations" (*gakkō hōjin*), "religious corporations" (*shūkyō hōjin*), "medical corporations" (*iryō hōjin*), and "special public corporations" (*tokushu hōjin*). Although legally nonprofit, the first two types of organizations are under strict control of the state. In addition, they are primarily domestic organizations and rarely take part in issues on ODA. The third, religious corporations, are not NGOs, as their main goal is proselytizing. The fourth type, special public corporations, is also legally nonprofit and was created by specific legislation through a government-appointed committee. It includes the Japan International Cooperation Agency (JICA) and the Bank of Japan (Amenomori and Yamamoto, 1998). For the purpose of this study, they will be treated as governmental agencies rather than NGOs.[5] The complex legal status of Japanese NGOs is indicative of the great diversity within the NGO community as well as of the great control that the developmental state imposes on different types of citizens' activities.

Marginalization of Civil Society and the
Developmental State

Perhaps the most important question related to Japanese civil society is why until recently were Japanese civil society organizations such as NGOs kept so weak vis-à-vis the state? And if NGOs have recently begun to gain influence in Japanese politics, what factors have contributed to the change?

The recent Japanese NGO movement is by no means the first citizens' movement in postwar Japan.[6] In particular, the late 1960s witnessed two important citizens' movements in Japan: environmental movement to address local pollution problems (so-called *jumin undo,* or local movement) and anti-Vietnam War movement (so-called *shimin undo*, citizens' movement) led by Beheiren (*"Betonamu ni heiwa o!" Shimin rengo* or the League for Peace in Vietnam).[7] However, these movements, although significant in their own capacity, did not last beyond their particular campaigns and their long-term impact on Japanese civil society was limited. First, in the 1960s, citizens' groups began to organize around environmental problems in heavily polluted regions of Japan (e.g., Minamata disease in Kumamoto prefecture, caused by methylmercury poisoning, and Itai-itai disease, or "ouch-ouch disease" in Toyama prefecture, caused by cadmium poisoning). These environmental groups adopted various strategies, including litigation, media campaigning, and lobbying of local governments, to bring about change in Japan's environmental policy (Kuroda, 1972; McKean, 1981). These groups succeeded in changing not only local policies but also national policies by winning litigations and making the central government responsible for the environmental problems in question (Pempel, 1982). There is no doubt that the environment movement had a significant impact on Japanese politics at that time; it altered local and national policies, highlighted the importance of individuals' rights over the profits of large polluting firms, and enlarged citizen participation in local politics. Yet, unfortunately, these positive impacts were temporary. The movement did not result in long-lasting environmental movements throughout Japan. The movement's major concerns were fundamentally parochial, such as pollution problems of the groups' own neighborhood, town, or city. The movement was mostly restricted to local issues and did not coalesce into a lasting national force. Once the local environmental problems were solved, the groups were disbanded, without attempting to address other environmental issues beyond their own regions (See for example, McKean, 1981; Steinhoff, 1989).

Similarly, while Beheiren's anti-Vietnam War movement made a significant contribution to citizen participation in politics in 1965–1974, the movement failed to develop into a larger antiwar movement to address issues other than the Vietnam War. Unlike the environmental movement, Beheiren was primarily concerned with Japanese foreign policy (e.g., U.S.–Japan relations). The group was formed by a group of Japanese leftist intellectuals such as Makoto Oda and Takeshi Kaiko to oppose U.S. involvement in Indochina and the Japanese support for that involvement. Beheiren leaders argued that despite the Japanese Constitution that prohibits Japan from getting involved in overseas wars, the country was collaborating with the United States by allowing the U.S. military bases in Japan to be used for launching attacks on Vietnam. In its near ten-year existence, Beheiren organized antiwar rallies throughout Japan, published numerous opinion papers, attended U.S. antiwar demonstrations, invited U.S. activists, published antiwar advertisements in major U.S. newspapers (e.g., the *New York Times*), and even protected U.S. military defectors (Oda, 1968). In their rallies and publications, Beheiren leaders urged Japanese people to learn and practice civil disobedience and cooperate with antiwar activists around the world. Yet, while Beheiren's main concern was foreign policy, the group was motivated mainly by nationalism (hostility to the U.S. use of Japanese soil for the prosecution of the war and the U.S.–Japan Security Treaty that allowed the U.S. military station in Japan) and pan-Asianism (opposition to Western colonialism in Asia). Thus, Beheiren's primary goals were removing Japan from the U.S. war effort, preserving Japan's national security that seemed endangered by the war, and terminating Washington's involvement in Vietnam. As a result, once these goals were met after the 1973 Paris peace accords, which resulted in the withdrawal of U.S. troops from Indochina, the antiwar movement faded away. Like the environmental movement, the antiwar movement was relatively short-lived and failed to develop into a larger peace movement to address other related issues (that may or may not directly involve Japan).

Why didn't these citizens' movements lead to a vibrant civil society in Japan in the 1960s and 1970s? At the individual or organizational levels, various factors may account for their failure. For example, these movements were focused on single issues that lacked long-lasting relations to other broader questions. As soon as a given problem that citizens' groups focused on was solved, the movement disappeared. Also, a lack of strong or charismatic leadership may be one of the reasons that these movements eventually fizzled. In addition, at the societal and state levels, the then-strong Japanese developmental state imposed structural constraints on citizens' activism and fostered passivity, thus hindering the growth of long-lasting, national movements or coalitions.

My use of the term developmental state is in line with Castells's (1997), referring to a development-oriented state that concentrates its entire energy on the country's industrialization and rapid economic development, while making noneconomic, political, or civic issues, such as expansion of citizens' rights, almost irrelevant. The developmental state enjoyed strong public support for development-oriented policies; having gone through the devastating World War II and subsequent poverty and social chaos, the majority of the Japanese people shared the government's view that economic growth was the foremost important national goal.

The developmental state model adopted in this study differs from Johnson's (1982) model of a "capitalist developmental state" on three accounts. First, unlike Johnson's model that focuses on bureaucracy–business relations and ignores state-civil society relations, the developmental state model here focuses on state–civil society relations, taking into account Japan's broad political economy. The model analyzes not only state–civil society relations but also close collaboration between major actors of the developmental state: that is, a developmental coalition of the bureaucracy, politicians, and the private sector. Although often filled with tensions and conflicts, with each group attempting to maximize its own benefits and power, the coalition was overall united on one particular point: support for Japan's rapid growth through export-led industrialization. As will be discussed later in the chapter, the leading actor of the coalition was the bureaucracy that planned and implemented economic policy in collaboration with politicians and the private sector. Japan's state-civil society relations cannot be understood without scrutinizing the role of the coalition, especially that of the bureaucracy.

Second, the developmental state in this study addresses not only the state's leadership in economic policymaking but also the role of the Japanese people, who wholeheartedly supported regime-sponsored development policies. In particular, it is important to examine cultural and psychological aspects of the Japanese who, together with state leaders, became integrated into developmental corporate culture (see Castells, 1997). Third, unlike Johnson's model that stresses a unitary state (especially a united bureaucracy) in imposing its preferences on the private sector, the developmental state in this study is more pluralistic, filled with intrabureaucratic rivalries. My analysis of the Japanese state does not reject Johnson's notion that the bureaucracy was strong and that it unanimously promoted Japan's economic development as a national goal in the early decades of the postwar era (especially in the field of ODA). But I disagree with his analysis over the degree to which different ministries maintained coordination among themselves to promote Japan's economic interests. Although each ministry perceived economic growth as Japan's ultimate national goal, the bureaucracy was not united as to the best *means* to pursue Japan's economic growth; intraministerial rivalries occurred regularly over how Japan should pursue its economic objectives. Each ministry promoted strategies for economic development best suited to the ministry's own organizational interests.

How did the Japanese developmental state inhibit a vibrant civil society? This leads to two further sets of questions, one focusing on the state and the other on civil society. First, what became the driving force of the developmental state? How did the state successfully promote industrialization and economic growth while at the same time marginalizing and subordinating civil society? To answer these first questions, it is necessary to examine the historical tradition of Japanese bureaucratic power and what role the bureaucracy played in promoting industrialization in the developmental era, as the bureaucracy served as the central actor in Japan's economic development. And second, how and why did the Japanese public accept the "iron triangle" of bureaucracy/ruling political party/corporate leadership? Where, in the public's eye, did the state's legitimacy lie? Why didn't civil society emerge to challenge state authority? To answer the questions, we need to analyze the cultural and psychological aspects of the Japanese people, who single-mindedly pursued economic development as a national goal.

The prominence of the Japanese bureaucracy is not a recent phenomenon. The bureaucratic tradition traces back to the feudal Japan of the Tokugawa era (1603–1868). During this time the *samurai* class (warriors)—ranked highest in the social hierarchy of the time—began to take on the administrative functions of the government. Although the *samurai* were not yet professional bureaucrats (for example, they did not receive a salary based on their bureaucratic work but instead received a modest government stipend for their *samurai* status), they paved the way for the emergence of modern Japanese bureaucracy. During the Meiji period (1868–1912), the feudal system was abolished and a modern imperial system emerged. The former *samurai* administrators took bureaucratic posts and officially became "servants" of the emperor under the new edicts of the 1880s.[8] The bureaucrats became politically responsible to the emperor, not to the parliament, and were virtually free of pressure from politicians. This emperor-centered bureaucracy was consolidated during the following Taisho (1912–1926) and Showa (1926–1989) periods. The bureaucracy became central in economic and military developments during the 1920s. Eventually, however, the military bureaucracy overpowered the civilian bureaucracy and exercised uncontrolled power by virtue of its independent access to the emperor.

In the post–World War II era, the Supreme Commander for the Allied Powers (SCAP) completely abolished the prewar military but decided to keep intact the economic bureaucracy. SCAP's decision was based on its view that Japan urgently needed to reconstruct its wartorn economy and that the economic bureaucracy was the only viable institution to carry out that task. The economic ministries thus regained power during the U.S. Occupation era (1945–52), filling in the power vacuum left by the military. Even though the Japanese military forces were reestablished and renamed the Self Defense Forces (SDF) in 1954 (formerly known as the National Police Reserve, established in 1950), the SDF gained far less influence and status than either its wartime predecessor or the postwar civilian bureaucracy.

Throughout the 1950s and 1960s, the economic bureaucracy further consolidated its power through successful industrialization strategies that focused on key industries. The bureaucracy promoted Japanese strategic industries through assistance from various administrative mechanisms. In particular, the Ministry of International Trade and Industry (MITI), which was established out of the former Ministry of Commerce and Industry after war, played the leading role in orchestrating the direction of economic change. MITI helped transform the Japanese economy from labor-intensive light industry to capital-intensive heavy industry. MITI's mercantilist policies included the imposition of high tariffs on imported goods from international competition to protect domestic industries and the provision of subsidies and other assistance to Japanese key industries. At the same time, MITI was not alone in promoting Japanese mercantilism in the developmental state. Each ministry—though bureaucratic turf battles existed between ministries (see Rix, 1980, 1989–1990, 1993)—attempted to accelerate industrialization in its own way. The Ministry of Finance (MOF), another key player in Japan's industrialization, designed financial and fiscal policies, including privileged finance and tax arrangements and infrastructure investment schemes to key industries. The core of the MOF policies was to provide Japanese firms with enough capital to accelerate industrialization. Similarly, MOFA, although not directly involved in formulating domestic economic strategies, also took part in the industrialization effort through mercantilist foreign aid and overseas direct investment policies. As discussed later, MOFA promoted foreign aid and investment to increase Japanese business opportunities in the 1950s– 1970s. MOFA also worked to ensure the acceptance of Japan by the international community as a member of the world's most advanced industrial countries. For example, MOFA succeeded in achieving Japan's entrance to the Organization for Economic Cooperation and Development (OECD) in the early 1960s. Each of these ministries maintained close communications with Japanese businesses under their jurisdiction, often through mutual participation in advisory councils and a practice called *amakudari* (descent from heaven), through which former officials took top positions in private corporations after retirement. In the end, these bureaucratic efforts—strategic planning, lucrative financial arrangements, increasing foreign aid and overseas investment, and close government-business communications—created massive production innovation and internationally competitive industries.

The success of the Japanese bureaucracy in contributing to successful economic transitions and economic growth was in large part due to the talent and dedication that individual civil servants brought to the Japanese bureaucratic system. Civil servants in Japan are highly skilled individuals who are the graduates of the nation's most prestigious universities. These bureaucrats are recruited through a competitive national examination system administered by the National Personnel Authority. Once employed, career bureaucrats usually go through extensive training in their respective ministries to acquire skills and knowledge. In Japan, it is possible to recruit and retain talented individuals in the bureaucracy despite the below–market salary they receive, because bureaucratic posts are considered prestigious and desirable. The bureaucratic prestige is reminiscent of that of the samurai administrators in the Tokugawa era, who also enjoyed social prestige despite the limited stipend they received from the government.

It goes without saying that the bureaucracy in the Japanese developmental state was in effect an unelected policy making power. The bureaucrats not only implemented policies but also developed them. They controlled important information and possessed expertise on specific issues. Since politicians were generalists, the bureaucrats provided them with expertise and knowledge in certain issue areas. The bureaucrats worked closely with politicians in policy making, especially with those in the Liberal Democratic Party (LDP), which ruled Japan uninterruptedly from 1955 through 1993. The bureaucracy became literally the LDP's "think tank" (Curtis, 1999b) and often wrote legislation on behalf of the party.

In addition, the bureaucracy fully supported key prime ministerial initiatives for economic development, such as Prime Minister Shigeru Yoshida's economic development doctrine of the 1950s (policy of economic rehabilitation within the framework of security protection from the United States), Prime Minister Hayato Ikeda's Income Doubling Plan of the 1960s, and Prime Minister Kakuei Tanaka's Plan for Restructuring the Japanese Archipelago of the 1970s (to industrialize Japan's rural areas by providing economic infrastructure). It was in the interest of the ministries to promote these political initiatives. For example, to pursue Tanaka's plan, the Ministry of Construction approved during the developmental era huge public work projects and doled out contracts to construction firms with close ties to the ministry and the LDP. To this day the public works are the concern of the ministry and LDP *zoku-giin* (policy "tribes"), policymakers with expertise on specific issues such as construction.

The bureaucracy maintained close communications with the LDP through personnel transfers. Many former civil servants became politicians, mostly in the LDP (e.g., prime ministers Yoshida, Nobusuke Kishi, Ikeda, and Eisaku Sato) and became conduits between the bureaucratic and political worlds. Thus, the relationship between Kasumigaseki (synonymous with Japanese bureaucracy, whose offices are located in the Kasumigaseki district in Tokyo) and Nagatacho (the Tokyo district in which the parliament is located) was, in general, close, even though conflict occasionally occurred between them, especially when politicians tried to gain more influence in policymaking vis-à-vis the bureaucracy.[9]

Coexisting with the developmental state was a civil society that was marginalized, subordinate to, and dependent on the state. Several factors account for these characteristics. First, the developmental state paid little attention to noneconomic affairs in the realm of civil society, such as respect for individuals' rights, since the state's primary goal was rapid economic development. The type of close collaboration that took place between the state and the private sector or between the bureaucracy and politicians never occurred between the state and civil society. Except for state-initiated, incorporated organizations under the paternal protection of the state, citizens' groups remained practically out of the developmental coalition of the state and the corporate sector.

Second, to maintain state control to promote economic growth, the developmental state regulated civil society activities by imposing strict legal restrictions on citizens' associations. In particular, the state exerted strong influence over citizens' activities through the maintenance of the aforementioned Uniform Civil Code promulgated in 1896. Article 34 of the code reads:

> An association or foundation relating to rites, religion, charity, academic activities, arts and crafts, or otherwise relating to the public interest and not having for its object the acquisition of profit may be made a legal person subject to the permission of the competent authorities. (Yamaoka, 1998, p. 24)

Under this code, incorporated associations were established only after gaining permission from the responsible bureaucratic agencies. In other words, their establishment depended solely on the judgment of the agencies with jurisdiction. In addition, as mentioned above, the state required each incorporated association to have starting capital of at least ¥300 million. Many citizens' organizations found it impossible to meet this target, thus giving up acquiring incorporated status under the law and falling into an incorporated (nonlegal) status that prevented them from gaining any type of tax exemption. Furthermore, even after the establishment of incorporated associations, the agencies maintained tight control over civic associations under their jurisdiction and were able to terminate the operations of these associations if they did not meet the standards set by the agencies. Incorporated associations functioned mainly as an arm of the state's welfare policy and had little basis for purely private activities, let alone any significant political role in changing state policy or curtailing state power (Yamaoka, 1998).

Performance legitimacy is another important factor that strengthened state authority vis-à-vis civil society. The state not only achieved its primary goal of catching up and surpassing many Western industrialized countries (at least in terms of GNP),[10] but also succeeded in distributing wealth relatively evenly among the people. During the developmental era, the majority of the Japanese felt they belonged to a vast middle class and viewed the state's performance highly, giving the bureaucracy—especially the economic ministries—further prestige and power. Many Japanese, who had never been wealthy, became satisfied with and accepted bureaucratic leadership in navigating Japanese economy and society.

Japan's weak civil society also derived from cultural aspects of Japan. In particular, three aspects of Confucian tradition deserve special attention: (1) respect for hierarchy and authority, (2) emphasis on conformity to group interests rather than individual needs, and (3) emphasis on order and stability. These values legitimized social hierarchy and state authority in Japan, emphasized citizens' obligations and responsibilities rather than their individual rights, and deterred challenges from citizens' organizations.

First, as explained by Nakane (1970), Japanese society emphasizes social hierarchy. In Japan, one's social status is not based on personal wealth per se, but rather on multiple factors including education, occupation, age, and gender. At the top of the social hierarchy is the bureaucracy often referred to as *okami* ("the above"; those above people). From the Meiji era through the developmental era, the people followed bureaucratic leadership believing that bureaucrats could best decide for society because they were the best and the brightest in Japan. Decision-making was considered a domain of the state. An individual's attempt to infringe the boundaries of their social status and socially assigned roles and to break in the realm of an activity deemed to belong to the state was considered disrespectful and disgraceful toward the authorities (see Yamamoto, 1999). The citizens' deference to the bureaucracy is most aptly summarized by a traditional Japanese phrase, *kansonminpi* ("respectful bureaucracy, despiteful common people"; bureaucrats exalted, common people despised), which implies that the public, due to its ignorance, should follow bureaucratic leadership (see DeVos, 1973).

Also, the social conformity of Confucian ideology helped the state subordinate Japanese civil society. Like many other East Asian societies, Japanese society stresses group conformity and consensus-building, as well as the importance of individual responsibilities for the welfare of community vis-à-vis individual rights. The individual is subordinate to the community. Social pressure to conformity helped to silence dissent and discourage individualism. Traditionally, the term "individualism" (*kojin-shugi*) has a negative connotation in Japanese, because it stresses selfishness and self-centeredness. Minority views were usually not tolerated in the conformity-emphasized society, and it required unusual courage and determination for individuals to deviate from social norms. As a result, the Japanese shied away from political participation. They had a keen sense of citizen duty but less of a sense that they possessed the right to make demands to authorities. And they were willing to follow state leadership that determined the goals of their community or nation.

Similarly, the Confucian value of order and stability also seem to silence dissent in Japan. Individuals and NGOs critical of the government were viewed by many Japanese as antigovernment and prone to cause social disturbance and instability. This view was reinforced especially during the Cold War era when many activist NGOs were regarded as communist or radical left-wing organizations.

While these Confucian values did not originate in Japan and are shared by many other Asians, the Japanese case is unique in that these values were fully incorporated into the state ideology of developmentalism; individuals were encouraged to support the hierarchical structure of the developmental state, in which they were obliged to follow state leadership by fulfilling their duties and sacrificing their rights for the welfare of their community and nation. In the developmental era, Japanese workers represented an extremely disciplined, selfless labor force. They worked diligently and willingly spent much longer hours at work than their counterparts in other industrialized countries, often exceeding 12 hours per day, six days a week, without any extra financial compensation for overtime. Their devotion to work can be explained by the belief that if they followed the state-corporate leadership, they would make Japan wealthy and eventually raise their own living standards. Devotion to one's work and self-sacrifice became a social norm. An individual "salaryman" became a selfless *kigyō senshi* (corporate warrior) or *moretsu-shain* (zealous employee) who completely sacrificed his private life—family, hobbies, and leisure—and made work the priority in his life. In this developmental culture, a notion of civil society, based on the concept of individual rights and liberty, was not on people's minds. Most people lacked either the time to concentrate on matters unrelated to their work, or the frame of mind, but also were deprived of the ability to think critically about state performance and the incredible sacrifices that they were making.

Other Japanese cultural—but nonConfucian—aspects are also worth noting. These aspects strengthened the developmental state by discouraging citizen activism while encouraging people's dependence on the government. The first is the concept of the *uchi* (inside) and *soto* (outside). The Japanese are generally group-oriented and traditionally tended to see sharp differences between in-group members and those outside the group. This *uchi-soto* concept discourages the Japanese from giving assistance to those who do not belong to their own groups (usually the family or immediate neighborhood). This traditional tendency was reinforced by the Japanese governments from the Meiji Restoration through World War II, all of which emphasized an ideology of *ie* (familyism) and filial piety. Families were legally required to take care of their own needy relatives. This tradition was maintained even after World War II and thus, until recently, Japan did not have many formal private associations to mobilize ordinary citizens to extend voluntary assistance to the needy on an indiscriminate basis. And when the Japanese found that they could not rely on their own family, they turned to the state for assistance, rather than organizing grassroots groups themselves.

Another cultural aspect is Japan's lack of Christian evangelical tradition. Unlike Western and some developing countries, Japan does not have a Christian Evangelical tradition based on volunteerism and charity. Although some Japanese converted to Christianity and became engaged in charitable work in the past hundred years, their influence was limited (only about 3 percent of the Japanese population is Christian) and values of Christian voluntarism and charity did not take deep root in Japan (Yamaoka, 1998). Thus social welfare was traditionally provided by *uchi* members and/or the state, not by Christian churches. Because of the lack of voluntarism to provide assistance indiscriminately, the Japanese people relied on the state at times of difficulty. Mainly through incorporated associations under strict control of the state, social welfare, although limited, was provided to the needy, albeit in a limited fashion.

Erosion of the Developmental State

The developmental state, which brought about spectacular economic success in Japan, was eventually eroded by two very powerful forces. One of these was internal, a maturation of industrialization that weakened the need for a developmental system. The second was external, a process of globalization that brought powerful new external forces to bear on Japan's political economy, society, and culture. Together, these factors have brought about contributed to profound structural and normative changes in Japan, contributing to the rise of Japanese civil society.

Globalization

Two aspects of globalization need to be examined: the acceleration of Japanese integration into the global economy and the acquisition of global norms and values. Globalization is a multifaceted phenomenon, which leads to economic, political, and cultural change. In Japan, globalization has challenged the structure of corporate-state cooperation as well as the traditional values that buttressed the developmental state.

First, Japan's economic rise of the last several decades and more thorough integration into the world economy have placed the Japanese state in a position of greater accountability to global norms and demands. In the processes of globalization, the state has come under great pressure to liberalize Japanese economy. Since the 1980s, other governments have been urging Tokyo to shift its focus from export-led industrialization to domestic consumption-based development. Liberalization of the Japanese economy and the abandonment of export-led growth are against the ethos of Japanese developmentalism. In the 1950s and 1960s, Japan still had a "catch-up economy," and Tokyo was not pressured by other governments to abandon its protectionist policies and change the pattern of development. Even though a trade dispute with the United States occurred in the 1960s over Japanese textile exports, the conflict never developed into a comprehensive bilateral trade war. Yet, in the 1980s, the situation dramatically changed. By then Japan had become one of the largest economies in the world and *gaiatsu* (external pressure) on Japan to open up its market for foreign goods intensified. Intense global criticism forced Tokyo to search for a solution. One result was the Maekawa Report, written in 1986 by a governmental study group chaired by former President of the Bank of Japan Haruo Maekawa (Study Group on Economic Structural Adjustment for International Cooperation). The report recommended that Japan promote economic development by cultivating the domestic market and that it abolish a tax exemption system previously designed to encourage domestic savings. The group argued that the Japanese should not excessively save, but should instead consume more so that more Japanese goods would be purchased at home.

This would in turn make the Japanese economy into more consumer-based, and lessen the threat of Japanese products on the world market (Nikkan Kogyo Shinbun Tokubetsu Shuzaihan, 1989). In the 1990s, *gaiatsu* further intensified, leading Japanese bureaucrats to believe that, if Tokyo failed to take action, it would face retaliation for Japanese goods abroad, especially from the United States where Congress adopted the "Super 301," retaliatory measures against countries with large trade surpluses.

Global pressure to open up Japanese market weakened state support for Japanese businesses and eroded the close state–corporate relationship. The Japanese bureaucracy was forced to gradually lift its grips on the private sector and to retreat from the market. Today, the Japanese private sector can no longer count on protection and provision of special privileges from the state at all times, but instead must compete with foreign firms. As Pemple (1998) explains, in the processes of globalization, the Japanese private sector has become polarized into highly efficient, truly global firms (such as Sony and Toyota) and inefficient, domestic-based firms (often small-scale to mid-size firms). Without state protection, the latter group can no longer compete with foreign firms. In ODA, for example, the high cost of labor in Japan has placed Japanese firms in an unfavorable position to win competitive aid contracts from the Japanese government. As a result, the participation of Japanese firms in ODA has been reduced dramatically.

Second, forces of globalization have been influencing cultural values and norms throughout the world, including in Japan. As the world has become more interconnected—with more access to global information via new technologies and more transnational travel for migration, tourism, and overseas education—new values and norms have been embraced. Indeed, the impacts of globalization have gone beyond changing lifestyles or "McDonaldization," but have affected people's values, belief systems, and normative orientations. Due to globalization of the media, individuals can actually see more international events through television and the Internet. Throughout the world, people realize there are other people in other parts of the globe who are working for the same cause. Realizing the interconnectedness of societies beyond national boundaries, they converge around shared norms across diverse cultures and think of their behavior in aggregate terms. With the help of new communications technologies, they may begin to work on shared issues with their counterparts throughout the world. The spread of new norms can (1) move people from narrow, self-serving, private orientation to engage in new forms of behavior and (2) create networks of like-minded individuals working on shared problems on a global scale (Rosenau, 1997).

This growing consciousness of global affairs and norms is matched by the acquisition of new organizing skills. The spread of global technology has helped citizens become more proficient at collecting and utilizing information. This "skill revolution," together with the acquisition of global norms, has changed the nature of political authority. Citizens are becoming more knowledgeable of issues they are concerned about and less deferential to traditional sources of authority (Rosenau, 1990; Rosenau & Fagen, 1997; Rosenau, 1997).

In parallel to this change in normative orientations, globalization also has weakened traditional values and belief systems. For example, the Confucian cultural values of social hierarchy and conformity are losing their grip on increasing numbers of globally influenced, independent-minded people in Japan (Larimer, 1999). Today, many Japanese do not have as much respect for social authority, such as that of the bureaucracy, as in the past. Global means of communications have accelerated this trend, creating horizontal relations among people who have begun to break away from established social norms and to communicate with each other as equals (see Rosenau, 1997; Castells, 1998).

Globalization also has influenced the way state leaders perceive the world. In the case of ODA, MOFA officials have acquired new ideas and approaches to development from the international community. As Japan has become the world's prominent economic actor, these officials have begun to heed the norms and values of a paradigm of sustainable human development, promoted by the international aid regime. In this paradigm, which emerged in the late 1980s, NGOs are considered the core of government aid programs to provide small-scale assistance to the needy in the developing world (Organization for Economic Cooperation and Development, 1992). MOFA has learned, though gradually, the importance of integrating NGOs into Japan's aid programs and has started working with Japanese NGOs.

Maturation of Industrialization

The other factor that has contributed to the weakening of the developmental state and strengthening of the civil society is the maturation of Japan's industrialization. As Japan became wealthy, it entered an era of postmaterialism. Having achieved the goal of becoming part of the industrialized world, people have begun to search for a new identity in the post-industrial age. Catching up with the West is no longer the national goal. Japanese people, especially the youth, have begun to look for non-material or spiritual meaning in life. Postmaterial value transformations that Inglehart (1990) observed in Western industrial societies have been also taking place in Japan. While older generations who grew up in wartime Japan have been concerned with traditional societal and material goals in the past, such as economic well-being, social security, and law and order, younger generations in Japan, having grown up in an environment in which these goals were relatively assured, are paying more attention to postmaterial goals of social equality, self-expression, personal freedom, and the quality of life. Today, many youth reject the self-sacrifice associated with developmentalism and developmental corporate culture characterized by *kaisha shijo-shugi* (company-firstism). Many young Japanese find it unthinkable to sacrifice in the same way as their parents' generation did for the sake of their firms and nation. These individuals would rather work no more than eight hours a day and spend their free time on hobbies and travel. Some choose to become *frīta* (freelancer) with flexible work hours, even though they have to compromise their income for this freedom.

In addition, the advance of Japanese industrial society has brought about and made evident the negative effects of developmentalism. Ironically, the developmental state has begun to crumble by the very source of power that drove the Japanese growth. The exclusiveness of the developmental alliance of the bureaucracy, politicians, and the private sector cultivated close working relations between them and fostered an environment where parochialism and corruption prevailed. In the 1990s, the public learned about a series of corruption cases involving not only politicians and business representatives but also elite bureaucrats who had previously been considered trustworthy. Some bureaucratic corruption cases were egregiously harmful (e.g., the HIV blood containment scandal in 1996), while others involved petty embezzlement. Large or small, the corruption scandals involving the bureaucracy enraged the public, reducing trust of the government and respect for state authority.

At the same time, the developmental alliance tried to maintain mercantilist trade policies to protect its own existing interests, running against the global trend of liberalization. Some bureaucrats (especially those in the former Ministry of Construction), LDP *zoku giin* (policy "tribes"), and construction firms attempted to provide the maximum level of public works, even when Japan's fiscal situation did not allow it. By passing large construction budgets, they sought to maintain and enhance their own power and financial advantages (through kickbacks and bribes). These self-interested and irresponsible actions aggravated the country's fiscal balance, angered the populace, and further weakened support for state authority. Together then, these widely publicized corruption scandals and ill-conceived economic and fiscal policies ended the performance legitimacy that the developmental state had enjoyed during the 1950s and 1970s.

In summary, the weakening of the state and corporate sector have created openings for a broader involvement of NGOs, both because NGOs are seen as less corrupt and thus more legitimate, and also because the tightening of budgets due to economic recession creates a demand for the deployment of cost-effective grassroots organizations in aid. This has created important political space for NGOs, which are seen as more capable of implementing community-based aid public achieving goal of rapid industrialization. In this situation, the pursuit of national economic development is no longer the sole goal of the Japanese people, especially the younger generation.

Historical Development of Japanese NGOs

Given the wide array of factors that have contributed to the decline of the developmental state and the rise of civil society, we can conclude that these changes are due to long-term, incremental transformations of Japanese society. No single incident or factor can account for the changes in the developmental state and civil society, or a shift in the power balance between the two.

At the same time, when we examine the historical development of Japanese NGOs, we can identify two important incidents that directly triggered the expansion of NGOs. These incidents are not isolated from the political, economic, and cultural changes that Japanese society has gone through, but instead they served to spark people—who were gradually becoming ready for citizen activism as a result of social transformations—to organize grassroots groups and take action. These triggering incidents are the Indochinese refugee crisis in the late 1970s and early 1980s and the 1995 Hanshin (or Kobe) Earthquake. While the first incident had a limited impact on Japanese society, as the population was not yet fully prepared for social activism, the second crisis had a tremendous impact on Japanese civil society. By the time the second crisis hit Japan, the developmental state was widely discredited, and large sectors of society were ready for social action. To understand the impact of these incidents on Japan's NGO growth, it is necessary to first examine the early stage of NGO development prior to the refugee crisis.

While many Western NGOs emerged in the 1940s and 1950s in order to assist to European rehabilitation after World War II, most Japanese NGOs, especially unincorporated associations, were started in the 1980s and 1990s, almost half a century later. The majority of the Japanese NGOs established prior to the 1980s were either Christian in origin (e.g., the Japan Overseas Christian Medical Cooperative Service [JOCS], established in 1960; the Asian Rural Institute, established in 1973; the Christian Child Welfare Association International Sponsorship Program, established in 1975) or incorporated associations with strong ties to the government (e.g., OISCA, established in 1961 and incorporated in 1969 under the authority of MOFA, MAFF, MITI, and the Ministry of Labor; JOICEF, established and incorporated in 1968 under the authority of MOFA and the Ministry of Health and Welfare [MOHW]) (Japanese NGO Center for International Cooperation, 1998b). Most early NGOs providing international assistance remained within Japan and invited people from the developing world, primarily from Asia, to Japan to receive technical training (Sugishita, 1998d).

An exception to this rule—a nonreligious, unincorporated NGO that implemented projects overseas—was Shapla Neer Citizens' Committee for Overseas Support (hereafter Shapla Neer). Shapla Neer was established in 1972 to assist the rural poor in newly independent Bangladesh. Other early NGOs that were unincorporated and nonreligions include the Pacific Asia Resource Center (PARC), established in 1973, and Amnesty International Japan, established in 1970. Unlike Shapla Neer, PARC and Amnesty International Japan concentrated their activities on domestic advocacy. PARC supports minorities' rights and environmental protection and publishes an English journal called *Ampo* (Japanese NGO Center for International Cooperation, 1998b). Amnesty International Japan promotes human rights internationally. Shapla Neer, PARC, and Amnesty International Japan were all critical of Japan's ODA and foreign policy. These three, while prominent, were among only a handful of nonreligious, unincorporated NGOs of their era.

However, as discussed earlier, several new factors contributed to the rise of Japanese NGOs, beginning in the late 1970s, including globalized communications, Japan's own economic development, and people's desire for a purpose beyond the accumulation of wealth. The first rapid expansion of Japanese NGOs began in the late 1970s and the early 1980s as a response to the Indochinese refugee crisis. The mass media, particularly television, appealed to Japanese with vivid images of Vietnamese, Cambodian, and Laotian refugees desperately trying to escape their countries. The images of their suffering were so powerful that they moved Japanese individuals—mostly youth in their twenties—to take action to provide assistance. These youth were concerned about the impact of the Vietnam War on the people in Indochina and wanted to do something to help the Indochinese refugees. Many traveled to Southeast Asia to do so. It was a "historical experience" (Matsui, 1990, p. 215) of ordinary citizens—students, doctors and nurses—to cross the national border for the first time to offer volunteer assistance to another people. From the Thai border camps emerged pioneer Japanese NGOs such as the Japan International Volunteer Center (JVC) and the Japan Sotoshu Relief Committee (JSRC).[11] At the same time, some Japanese volunteered in their home communities to give assistance to Indochinese refugees coming to Japan. While most of the early work with Indochinese refugees in Japan fell on international NGOs (INGOs) such as Caritas Japan and the Salvation Army Japan, some Japanese NGOs, such as the Japan Red Cross Society (JRCS), also provided refugee assistance (Havens, 1987). Also, the Association to Aid Refugees (AAR), the first Japanese relief organization specializing in assistance to refugees, was established in 1979 to help Indochinese refugees in Japan.

The impact of the Indochinese crisis on Japanese civil society was limited but significant. Although the number of newly established NGOs as a result of the Indochinese crisis was small (approximately 20 NGOs), these new groups carried out nationwide campaigns to address to the general public on the importance of assisting the needy outside Japan. These NGOs maintained high visibility and stimulated people either join them or organize similar groups. The Indochina crisis did not lead to a fullscale NGO movement in Japan, but it did serve as a catalyst for later NGO activism.

Since the Indochina crisis, the organizations engaged in assistance to Indochinese refugees have gradually started addressing other issues related to development and poverty. For example, early NGOs such as JVC, JSRC, and AAR first worked on emergency relief activities for Indochinese refugees on the Thai–Cambodian border camps or in Japan. They have since expanded their scope of activities to address root causes of poverty and vulnerability to natural disasters. These NGOs now provide developmental assistance in areas such as environmental protection, agricultural development, social welfare, and primary education.

Since the early Japanese NGOs launched their activities in Southeast Asia, this region has remained important for both old and new NGOs. Like the first-wave NGOs, such as JSRC and JVC, which concentrated their activities in Thailand (especially the refugee camps at the Thai–Cambodia border), many of the newly established NGOs have focused on Southeast Asia, especially Thailand, the Philippines, and Indonesia. Indochina, particularly Cambodia, also has attracted many Japanese NGOs since the early 1990s. In contrast to the 1980s, when very few of them operated inside Cambodia, the 1990s witnessed a surge of interest as Japanese NGOs opened regional offices and began relief and development work in Cambodia. Their sudden increase in activities was due to the peace settlement of Cambodia in the early 1990s and the easing of restrictions on foreign NGOs by the Cambodian government. Outside Southeast Asia, Japanese NGOs also focused their efforts on South Asian countries such as Nepal, India, and Bangladesh in the 1980s and 1990s (Japanese NGO Center for International Cooperation, 1998a).

Although Asia remains the area of greatest Japanese NGO involvement, NGO activities are becoming more globalized. In particular, aid to Africa rapidly increased in the 1990s, with a growing number of NGOs launching agricultural, educational and social welfare projects in that continent. Latin America (e.g., Bolivia) and the Middle East (e.g., Palestine) also have received increased attention from the NGO community, with some NGOs such as JVC launching projects in these regions.

In addition to the diversification of Japanese NGO activities, the composition of NGOs has changed. When the Indochinese refugee crisis emerged in the 1970s and 1980s, the overwhelming majority of Japanese NGO members were university students and other college-age activists. In the 1990s, while young people remained the majority, housewives and retirees began to participate as volunteers or full-time workers, joined by some dissatisfied company employees who quit their jobs to devote themselves to NGO work.

Another important phenomenon, especially since the mid-1980s, is the expansion in Japan of local branches of international organizations headquartered abroad. For example, in 1986, Save the Children Japan was established, and in the following year CARE Japan and World Vision Japan were initiated. In 1989, Greenpeace Japan followed suit. In 1992, Médecins sans Frontières Japan (MSFJ) was launched and in 1999 Oxfam Japan was initiated. The opening of these INGO offices in Japan reflected the Japanese public's growing support for international aid, development, and environmental protection.

While the Indochina refugee crisis had an important impact on the growth of Japanese NGOs in the late 1970s and early 1980s, Japanese civil society was further mobilized in the mid-1990s by another tragedy, this time within Japan itself: the Great Hanshin Earthquake of 1995, which killed more than six thousand people and made 30,000 people in the Kobe region homeless. The Japanese government dithered in its response to the earthquake and failed to mobilize domestic resources quickly enough or even to allow international governments and organizations to deliver emergency assistance.[12] In response, a great number of individuals—estimated at more than 1.3 million—rushed to help the victims with much-needed food, medicine, and supplies. The earthquake became "a watershed event for the development of a civil society in Japan" (Japan Center for International Exchange, 1996), fueling intensive discussion on the role of civil society and creating a broader awareness of the need to foster citizens' groups. The Great Hanshin Earthquake became a catalyst for both the growth of preexisting citizens' groups and the launching of many new groups. And since then, many NPOs engaged in earthquake relief operations have extended to other project areas such as international aid, development, education, and environmental protection.

Finally, a growing worldwide awareness of environmental issues has also encouraged Japanese NGO activities. For example, approximately 350 Japanese individuals participated in the NGO meetings held concurrently with the United Nations Conference on the Environment and Development (UNCED) in Rio de Janeiro 1992. This marked the first time that so many Japanese NGOs had participated in an international conference outside of Tokyo.

In the last two decades, the growth of NGOs devoted to international aid and development has been dramatic (see Figure 1.1). In 1980, only 59 NGOs were listed in a directory of Japanese NGOs engaged in international cooperation complied by a Japanese NGO network. In 1993, the number reached 290 and, in 1996, 368[13] (Japanese NGO Center for International Cooperation, 1994; Saotome, 1999). As most Japanese NGOs are unincorporated and not registered with the government, the exact number of them is difficult to determine and there are likely many more beyond those listed in the directory.

This prolific and unprecedented growth among NGOs has brought forth a new, potentially powerful civil society, which for the first time is beginning to influence the decision making of Japanese ODA. Japanese citizens' groups have become a main engine in Japan's ODA reform movement. Many Japanese NGOs share the concept of sustainable human development promoted in the international aid community. They value grassroots-based development in the social sector. In the domestic political scene, they are the main proponent advocating aid programs that addresses human, environmental, and social concerns in the developing world.

The growing number and influence of Japanese NGOs has significant implications for state–NGO relationship as well as for Japan's ODA policy. With the rise and growth of Japanese NGOs, state officials now take the NGO movement more seriously. This has created more active dialogue between the state and NGOs and a new role for Japanese NGOs in helping shape Japan's ODA policy. At the same time that the NGO movement

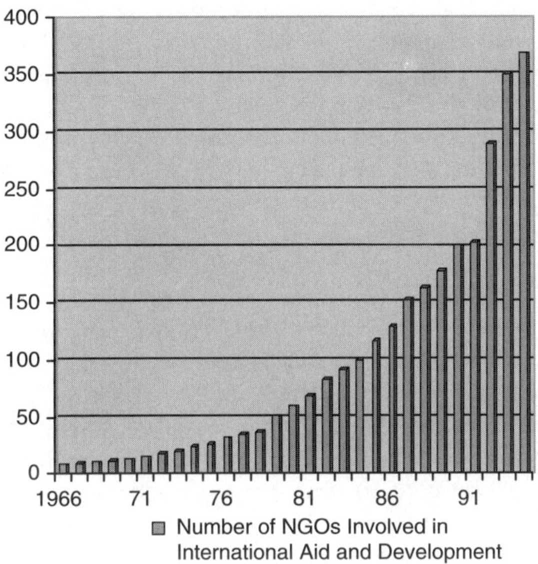

Figure 1.1   Growth of Japanese NGOs involved in International Aid and Development, 1966–1996

Table 1.1   Year of establishment of NGO in international aid from pre-world war II to 1996

Year of establishment	Number of NGOs established	%
Before World War II	2	0.5
1945–the 1950s	4	1.1
1960–1964	3	0.8
1965–1969	4	1.1
1970–1974	11	3.0
1975–1979	22	6.0
1980–1984	46	12.5
1985–1989	86	23.4
1990–1993	143	38.9
1994–1996	⋆47	12.8
Total	368	⋆⋆100.1

(Japanese NGO Center for International Cooperation, 1998a)

⋆ The number of new NGOs fell in 1994–1996, due to the recession in Japan.

⋆⋆ Total varies from 100, due to rounding.

has become larger and more influential, it also has become more diversified and fragmented. Japanese NGOs now represent a diverse range of interests, activities, and perspectives on development and aid and vary greatly in their relations with the state.

In summary, over the 25 years since the beginning of the Indochina refugee crisis, hundreds of new NGOs have been established, NGO activities have expanded, and NGOs have become more globalized, reaching out to many regions in the developing world. While the Japanese NGO movement is still relatively young, it has acquired a growing public profile and greater public trust in its activities. The movement is starting to exercise its influence in the area of foreign aid.

NGOs and ODA

Until the end of the 1980s, NGOs had little cooperation or even contact with state aid officials. For decades, Japanese civil society had virtually no room to participate in either decision making or project implementation in Japanese ODA. Foreign aid served as a diplomatic instrument of the developmental state to promote economic development at home. Aid was used to help Japanese firms acquire overseas markets: aid contracts were given primarily to Japanese firms, and aid projects were created in areas with the greatest economic potential for Japanese businesses. This landscape began to change in the late 1980s. Parallel to the weakening of the developmental state, the legitimacy of economic-centered Japanese aid programs has become the subject of intense public scrutiny (Inman, 1998).

Japanese bilateral aid began in the 1950s with war reparations programs in former colonies in Southeast Asia, based on the San Francisco Peace Treaty of 1952, which stipulated that Japan fulfill its international obligations to war indemnities (see Appendix for the history of Japanese aid). The developmental state turned the reparations obligations to opportunities, by utilizing the reparations to promote the country's export led industrialization. The state required procurement of reparations to be tied to Japanese goods and services in order to help Tokyo's own economy recovery and expand Japanese exports. As a result, Japanese firms benefited tremendously from the reparations. And even after the reparations, Japanese aid remained highly business-centered. With the advent of the oil crises in the 1970s, Japan used aid to secure oil supplies. Japan's aid to the Middle Eastern region suddenly increased. Thus, in the 1950s–1970s, Japanese ODA served to promote Japan's own postwar reconstruction, exports of Japanese goods and services, and resource acquisition, through tied aid schemes.

Japanese aid primarily consists of two types of programs and projects: those based on grant aid and those based on loan aid. As in many other countries, Japan's grant aid is usually tied. Japanese loan aid was almost all tied until the 1980s, when a partially untied system called LDC-untied aid was introduced in response to international criticism that Japanese aid was primarily benefiting Japanese businesses rather than people in recipient countries. Yet, this new scheme continued to greatly benefit Japanese firms, because it excluded participation of firms from advanced economies in aid bidding. The system restricted the competition for bids to only Japanese firms and firms from less developed countries (LDCs). Since LDC firms lacked advanced technologies to carry out Japanese aid projects—usually large-scale economic infrastructure construction—they were unable to win bids. By concentrating on infrastructure and business-centered "hard" aid (or *hardware aid*) through loans, the Japanese state showed almost no interest in incorporating people-centered "soft" aid (or *software aid*)[14] during the peak of the developmental era.

Change came gradually in the 1980s. To meet international norm to increase "grant element" in each country's aid program, the state adopted untied loans, opening the door to Western companies to participate in Japanese aid. Then, in the second half of the 1980s, Japanese NGOs grew in number and began high profile campaigns against certain infrastructure-based ODA by mobilizing public opinion through media appearance, publications, seminars, workshops, and symposiums (Nakauchi, 1996; see Chapter 4).

To respond to criticism at home and outside Japan, MOFA began to reform Japanese aid by increasing soft aid (see Ministry of Foreign Affairs, 2000b). The reform involved a shift in target sector of aid (e.g., from economic institutions to health care); a shift in emphasis within particular target sectors (e.g., from building hospitals to training community health practitioners); and a new emphasis on the Least Less Developed Countries (LLDCs). These shifts in emphasis ultimately required MOFA to reach out to NGOs to take part in Japanese ODA.

The state developed various systems to incorporate NGOs in aid. As discussed in detail in Chapter 5, the state started a couple of grant programs in 1989 to assist NGOs with small-scale grassroots projects in the developing world. Then, in the early 1990s, the MOFA established a division within the ministry to specialize in MOFA–NGO relations. In the mid-1990s, the bureaucracy started inviting NGO representatives to take part in policy dialogues with bureaucratic leaders. Many NGOs, in hopes of influencing aid policy and improving the state grant programs, welcomed the opportunities to exchange opinions with officials. As a result, NGOs now meet regularly officials from MOFA, JICA, and MOF.[15] In addition, NGOs have begun to take part in project evaluation and implementation of Japanese aid.

The changing relations between the bureaucracy, in particular MOFA, and NGOs in ODA reflect broader changes occurring inside and outside of Japan, primarily due to the forces of globalization and the industrial maturation of Japanese economy. On the one hand, NGOs have acquired global norms (e.g., human rights, sustainable development), skills, and knowledge and information, and they have become more assertive in demanding aid reform. Japanese firms, once fully integrated into the aid system, drifted away from it, since they cannot win aid bids in international competition. Furthermore, MOFA officials themselves have learned about global norms of aid through multilateral donor conferences and meetings, which have impacted the way they perceive development. They have learned that the international aid regime has moved toward sustainable human development, with an emphasis on human development, social welfare, sustainability, and ecological protection, rather than economic infrastructure and trickle-down economic effects.

On the other hand, negative effects of Japan's industrialization have come to the surface. Fiscal deficits have reached a record high, thus forcing the bureaucracy to cut down aid expenditures and to shift emphasis from hard aid to soft aid; the latter is labor intensive and is considered more cost-efficient than the former. Implementation of soft aid has made it necessary for MOFA to reach out to NGOs, because the ministry and JICA lack enough personnel for aid implementation. Furthermore, MOFA has faced another problem with infrastructure aid programs. The 1990s has witnessed a surge of corruption cases involving the developmental coalition of the bureaucracy, the corporate sector, and politicians. Seen as the hotbed of corruption, infrastructure projects at home and abroad have become the target of public criticism. Thus, MOFA has found it necessary to emphasize soft aid with the involvement of NGOs to win public approval of Japanese ODA.

Table 1.2   Contrast of hard vs. soft aid

Hard aid	Soft aid
Emphasis on industrialization	Emphasis on human resources
Infrastructure-oriented	People-oriented
Top-down (trickle down)	Bottom-up
One-shot	Long-term and sustainable
Large-scale	Small-scale
Capital-intensive	Labor-intensive
Costly	Cost-effective
Carried out by firms (e.g., construction and trading firms)	Carried out by NGOs

Characteristics of Japanese NGOs

Strengths and Weaknesses of Japanese NGOs

Today, Japanese NGOs enjoy more latitude and influence in ODA policy making than ever before. Several special strengths of Japanese NGOs have won them the support of the public and MOFA. First, their small size and flexible administration allow them to avoid the complex procedures and politics that slow government decisions. While the state bureaucracy takes several years to launch a new program, Japanese NGOs can initiate an operation with greater speed and ease.

A second strength of Japanese NGOs is their good reputation. Most NGO members are highly dedicated to their work, despite low salaries. The public has a dramatically different attitude toward NGO members, who are seen as selfless and sincere, than they do toward politicians and bureaucrats, who have been tainted with corruption scandals. This positive reputation often extends abroad as well. In many Asian nations, Japan is still held in suspicion due to Tokyo's expansionist policies of the first half of the twentieth century, especially during World War II. Japanese NGOs are seen as "Japan-lite," representing Japan but causing less suspicion than might official Japanese political representatives or businesses. Due to their independence from the government, Japanese NGOs can even work in countries that lack diplomatic relations with Tokyo. And almost all NGOs in Japan are either nonreligious or, in a few cases, are affiliated to Buddhist groups (such as Shanti Volunteer Association [SVA], established by Soto Zen Buddhists) or nonmissionary Christian groups. The fact that virtually no NGOs in Japan are affiliated to proselytizing religious groups also eases people's fears in recipient countries.

A third strength, related to the above, are the excellent grassroots ties and involvement of many Japanese NGOs. This stems in part from the people-centered nature of NGO activity. Through hands-on assistance projects, NGOs often work side by side with local people to transfer knowledge, skills, and expertise to the local community. The grassroots approach gives Japanese NGOs a familiarity with the people, their customs, language, and conditions that is unavailable to state officials. The grassroots connections of Japanese NGOs are enhanced by the particular values that permeate many Japanese aid and development organizations, compared for example, to more established, wealthier NGOs in the United States or Europe. Unlike Japanese business or government representatives or Western NGO executives, most of whom wear suits and ties and live in large homes in expensive neighborhoods while on overseas assignment, many Japanese NGO workers prefer an ascetic lifestyle that keeps them close to the poor in developing countries. These Japanese NGO workers tend to wear jeans and t-shirts, eschew their own cars or drivers, and live in modest housing, all of which strengthens their ability to work closely on grassroots projects with the rural poor.

Due to these strengths, the public and the government have come to realize that NGOs have the potential to play a constructive international role in addressing important issues that the government itself cannot adequately address. Yet, Japanese NGOs also have a number of weaknesses that hinder them from fully achieving their goals. First, most of the NGOs have no legal status but instead operate as informal associations or clubs. This lack of legal status prevents them from renting offices in Japan or borrowing money from financial institutions. Individuals in the organizations have to use their own names to rent offices or borrow money, which creates obstacles to establishing and maintaining efficient operations.

A second serious problem faced by many Japanese NGOs is a lack of funds. Government funding totals less than 10 percent of the revenue of most NGO budgets (Japanese NGO Center for International Cooperation, 1998a), and there is very little private sector funding, especially for unincorporated associations. The majority of NGO income necessarily depends on individual donations, membership fees, and sales of publications and other goods. However, these sources of revenue are hampered by the small size of Japanese NGOs, which average 1,560 members, according to a 1998 survey (Japanese NGO Center for International Cooperation, 1998a).[16] Also, since most NGOs are unincorporated, they lack a tax deductibility privilege for contributions they receive (Coalition for Legislation to Support Citizens' Organizations, 1998). Even those recently registered with the state as specified nonprofit activity associations under the 1998 NPO law have not yet been granted any special tax status. Finally, the fact that most Japanese NGOs are relatively young means that they have not had time to build up their operations, staff, and assets.

Consequently, Japanese NGOs are poor. According to a 1998 survey by JANIC, 72 percent of 217 NGO respondents have annual budgets between ¥3 million and ¥50 million (US$25,000–US$416,600), with an average of ¥23.88 million (US$199,000) (Japanese NGO Center for International Cooperation, 1998a).[17] Maintaining an office in Tokyo—much less conducting overseas operations—is difficult on such a small budget. Even the richest Japanese NGOs are much smaller in scale than Western NGOs. For example, in 1996, SVA, the fifth richest Japanese NGO in JANIC's study (see Table 1.3), had only ¥887.67 million (US$7.4 million)[18] (Japanese NGO Center for International Cooperation, 1998a), still miniscule compared to non-Japanese NGOs such as CARE USA (US$340 million in

Table 1.3   Top 20 NGOs with largest annual budget, 1996 (¥ million)

Name of NGO	Budget
1. Plan International Japan (PIJ) [I]	3,903.58
2. OISCA [I]	1,248.47
3. Japanese Organization for International Cooperation in Family Planning (JOICEF) [I]	934.29
4. World Vision Japan (WVJ) [U]	887.67
5. Shanti Volunteer Association (SVA) [U]	715.44
6. Japan International Food for the Hungry (JIFH) [U]	540.16
7. World Wide Fund for Nature Japan (WWF Japan) [I]	504.32
8. Association to Aid Refugees (AAR) [U]	498.86
9. Japan International Volunteer Center (JVC) [I]	407.76
10. National Federation of UNESCO Association in Japan (NFUAJ) [I]	395.88
11. Association of Medical Doctors of Asia (AMDA) [U]	341.16
12. Christian Child Welfare Association International Sponsorship Program (CCWA) [I]	301.62
13. Asian Health Institute (AHI) [I]	291.01
14. Médecins sans Frontières Japan (MSFJ) [U]	243.34
15. Amnesty International Japan (AIJ) [U]	235.79
16. Save the Children Japan (SCJ) [I]	234.90
17. Japan Overseas Christian Medical Cooperative Service (JOCS) [I]	229.19
18. Japan Silver Volunteers (JSV) [I]	223.36
19. Kanagawa Women's Space (MsLA) [U]	206.33
20. Minsai Center [U]	199.78

[I]: Incorporated association. [U]: Unincorporated association.
(Japanese NGO Center for International Cooperation, 1998b)

FY1998) (CARE International, 1999) or Oxfam UK (US$150.49 million in FY1996)[19] (Oxfam, 1997). Only 32 of 217 Japanese NGOs in the JANIC survey had annual budgets exceeding ¥100 million ($833,000)[20] (Japanese NGO Center for International Cooperation, 1998b).

The same JANIC survey identified the richest 20 NGOs in Japan and found that 11 of the richest NGOs in the survey were incorporated, six were Japanese branches of INGOs (i.e., PIJ, WVJ, JIFH, WWF Japan, AIJ, SCJ), and four were Christian organizations (i.e., WVJ, JIFH, CCWA, JOCS) (see Table 1.3). This indicates how difficult it is for the majority of Japanese NGOs—which are indigenous, nonreligious, and unincorporated—to grow in size and budget. The richest ten NGOs accounted for approximately ¥10 billion, approximately 52 percent of the total of the budget of the 217 NGOs in the survey (Japanese NGO Center for International Cooperation, 1998b).

A third problem confronting Japanese NGOs is a lack of qualified personnel. Although the situation is slowly improving, Japanese NGOs have had difficulty recruiting qualified individuals with managerial and technical skills and knowledge of development and economics. The difficulty in recruiting such individuals stems from the low salaries that NGOs provide and the lack of prestige in working for NGOs. Many Japanese admire NGOs—from afar—but they wouldn't want their own relatives to work for them. Qualified individuals tend to seek employment in the more prestigious, better paid corporate or government sectors or intergovernmental organizations (IGOs) such as the United Nations. This situation contrasts sharply with that of many developing countries, such as Cambodia, Indonesia, Egypt, and Palestine, where INGOs may offer salaries and prestige that far surpass that of government posts. Well-established NGOs in Europe and the United States can also offer competitive salaries to highly qualified technical personnel.

The inability of Japanese NGOs to attract and hire qualified personnel hinders their professional development and expansion. Most hire only a handful of paid staff, usually fewer than ten people (Japanese NGO Center for International Cooperation, 1998a), and rely on unpaid volunteers who have no special skills. While necessary for NGO work, volunteers with little knowledge and expertise do not typically provide professional leadership. The majority of Japanese NGOs do not even hire professional accountants but rely on untrained staff to manage finances. Because of the shortage of professional staff, most NGOs lack the ability to get beyond their own projects and microlevel issues. Preoccupied with managing their own work or lacking expertise on broad economic and political issues, many NGOs fail to pursue broader policy issues. They concentrate on small-scale projects but often fail to comprehend the linkage between micro projects and macro policies in target countries or regions. Influencing policy requires careful data collection and analysis, broad knowledge of political and economic development, and mass public relations and campaigning, all of which require skilled professional staff.

NGO Coalitions

One way that Japanese NGOs are trying to overcome their weaknesses is through mutual cooperation and collaboration. The large number of NGO coalitions that have emerged since the late 1980s indicates both the increased activism of Japanese NGOs, which necessitates NGO networking, and also the emerging diversity within the NGO community, which requires a variety of network groups.

In 1987, several Japanese NGOs, mainly unincorporated associations active in international development and aid, established the Japanese NGO Center for International Cooperation (JANIC). The center's main purposes are: (1) to promote networking and collaborative activities among NGOs, (2) to strengthen the institutional capacity of NGOs, (3) to educate Japanese public about the role of NGOs, and (4) to encourage citizens' participation in international aid and development (JANIC, 1997b). To attain these goals, JANIC disseminates information on aid and development, hosts public lectures and symposia, and conducts training sessions for NGO staff and volunteers. JANIC also represents the Japanese NGO community in NGO–MOFA council meetings and in other negotiations with MOFA and ministry officials (see below).

In addition, JANIC works with domestic-oriented NPOs to expand the legal rights of unincorporated associations as a whole. In the mid-1990s, JANIC took a leadership role in forming the Coalition for Legislation to Support Citizens' Organizations (known as "C's") for the establishment of an NPO law to give unincorporated associations an incorporated status and tax exemption. The coalition became active in reviewing diverse legislative proposals for such a law, lobbying politicians and bureaucrats, organizing media briefings, publishing reports on the legislative process, and presenting the coalition's own proposal for the NPO law (Coalition for Legislation to Support Citizens' Organizations, 1998).

As of September 1997, JANIC consisted of more than 50 NGOs and was governed by a board of trustees and a secretary general (Japanese NGO Center for International Cooperation, 1997b; see Table 1.4). JANIC tries to include a wide range of Japanese leftist, centrist, and progovernment NGOs. Independent NGOs in JANIC include JVC, Shapla Neer, and the Services for the Health in Asian and African Regions (SHARE). A well-known moderate NGO in the organization is Shanti Volunteer Association (SVA). NGOs with strong ties to the government include the Association of Medical Doctors of Asia (AMDA) and JOICEF. JANIC promotes coordination and unity among diverse NGOs to present the broadest possible front in negotiating with state officials. Its diversity is seen as a strength by some and as a threat by others, especially by some leaders of progovernment NGOs who dislike the strong leftist influence in JANIC.

To complement JANIC, which oversees NGOs all over Japan, regional NGO coalition groups have emerged in several major Japanese cities. In 1987, the Osaka based Kansai NGO Council was established. The main objectives of this council are to accelerate coordination among NGOs in the Osaka region, conduct advocacy activities to reform ODA policy, educate the public about the importance of NGO

Table 1.4   Key representatives in JANIC, 1997

Managing director/ *Secretary-general*	*Michio Ito (JANIC)*
Trustees	Terumasa Akio (OISCA), Koyu Furusawa (Japan Center for a Sustainable Environment and Society), Tsutomu Hotta (Sawayaka Welfare Foundation), Chanthason Inthavong (Association to Send Picture Books to Lao Children), Sukesada Ito (International Labor Organization)★, Yoshiyuki Kawaguchi (Shapla Neer), Michiya Kumaoka (JVC), Keizo Shibata (Seikatsu Club Kanagawa), Taiji Yamaguchi (CARE Japan), Mikiko Yamazaki (Tokyo Volunteer Center Auditors)

(Japanese NGO Center for International Cooperation, 1997a)
★ ILO is not an NGO but is involved in JANIC.

activities, and encourage public participation in NGOs. The Kansai NGO Council has nearly 30 member NGOs and its activities include offering courses on development and aid (through a program they call "Kansai NGO University"), facilitating information exchange among NGO members, providing training sessions for NGO personnel, and conducting research and investigation (Kansai NGO Council, 1999). Similarly, a Nagoya NGO Center was established in 1995 to promote networking among NGOs in the Nagoya region and advocacy for NGO development. Besides these major regional NGO councils, there are several small-scale regional NGO network groups (with about ten NGO members per group) located in large other cities, including the Kyoto NGO Council, the Kobe NGO Council, and Fukuoka NGO Network (Japanese NGO Center for International Cooperation, 1998a). These regional councils cooperate with each other and with JANIC.

A decade after the creation of JANIC and the Kansai NGO Council, another NGO network group, the Japan Association of NGOs and NPOs (JANAN), was established to facilitate the exchange of ideas, knowledge, and human resources among not only NGOs but also NPOs. JANAN especially encourages the networking of NGOs/NPOs in rural Japan, as many NGOs outside the major cities are isolated and lack sufficient opportunities to exchange information. While JANIC, the Kansai NGO Council, and the Nagoya NGO Center promote coordination among NGOs and advocacy to reform ODA, JANAN, in contrast, attempts to forge friendly relations and promote collaboration on a wider basis among NGOs, the state, the corporate sector, and academia (Sugishita, 1998c). Some conservative NGOs who find JANIC too leftist are active members of JANAN.

Like-minded NGOs have also formed networking groups in relationship to activities in certain countries or sectors. For example, Japanese NGOs working in Cambodia established in 1992 a People's Forum on Cambodia Japan. This network facilitates communication and cooperation among NGOs engaged in humanitarian aid to Cambodia. Also, NGOs concerned with environmental deterioration in the Mekong River Basin in Indochina formed a Mekong Watch Network Japan (hereafter Mekong Watch) in 1994. The group consists of independent NGOs and NGO coalitions such as Japan International Volunteer Center (JVC), the Pacific Asia Resource Center (PARC), and the People's Forum on Cambodia Japan. Other region-based NGO network groups include the Africa Japan Forum, the Japan NGO Network on Indonesia, the Nippon NGO Network for Nepal, and Burma People's Forum. Many issue-based NGO network groups are engaged in environmental protection. For example, People's Forum 2001 Japan was established in 1993 to follow up on issues raised at the 1992 UNCED. Another environmental NGO coalition group is the Japan Tropical Forest Action Network, established in 1987 to promote antideforestation campaigns through documentation, rallies, and press conferences (Honnoki USA, 1992; Japanese NGO Center for International Cooperation, 1998b).

Relations with Foreign NGOs

Japanese NGOs also forge links with their Western and developing country counterparts to address transnational problems related to refugees, the environment, sustainable development, and landmines. In Cambodia, JVC joined forces with Oxfam UK, supporting the latter's rural water supply program in the early 1990s (Cooperation Committee for Cambodia, 1994). In Vietnam, JVC again collaborated closely with Oxfam UK, sending its members to the British NGO for training. JVC has also taken a leadership role in forming and running the Cooperation Committee for Cambodia (CCC), which brings together a wide range of NGOs from developed and developing countries to work toward rehabilitation and reconstruction of Cambodia.

The transnational linkages between Japanese NGOs and non-Japanese NGOs are further exemplified by NGOs from other countries with regional offices in Japan, such as Save the Children, Greenpeace, and Friends of the Earth. These regional offices in Japan maintain close communication channels with their counterparts overseas, acquire necessary skills and information from overseas counterparts, and plan joint programs with other regional chapters throughout the world. For example,

Save the Children Japan (SCJ) has a joint project with its American counterpart in northern Vietnam. This project began in 1995 to improve the health of young children in the region and SCJ and Save the Children USA work in partnership to teach basic concepts of nutrition and health to children and their parents (Sugishita, 1998b). Likewise, Médecins sans Frontières Japan (MSFJ) work closely with Médecins sans Frontières France (MSFF). When MSFJ sends Japanese doctors abroad, they usually join in the French organization's operations (Sugishita, 1998a).

Working with Western NGOs is advantageous to Japanese NGOs, which still lag far behind their Western counterparts in organizational skills and resources. Many Western NGOs maintain large professional staffs and produce extensive, well-researched policy proposals. Due to the shortage of personnel, Japanese NGOs find it beneficial to cooperate with Western NGOs, from which they can acquire necessary information and learn organizational skills.

Many Japanese NGOs also establish partnerships with developing country NGOs, often providing financial and material assistance. Some invite developing country counterparts to Japan for training. Others transfer their own projects in developing countries to local NGOs after the projects are launched and stabilized. Considering local NGOs indispensable to implement projects, many Japanese NGOs work closely with local counterparts through regular meetings or joint projects. Such cooperation is most prominent in Cambodia, where Japanese NGOs interact with Cambodian as well as Western NGOs to promote grassroots development through the aforementioned Cooperation Committee for Cambodia (CCC). Local NGOs are valued for their knowledge of local culture, customs, politics, and contacts, and are helpful for project identification, design, and implementation.

At the same time, some Japanese NGOs (e.g., AMDA), for competitive reasons, are adverse to working with Western NGOs.[21] These Japanese NGOs aim at winning as many contracts as possible from international organizations such as UN agencies, and thus see Western NGOs as competitors rather than partners.[22]

NGOs and Democracy

NGOs have increased in size and strength, formed new coalitions and networks, and redefined their roles and purposes. The emergence of an NGO movement as a player in national policy making thus forces a reconsideration of previous notions of civil society and pluralism within Japanese politics.

A central question regarding Japanese NGOs in this study involves issues of democracy. Do NGOs promote democracy? Does the retreat of the developmental state give political space for NGO activism and essentially help consolidate Japanese democracy? Democracy requires an active civil society, because it is through public discussion and involvement in politics that societal goals are defined. Without wide public involvement in the process, democratic consolidation cannot be achieved. Yet, what is crucial is not only the level of civil society participation in the political process but also the quality of that participation. To scrutinize this point, it is necessary to examine the key functions and features of civil society and NGOs in regard to democracy.

One of the most crucial functions of civil society organizations including NGOs is to act as a counterweight to the state. By checking, monitoring, and publicizing the state's abuses of power or violations of law and mobilizing the general public to protest against the state, civil society organizations can restrain the state's exercise of power and contain corruption. This "checking and limiting" (Diamond, 1999, p. 241) function of civil society is important for consolidating and maintaining democracy in Japan, where the state has generally enjoyed public deference and has been largely free from public scrutiny of its abuses of power. By subjecting state officials to public scrutiny, civil society can control abuses of power, make the state accountable to the public, promote institutional reform, and sustain democracy.

The state and civil society, however, are not locked in to an antagonistic, zero-sum struggle. While civil society organizations criticize state mismanagement or demand the state be accountable to the general public, cooperation between civil society and the state is also possible. As seen in MOFA–NGO relations, such cooperation is increasingly common in Japan. But working with the state requires a balancing act on the part of civil society organizations, between maintaining autonomy and promoting cooperation with the state to pursue shared goals. The danger of co-optation looms large for organizations that move too quickly toward cooperation while failing to guard their independence.

Another important function of civil society is creating channels other than political parties for the articulation and aggregation of interests for political reform. This function is important in Japan, where many people support neither the dominant party LDP nor opposition parties and are thus excluded from formal party channels. By generating opportunities to express popular opinion through informal, nonpartisan mechanisms, civil society can promote broader political participation—an important foundation for democracy. But it is important to remember that civil society does not necessarily pose a threat to political society. Civil society organizations do not replace or substitute for political parties. Rather, they supplement political parties and promote democracy by "stimulating political participation, increasing the political efficacy and skill of democratic citizens, and promoting and appreciation of the obligations as well as the rights of democratic citizenship" (Diamond, 1994, pp. 7–8).

While civil society groups can promote democratic governance, by checking and limiting state power, demanding state accountability, and improving interest articulation, not all civil society organizations necessarily foster democracy. An important concept of democratic civil society concerns autonomy (Brysk, 2000). First, if civil society organizations are not fully autonomous from the state—especially if they become dependent on state subsidies for their operations—they run the risk of being subverted or hijacked by the state to its own agenda. Many Japanese organizations suffer a serious shortage of financial resources and thus seek state funding. If they overzealously pursue financial resources from the state, they are likely to be co-opted or become instruments of state propaganda. This will not only hurt their institutional effectiveness but also do serious harm to the development of civil society. These organizations can aggravate existing patterns of political contestation between the state and civil society (by further strengthening the state) and within civil society itself (by empowering co-opted NGOs and by marginalizing independent NGOs that challenge state authority).

Second, to promote democracy a civil society organization needs to maintain autonomy from an individual leader, founder, or ruling faction as well. If a civil society group is run by a personalized ruler and is subordinate to the whims of his/her own narrow interest, its ability to develop a democratic culture is seriously undermined (Diamond, 1999; Brysk, 2000). Some Japanese organizations are run by personalistic individuals who tend to dominate decision-making processes (Wong, 2001). Although strong leadership is necessary for effective promotion of group interests and goals, this should not be mixed up with undemocratic, particularistic, domineering behavior. To promote democracy, a civil society organization needs to be internally democratic and promote goals and methods broadly shared by its equally treated members.

Another important factor for the promotion of democracy is accountability. Unlike legislators, civil society actors are not elected by popular votes. Thus, a question arises as to whom they represent and to whom they are accountable. Moreover, even if a civic organization can clearly identify its constituents, it still needs to address various issues of accountability, especially as related to organizational funding. For example, many Japanese NGOs are small in scale and lack professional accountants and other professional technical staff to carry out projects. Yet, they have recently started receiving state funding to carry out projects to alleviate poverty in the developing world. With a sudden inflow of state funding, they have become overburdened with new responsibility to monitor an increasing number of projects. As a result, instances of financial mismanagement are on the rise.[23]

Related to accountability is the issue of transparency, another important requirement for deepening democracy. Civic organizations need to provide the general public with information about themselves, including the sources and amounts of organizational funding, types of activities, and internal and external assessments of their programs and projects. While Japanese NGOs often make demands for state transparency regarding Japanese ODA projects, these same NGOs are often secretive about their own activities or funding sources. They are neither subject to outside audits nor do they openly publicize their annual reports. This double standard undermines the legitimacy of NGOs and prevents them from effectively confronting the state for its abuses of power. Democracy requires transparency; civic organizations that refuse to share information do not contribute to democratic consolidation.

As Brysk (2000) argues, democracy depends on democratic civil society. Clearly, if a civil society organization does not value democratic principles or has undemocratic methods to carry out its agenda, it can undermine efforts at democracy. Thus, building an active civil society is not enough. It is also necessary to create a democratic civil society for democratic consolidation.

The following chapters will examine how NGOs interact with state leaders, especially MOFA, and how these NGOs participate in Japanese ODA. By examining their participation in aid within a framework of the broad political economy of Japan—with a focus on changing economic structures, new forces of cultural change, and a new relationship between the state and citizenry—I will address the question of democratic consolidation in Japan.

C H A P T E R   T W O

Globalization and Pluralism

In recent decades, globalization has affected every aspect of Japan's economic, political, and cultural spheres. Forces of globalization—as evidenced by the expanded transnational movement of tangible goods, capital, and people, as well as intangible goods such as norms and ideas—have changed the way Japanese firms operate, the way the state implements economic policy and interacts with the corporate sector, and the way citizens think and act. Moreover, globalization has weakened state authority by eroding the state's ability to manage global trade and movement of capital, thus undermining the ideology of the developmental state (i.e., economic mercantilism). A consequence of these changes has been the creation of new political space for citizens and an altered power balance between the state and civil society.

This chapter examines how processes of globalization have contributed to pluralism on the Japanese aid scene. In particular, it analyzes how processes of globalization have impacted the three main actors in Japanese foreign aid policy making—the state, the corporate sector, and NGOs—and contributed to a weakening of the developmental state and mercantilism in Japanese foreign aid policy. The analysis focuses on three aspects of globalization that have substantially influenced state–civil society relations and Japanese aid policy: the weakening of a developmental alliance of the state and corporate sector as a result of economic globalization, the rise of NGOs due to normative change and skill development of individuals, and change in a normative orientation on the part of state (i.e., Ministry of Foreign Affairs, MOFA) officials.

Economic Transformation and Corporate Failure

> Let's be honest: For the past 50 years Japan was just the most success-
> ful Communist country in history. It was only a matter of time before
> the forces that brought down the Berlin wall and the Soviet Union
> felled the wall around Japan as well. (Friedman, 1999)

For the past decades, forces of globalization have engulfed economic institutions and systems throughout Japan. Most salient economic changes affecting Japan's economic activities include: liberalization of the Japanese economy, polarization of the Japanese economy with super competitive and super weak Japanese firms, and the erosion of the developmental alliance of the state and business sector. These changes have been seen in nearly all aspects of economic life in Japan, and certainly, clearly seen in the area of ODA. The following analysis will focus on the impacts of globalization on the Japanese economy in general and on Japan's ODA in particular. The discussion will demonstrate that globalization has had profound impacts on the Japanese economy, significantly weakening the developmental alliance between the state and the corporate sector: the state can no longer protect Japanese firms in the age of globalization. These changes are manifested in Japanese aid in which the developmental state can no longer adhere to protectionist policies.

Globalization and Japanese Economy

In the processes of globalization, Japanese economy has been gradually but surely liberalized. For instance, in the mid-1980s, Japan eliminated all tariffs on semiconductors and parts of computers. In the 1990s, foreign investments are increasingly welcomed in Japan, primarily in financial sectors but also in manufacturing. Since the collapse of the "bubble economy" in 1991, foreign investment has been occasionally solicited by cash-starved Japanese firms, and foreign management techniques have been sought to accelerate corporate restructuring. For example, the French automaker Renault took a large part of Nissan. GE Capital, AIG, Merrill Lynch, and Goldman, Sachs bought up Japanese financial institutions, strapped for cash and management techniques, and they are now working toward restructuring (Friedman, 1999). Although developmental state regulations and certain commercial practices in the inefficient domestic sectors (e.g., protectionist policies, oligapolistic networks, fixed prices, and cartels) still persist (Carlile & Tilton, 1998), the trend toward liberalization is becoming increasingly irreversible in the age of globalization. The state is now running out of cash to prop up these inefficient sectors that lack international competitiveness as a result of long protection from the state, and the state is losing the ability to protect them by preventing foreign competitors from coming into the Japanese market. With the opening of the domestic market, the state can no longer provide protection to many sectors in Japan but instead is increasingly forced to let them compete with foreign firms. It has become clear that it is a matter of time that these protected sectors would face full competition with foreign businesses in the Japanese market and that market forces, not the state, are going to decide where capital and labor should go in the Japanese market.

In parallel to foreign firms coming into the Japanese market, many more Japanese firms—usually efficient and globally competitive—have left Japan, marking a significant exodus of labor and capital into the global market. More important, the exodus of Japanese firms have contributed to furthering the polarization of Japanese firms: super efficient Japanese firms making substantial profits abroad, and super inefficient ones that remain in Japan and still try to rely on state protection. The 1985 Plaza Accord, which rocketed the value of the yen vis-à-vis the U.S. dollar, triggered the exodus of many Japanese export industries (e.g., automobile, electronic appliances) toward other parts of Asia (e.g., China and Southeast Asia), North America, and Europe. The value of the yen jumped from ¥240 per U.S. dollar at the time of the Plaza Accord in September 1985, to nearly ¥200 per U.S. dollar in just three months after. Furthermore, the yen's appreciation did not stop there. In 1988, the average exchange rate was ¥128 to the dollar, and at one point in 1995 it further rose to ¥90/$1 (Bank of Japan, 1999; Economic Planning Agency, 1999). Given the mounting production costs at home (in the dollar terms due to the appreciation of the yen), it was inevitable for these firms to go abroad, to cut costs and remain competitive on the international market.

While the Plaza Accord was a triggering factor of the exodus of the export industries, it is important to remember that they had already faced problems with the high costs of operating in Japan prior to the Plaza Accord—with high labor costs, political bribes, high entertainment costs, and state regulations. These were the by-products of economic strategies adopted by the developmental state (see Chapter 3). By any account, it became apparent that these developmental strategies were increasingly debilitating the exporting sectors. The Plaza Accord has impelled the already distressed export industries to leave Japan for their own survival. By going abroad, these firms have adopted global market conditions and have undergone internal adjustments to enhance their competitiveness.

As the successful industries began to foster global networks, their interests became diversified. They no longer decide their strategies according to national economic goals, nor do they seek state protection or guidance. The interests of successful, efficient, and global Japanese multinational firms and the interests of the Japanese state do not necessarily converge any more. These industries have begun to see state economic intervention as a nuisance and now act independently of the state. In other words, as Ohmae (1995) points out, the state no longer holds a firm grip on the Japanese economy or on Japanese multinational corporations. Pempel (1998) refers to this phenomena as "regime shift," a shift from "embedded neomercantilism" (p. 15) to more laissez-faire policies in line with global market forces.

These changes—the liberalization of the Japanese economy, the globalization of efficient Japanese firms, and the upcoming struggle of inefficient Japanese firms in competition with foreign firms—indicated that the Japanese state has little room to maneuver in controlling or "guiding" Japanese firms or intervening in the domestic economy. On the one hand, globalized Japanese firms no longer want state protection. On the other hand, the state cannot provide protection to domestic, inefficient firms even though they want such protection, both because the state does not have financial means enough to prop them up and because it cannot prevent the entrance of foreign firms into Japan. One of the most serious consequences of these changes is the erosion of the developmental alliance between the state and the corporate sector. Japanese firms cannot always rely on state protection against foreign competitors. More detailed discussion on these inefficient weak sectors will be done in Chapter 3.

Globalization and ODA

In the case of ODA, market liberalization has clearly been underway, as seen in tendering processes of both types of Japanese aid: loan and grant aid. First, since the 1980s, MOFA has attempted to make tendering for aid loans open to international competition. Today, the majority of Japanese loan aid projects and programs (99 percent) have been open to international competition involving firms from any parts of the world. This means that Japanese firms have to compete with firms from the United States, Europe, East Asian Newly Industrialized Countries (NICs), and developing countries, for loan aid projects and programs. The decrease of the participation of Japanese firms in ODA loan projects, as a result of the untied policy, is staggering. In 1986, Japanese firms won more than 65 percent of OECF project bids under a limited untied aid policy (with the participation of firms from Japan and LDCs). In the mid-1990s, Japanese firms won only 27 percent. They have lost to firms from outside Japan—not only from the United States and Europe, but also from NICs such as South Korea and Taiwan—that could offer lower costs for proposed projects (Ministry of Foreign Affairs, 1997).

Second, while the majority of grant aid projects and programs are tied to the procurement of services and goods from Japanese firms, a practice commonly adopted by other donor governments, Japan has partially opened the grant aid market to foreign firms. In response to *gaiatsu* for a more open aid system, MOFA has recently taken a measure, as in the loan aid, to increasingly open Japan's grant aid market. Foreign firms can now participate partially in untied Development Study (DS) program overseen by the Japan International Cooperation Agency (JICA). The DS program consists of country studies, Master Plans, Feasibility Studies, and other similar reports. Under the new system, foreign participation is allowed as long as it does not exceed 50 percent of the total DS cost (United States Department of Commerce, 1995). In FY 1996, for example, 56 foreign consulting firms were hired for DS. Among these, U.S. firms were the majority (Kidder, 1998). Although this is a limited measure—most grant aid and technical cooperation aid is still tied to Japanese firms—Japanese firms now face competition not only in loan aid but also in some grant aid programs.

It is assumed that Japan's grant aid will follow suit of its loan aid to open the market to foreign competitors due to international pressure, particularly from the Development Assistance Committee (DAC) of the Organization for Economic Cooperation and Development (OECD) and the United States. Since the late 1990s, some DAC member states have been promoting untied policy for grant aid. In 1998, for example, some DAC member states, led by the United States, began to argue that all DAC members adopt untied grant aid policy for capital, infrastructure-based project aid to least-less-developed countries (LLDCs). DAC advocates for untied grant aid policy argue that for the promotion of the 1996 DAC New Development Strategy, a policy based on the sustainable human development paradigm, LLDCs should achieve "ownership" of development. This is to be achieved by learning to determine procurement for their own needs through selecting services and goods in an open competitive market. As of mid-2001, DAC has not ruled that all member donor countries, including Japan, have to untie grant aid. Yet, the fact that DAC members have brought up the issue several times itself indicates a strong possibility of moving toward untied aid policy among donor countries. If DAC decides to adopt untied policy for grant aid, MOFA will be obliged to follow.

Almost all Japanese firms involved in the aid industry are inefficient ones that have been heavily dependent on a closed grant aid market. The Japanese ODA industry consists of three main types: trading companies (*sōgō shosha*), general construction firms (commonly called *zenekon*), and consulting firms. First, trading companies participate in Japan's ODA through the procurement of machinery and other goods. Compared to the other types, these firms are relatively competitive on the international market, but they have recently faced increasing difficulty in winning market shares abroad (*Asahi Shimbun,* 2001a). The key players in this category are six major *sōgō shōsha:* Nissho Iwai, Mitsubishi, Sumitomo, C. Itoh and Co., Marubeni, and Mitsui. Second, construction companies are involved in ODA infrastructure projects and vehemently oppose market liberalization and increase in soft aid. The key construction firms active in ODA are Hazama, Obayashi, Taisei, Shimizu, Toda, Kitano, and Fujita. These firms are also involved in domestic public works and heavily protected by the state. Third, the major consulting firms involved in ODA include Nippon Koei, Pacific International, Sanyu Consultants, and Yachiyo Engineering. Many of the consulting firms belong to quasi-governmental associations, such as the Engineering Consulting Firms Association (ECFA),[1] to promote overseas business activities. Because consulting firms are having great difficulty winning aid bids for intergovernmental organizations such as the World Bank and the Asian Development Bank, these firms are highly dependent on Japanese ODA (especially tied aid). Their major clients are JICA and the Overseas Economic Cooperation Fund (OECF). In 1996, 31.3 percent of the monetary output of the ECFA members (109 firms in total) went to JICA-related projects, and 47.1 percent to developing country governments for projects that were mostly financed by OECF loans (Engineering Consulting Firms Association, 1996/1997).

The participation of Japanese firms in ODA stems from the historical development of Japanese aid. Japanese ODA started with World War II reparations in Southeast Asia, which were designed in part to benefit Japanese firms involved in procurement and infrastructure construction. The dearth of government personnel also explains the scale of Japanese industrial involvement in ODA. Collaboration between the government and the private sector is further encouraged by Japan's "request-base policy" (*yōsei-shugi*), which demands that recipient countries assess their development needs on their own and make requests for ODA to the Japanese government. Many recipient countries lack the knowledge and expertise to measure their own needs, so they rely on Japanese consulting firms to advise them on the kinds of programs they should request from the Japanese government. Many Japanese consulting and trading firms have worked proactively to find and even formulate projects for Japanese aid funding. The practice of identifying and formulating projects to propose for ODA funding is informally known as "seed planting." Seed planting may involve years of advance field research and proposal writing. Some Japanese firms even intentionally submit ODA proposals that they know will be rejected by the Japanese government in the hopes that proposal will be accepted in a second or third attempt later. This means that they put their name to a project to claim ownership of the project later. Although not all Japanese aid projects involve seed planting, the most profitable projects, such as capital-intensive loan projects, do tend to involve this informal practice. Seed planting is frequently criticized by the U.S. government and other donor governments for creating anticompetitive, nontransparent tendering and implementation processes. It is also criticized as putting the cart before the horse, making projects driven by Japanese business needs rather than by the needs of the poor in recipient countries (United States Department of Commerce, 1998). In many cases, Japanese firms themselves formulate an entire proposal on behalf of recipient governments because the latter are often unfamiliar with the Japanese ODA system.[2]

However, Japanese firms have been finding it increasingly difficult to win Japanese aid contracts since the late 1980s, when MOFA adopted an untied loan policy. The major hurdle of Japanese firms in competition with foreign firms in aid bids is the high costs of labor and production in Japan, which has placed Japanese firms in an unfavorable position to win competitive aid contracts. Anxiety among Japanese firms has further increased in the area of grant aid. Japanese firms are particularly apprehensive of the DAC's demand on the Japanese government, since they know that MOFA cannot easily reject foreign pressure (*gaiatsu*) and that, if grant aid becomes untied, they will have difficulty winning grant aid contracts (International Development Journal, 1998f).

The situation for Japanese businesses in the aid industry has further aggravated, as JICA, which is in charge of bidding, began to promote a policy of selecting a contractor based on the proposed cost for a project. This decision, which seems highly rational given shrinking aid budgets (see Chapter 3), has made it difficult for Japanese firms to win profitable grant aid projects. Competition in aid bids has become intense and firms have been pressured to propose low-cost projects. The practice of price destruction (or *danpingu,* "dumping") has become prevalent; companies sell their services at below market value to gain a foothold in the aid and development market. For example, a company may put in a below-cost bid for a contract in Vietnam as a way to gain entry into what is viewed as a country with long-term economic potential. Established Japanese firms facing all-out cost competition complain that JICA should not make the proposed cost the only criterion but should adopt additional criteria, such as the technological sophistication projected in a company's proposal (International Development Journal, 1998c).

The attitude of Japanese firms toward ODA has become ambivalent. On the one hand, many firms unable to undertake aid projects have been drifting away from aid business. They have been forced to reduce the number of their employees specializing in ODA or to leave the aid field. According to Araki (1999), the process from project identification to project implementation usually takes seven to eight years and requires the work of at least five full-time employees. Araki claims that it is too costly for many firms to invest that much time and labor in identifying and formulating projects that may not bear fruit as funded ODA projects.

On the other hand, many firms are still highly interested in grant aid that involves limited foreign competition, knowing that grant aid projects, although much smaller in scale than loan aid projects, often lead to other business opportunities in recipient countries. A representative of Hazama Construction admits that participating in grant aid is valuable in a country in which his firm is not familiar with the local business environment. By participating in ODA, the firm gains an opportunity to learn about tax and other legal systems of the country without risking its business operations because of guarantees of the Japanese government (cited in International Development Journal, 1998k).

The firms that are still interested in Japanese ODA have gone on the offensive against MOFA and their international competitors. Japanese firms have complained vociferously about their failure to win contracts for ODA loan projects because of international competition. They have put much of the blame for their failure on MOFA that tried to meet international standards to open the Japanese aid market. In addition, they have criticized MOFA for shifting the ODA focus from infrastructure to soft aid, arguing that Tokyo should continue prioritizing projects it excels in, like building bridges and power plants (Fujisaki et al., 1996–1997). Lacking expertise in the social development sectors such as education and health, most Japanese firms reject the idea of reducing large-scale economic infrastructure projects (see below).[3]

With these complaints, Japanese firms have begun to lobby against MOFA's aid policy that has shifted toward open bidding systems and increased soft aid. In 1996, Japanese construction firms formed a study group together with Keidanren. The official purpose of this group is to reevaluate the bidding system of Japanese loan aid in order to "improve" the mechanism, which, the group argues, requires a change in the current bidding criteria. The group maintains that the bidders' technological capacity should become one of the main criteria in the selection for a bid (*Asahi Shimbun,* 1997b). The group, however, obviously aimed at excluding firms from developing countries by de-emphasizing costs of given projects, by which Japanese firms fare poorly. A shift of focus from on cost to on technology would favor Japanese firms, since they are technologically more advanced than those of developing countries.

The Japanese private sector has succeeded a few times in pressuring MOFA to create or restart some aid projects favorable to them. In 1997, Japanese firms won a small victory in creating a new loan program that excludes Western firms to participate in. The private sector, in coalition with MITI, succeeded in persuading MOFA to start a new loan aid program based on LDC tied aid, that is, allowing only firms from Japan or developing countries to bid on loan projects and eliminating competition from firms in the United States, Europe, and the NICs. The program makes available environmental loans at 0.75 percent interest. Although the OECD is generally opposed to tied aid policies for loans, it makes exceptions in cases when aid is given on beneficial terms to the recipient country, and the low interest rate of these loans thus allows the project to satisfy OECD guidelines. The new environmental loans are intended to boost Japanese firms' involvement in Japanese aid and to gain support for ODA from the private sector (*Japan Times Weekly International,* 1998b; *Kyodo News International,* 1998).

Japanese firms also have attempted to reverse the trend toward "softnization" of ODA by emphasizing the importance of infrastructure aid. With the help of MITI, the Japanese corporate sector has succeeded in persuading MOFA and MOF, which is against expanding ODA for fiscal reasons, to introduce a special ODA loan program worth ¥600 billion (US$5 billion) to finance infrastructure projects in East Asia for a three-year period as part of rescue plans for the crisis-hit region. This loan aid is especially profitable to Japanese firms because it is virtually tied to Japanese procurement. Under the tied conditions of the loans, Japanese firms have begun to carry out almost all the contract work. Like the low interest environmental aid introduced in 1997, the special loans were concessional in nature, with an 0.75 percent interest rate for a 40-year term, thus they met the OECD guidelines (*International Herald Tribune,* 1998). The Japanese ODA industry achieved another small victory in persuading MOFA to partially resume ODA to Myanmar in 1998, despite strong disapproval from human rights organizations, U.S. and European policy makers, and the Burmese prodemocracy leader Aung San Suu Kyi (*Asahi Shimbun,* 1998c; *Japan Times Weekly International,* 1998a). The aid resumption was to cover emergency repair work at Yangon International Airport (US$19.2 million) as part of a loan project for the expansion that began in 1986 but was suspended in 1988 when the military suppressed prodemocracy demonstrations. Taisei Construction and Marubeni, a major trading house, originally won contracts for the work and have now begun to resume the work. According to the *Nikkei Weekly,* Japanese firms have been urging the Japanese government to fully resume ODA to Myanmar. For example, Iwao Toriumi, president of Marubeni and chairman of Keidanren's Japan–Myanmar Economic Committee, promised Burmese officials that the Japanese private sector would pressure MOFA to fully resume Japan's ODA (*Nikkei Weekly,* 1998e).[4]

In this way Japanese firms have from time to time have succeeded in pressuring MOFA to eliminate foreign competition, create infrastructure-based aid projects, and restart a controversial aid project. However, it is important to emphasize that the private sector has not succeeded in changing the overall trend of Japan's aid promoted by MOFA: more international competition and more soft aid. Although Japanese firms try hard to lobby MOFA, they find it difficult to gain sympathy from the ministry for their needs.[5] In fact, it is becoming increasingly apparent that MOFA and JICA, MOFA's aid implementing agency, are distancing themselves from the corporate sector by ending their support for or tacit approval of the aid practice by the business sector (e.g., *dangō* or price rigging).

MOFA has adopted an incremental liberalization policy, and no longer attempts to protect Japanese industries it once supported during the developmental era. MOFA officials are well aware that tied aid, for example, can bring money back to Japan, but that would tremendously hurt the country's reputation as a generous aid power. MOFA, whose main constituency is foreign governments, does not want to take a risk.

Now that MOFA does not support mercantilist aid policy any more, the only ally in the bureaucracy that the private sector can find is MITI, which is often sympathetic to Japanese firms losing aid bids. Representing the voice of the frustrated Japanese business community, MITI Minister Kaoru Yosano once told the Japan Trade Association that he would like to restart tied aid policy for ODA loans. His speech reflected Japanese firms' deep-rooted resistance to the untied aid policy that is promoted by MOFA (*International Development Journal,* 1998f). Yet, MITI lacks the power and willingness to pressure MOFA enough to reverse the current trends toward untied aid, noninfrastructure projects (i.e., grassroots aid projects), and NGO involvement. This is partly because

MITI has lost much of their clout in the area of ODA in the last decades, reflecting the ministry's overall standing within the government, and partly because the ministry's international bureau now favors liberalization of the Japanese economy.

For decades, Japanese firms in the ODA industry enjoyed nurtured relations with the bureaucracy. However, as the winds of globalization are blustering through Japan, the old-style state-corporate relationships are rapidly unraveling. Although companies are still seeking state protection against international competitors and have achieved a few "successes" in regaining untied aid programs by pressuring the government to eliminate international competition or start tied aid programs, they can no longer rely on bureaucratic protection from MOFA, or even from MITI. Japanese firms are becoming frustrated with the bureaucracy for not providing protection against foreign competitors, but they know that they are fighting a losing battle. Those that aggressively lobby against MOFA are simply hoping to slow the processes of opening aid market or of increasing soft aid, but not expecting they could reverse the whole trends to get back to the "old good days." Thus, state-corporate relations have become increasingly distant, indicative of the erosion of the developmental alliance of the state and the corporate world.

Global Norms, Skill Revolution, and the
Growth of NGOs

Globalization is a multifaceted phenomenon that affects not only economic affairs but also cultural, political, and social matters on both the macro and micro levels. In fact, globalization means a growing interconnectedness throughout the world, with a multiplicity of interactions among individuals, groups, companies, governments, and others, and involving transfer of people, goods, information, intangible ideas, or norms. Indeed, globalization affects every aspect of our lives, including how we think (e.g., the way we see ourselves, our communities, nations, states, and the world) and how we behave (e.g., at the individual and collective levels). Globalization forces are so powerful that they can standardize the way people think and act. In many respects, individuals have been impelled "toward engaging in similar forms of behavior or participating in more encompassing and coherent processes" (Rosenau, 1997, p. 81).

What drives people to act in similar fashions is global norms, or more precisely (1) acquisition of global norms, such as humanitarian responsibility, respect for human rights, the promotion of democracy, freedom from conquest, and ecological protection; and (2) change in normative orientations and behavioral change. Acquisition of global norms takes place through a process of *learning* of new ideas or information, which can generate *knowledge.* The term knowledge refers to "the sum of technical information and of theories about that information which commands sufficient consensus at a given time among interested actors to serve as a guide to public policy designed to achieve some social goal" (E. B. Haas, 1990, pp. 367–368).

Knowledge is powerful because it can lead to new perspectives on a given problem (i.e., change in normative orientation) and to new patterns of behavior. Throughout the world when people learn about human sufferings, environmental destructions, and poverty in other societies, individuals may change their behaviors and practices accordingly. For instance, to contribute to environmental protection, individuals may reevaluate their lifestyle and start recycling or riding a bicycle rather than driving a car. Also, they may organize NGOs to give medical assistance to refugees or people in need across nation-state boundaries. The spread of knowledge and global norms is of critical importance for understanding civil society activism, because with new knowledge and norms, individuals may alter their previous opinions, perceptions of reality, and behavior—without recourse to law or the threat of physical coercion (Wapner, 1996)—and act in aggregated terms to bring about change in governance within their community, society, and state, and even at the global level.

In Japan, cosmopolitan norms such as environmental protection, humanitarian assistance, human rights, and democracy have become more widely accepted. Today, with the advent of satellite dishes, fax machines, and the Internet, the public has had more opportunities to learn about global norms. People have more access to the views of people outside Japan, including the views of social and human rights activists from around the world, and have more opportunities to actually see the lives of people outside Japan than in the past, often receiving vivid television images of mass suffering, starvation, civil war, or human rights abuses. The media messages are often so powerful that they can have a strong impact on individuals. People can learn about suffering in other parts of the world instantaneously and may be spurred to act, challenging their consciousness as human beings. To the Japanese born before World War II, images of war, starvation, and death may remind them of their bitter memories of the war and make them feel empathy toward those suffering now. The generations born after the war ("*senso o shiranai sedai*" or generations that don't know war) may have more overseas experiences than the older generations, through overseas travel, work, and study, and may be more flexible to accept views expressed outside their own country. What seems common among the old and young are increasing appreciation of global norms, such as poverty alleviation, and a growing awareness of their responsibility as world citizens to provide humanitarian support for people, regardless of nationality or citizenship.

Many Japanese NGOs consist of these individuals who have come to embrace various global norms and who feel responsible to contribute to solving global problems. Many NGO members tend to have strong interest in international affairs and are willing to learn new ideas and perspectives from abroad. They have witnessed or heard about, directly or indirectly through the media or publications, dismal poverty and unequal power structures in the developing world, and have come to sympathize with the marginalized in developing societies. Many NGO members have developed a sense of belonging to the global community, rather than just to the family or a parochial community, and have divested themselves of the traditional mentality of *uchi-soto* (insider vs. outsider) that distinguishes the Japanese from non-Japanese. In the past, the Japanese were exclusive toward foreigners and were hesitant to assist them. Today, many NGO members are eager to assist the needy overseas. Clearly these NGO members are not nationalistic, but rather cosmopolitan in orientation due to acquisition of global norms.

Many NGO members not only provide assistance in the developing world but also serve as conduits of global norms in Japan. Through public lectures, workshops, participation in conferences, publications, media appearances, NGOs advocate global norms to individuals who have not learned about them. NGOs provide information about global norms, which can lead to knowledge on the part of the learners.

Yet knowledge, which can bring about changes in normative orientations and behavior, requires individuals to gather, interpret, and evaluate new information or ideas on their own. Individuals who lack these skills have difficulty in generating knowledge and changing normative orientations and behavior.

These skills have been increasingly acquired by individuals throughout the world in the course of globalization, especially due to the development and widening use of technologies. According to Rosenau (1997), individuals have gone through a "skill revolution" in the processes of globalization, which has made them both more analytically competent in assessing events of global and local affairs and more emotionally skillful in applying values, or transnational norms spread by globalization, toward improving the collective welfare of the world. Through the skill revolution, individuals have learned the aggregation of local actions can produce national and global outcomes.

The skill revolution has not only made individuals more analytically and emotionally skillful but also has helped them become better political organizers. In the case of Japanese NGOs, newly acquired skills of NGO members have assisted them in identifying their interests and organizing themselves to pursue them. In particular, they have taken advantage of information technologies to communicate and orchestrate their efforts in aggregate terms. They regularly use the Internet and fax to network among themselves and with foreign NGOs around the world. In a campaign to ban landmines in 1997–1998, for example, Japanese NGOs used the Internet to communicate with the International Campaign to Ban Landmines (ICBL), the key umbrella organization consisting of hundreds of local NGOs that collectively promoted a ban treaty on antipersonnel landmines throughout the 1990s (see Chapter 4). Also, in campaigns for ODA reform, most communications among Japanese NGOs take place via e-mail and fax. The majority of NGOs have publications on the World Wide Web, often in both English and Japanese. Thanks to transnational networks and the use of telecommunications, many NGO members are often more knowledgeable about specific issues and needs in developing countries than Japanese bureaucrats who work in their Tokyo offices and are often out of touch with what is happening at a micro level in the developing world.

In addition, transnational linkages between Japanese NGOs and those overseas are further strengthened by international NGOs with regional offices in Japan, such as Amnesty International, Save the Children, Greenpeace, and Friends of the Earth. These regional offices in Japan maintain close communication channels via the Internet with their counterparts overseas, acquire necessary skills and information from them, and consolidate their efforts together throughout the world.

Finally, and most important, the diffusion of transnational norms and the skill revolution of individuals have enabled people to act less deferential to authority. They have been empowered to challenge, ignore, or circumvent authority and have begun to question traditional Confucian values of hierarchy and group harmony that were considered necessary to promote the national goal of economic development. In the processes of globalization, individual attitudes toward the state and their perception toward their own role in Japan and the world have greatly changed: people have come to realize that individuals have the right to challenge authority and that does not mean selfishness or self-centeredness.

This means that people have begun to shift some of their loyalties from national authority to global nonstate collectivities.

In short, globalization has triggered the rise and growth of Japanese NGOs that serve as a conduit for global norms and values. With their increasing capacity, due to access to information technology and the development of individual and collective skills, Japanese NGOs are now capable of challenging and pressuring the state to broaden its aid agenda to address issues such as environmental protection and poverty alleviation.

Global Norm and MOFA

Globalization affects attitudes and behaviors of not only individuals or NGOs but also state institutions. Japanese state officials, especially those in the Ministry of Foreign Affairs (MOFA) have gone through an important change of attitude toward development issues since the late 1980s. This change is worth discussing in depth, as it is, in my opinion, one of the main reasons that NGOs' influence has increased in aid policy making.

MOFA's attitude change results from acquisition of a global norm, that is acquiring new knowledge through learning at both individual and organizational levels. E. Haas (1990) argues that individuals in an organization can share knowledge with other members in a learning process and, in this way, new consensual knowledge can be transmitted throughout the organization. Based on the observation of individuals affiliated with intergovernmental organizations, E. Haas (1990) notes on organizational learning:

> As members of the organization go through the learning process, it is likely that they will arrive at a *common* understanding of what causes the particular problems of concern. A common understanding of cause is likely to trigger a set of larger meanings about life and nature not previously held in common by the participating members. Put succinctly, learning implies the sharing of larger meanings among those who learn. (p. 24, italics in original)

The knowledge/norm MOFA has acquired in the field of ODA is about a new development paradigm,[6] called sustainable human development. This paradigm was originally developed by a community of economists and foreign aid specialists (or an epistemic community on development)[7] and has been promoted by the international aid regime[8] since the late 1980s (United Nations Development Program, 1995). In this paradigm, foremost priority is given to sustainable development—including human resource development and improvement of health and living conditions—rather than to economic development per se, which would supposedly trickle down benefits to people in need. The new paradigm stresses the importance of grassroots aid and the role of NGOs in providing such assistance to people in the developing world. NGOs are considered indispensable actors in this paradigm because as grassroots organizations they can work closely with people in need and deliver public services to hard-to-reach populations.

Foreign pressure *(gaiatsu)* plays an important role in encouraging MOFA to learn about sustainable human development and innovate and reform Japanese aid programs. The major criticism of Japan's aid was concentrated on the fact that it was too much influenced by a narrow definition of its own economic interests and lacked a clear rationale of giving aid to poor countries. The leading proponent among DAC members of Japanese aid policy change has been the U.S. government (i.e., the State Department and the Agency for International Development, or USAID).[9] Although there was genuine concern for improving the quality of Japanese aid among U.S. aid officials, Congress members felt that Japan was not doing as fair a share as an economic power should, as their aid narrowly focused on economic infrastructure projects. An American policy maker who participated in a comparative study on U.S. and Japanese aid programs on behalf of the U.S. Congress expressed his concern over the strong link between Japanese aid and trade:

> Historically, promoting trade interests has been an important motivating factor behind Japanese assistance, producing a program that provides comparatively great commercial benefits due to its sectoral and geographic concentration. Japanese economic assistance is heavily oriented toward infrastructure projects. Such projects can provide significant commercial benefits, as they tend to require procurement of high value added goods with subsequent need for maintenance and repair, and can open new markets for donor country firms. Also, Japanese assistance is provided primarily to Asian countries, where it reinforces existing Japanese trade relationships. Japan requires recipients to procure significant portions of assistance-financed goods and services in Japan. Certain other aspects of the Japanese system also help to ensure that commercial benefits will accrue to Japan, primarily through a relatively high degree of private sector involvement in development assistance project planning and administration. (United States General Accounting Office, 1990, p. 1)

American aid, largely spent in cash transfers and small-scale projects in health, education, and agriculture, tended to lack a direct commercial orientation and brought relatively limited benefits to American firms. In contrast, about 45 percent of Japanese ODA was spent on economic infrastructure projects in sectors with strong commercial potential, such as energy, transportation, and telecommunications. These capital-intensive projects usually required equipment, machinery, and other industrial goods of significant commercial value, presumably creating "enormous multiplier effects on future private as well as public sector export markets" (Bloch, 1989, p. 63). Moreover, Japanese capital projects usually took place mainly in middle-income countries in Asia, where commercial returns were high. Conversely, Japanese aid has a relatively low level of social-sector assistance (e.g., education, health and population, administration) and program assistance (e.g., balance of payments and structural adjustment support). Since the 1970s, the United States has encouraged other

Table 2.1 Grant share of ODA of DAC countries in 1995–1996

Country	Grant share (%)
Australia	100.0
New Zealand	100.0
Ireland	100.0
Switzerland	100.0
Portugal	100.0
Luxembourg	100.0
Sweden	100.0
The Netherlands	99.8
Norway	99.2
United States	98.4
Finland	97.9
Canada	97.1
Belgium	96.9
United Kingdom	96.7
Denmark	96.6
Italy	94.9
Austria	87.2
France	82.7
Germany	78.6
Spain	71.0
Japan	41.4
DAC Average	76.9

(Ministry of Foreign Affairs, 1999b)
Note: Figures exclude debt relief.

donor governments to reduce linkages between foreign aid and trade promotion. In this effort, the U.S. government has pressed the Japanese government to take more initiative to find solutions to global problems, adopt more soft aid, and increase the percentage of aid available as grants.[10]

Another major criticism of Japan's ODA is focused on Japan's aid philosophy. The Japanese government is frequently criticized for promoting its own top–down development model with strong state leadership in close collaboration with the private sector, and for being harsh on poor aid recipient countries by promoting loan aid (usually used for building economic infrastructure) rather than grant aid (usually used for social welfare) to enforce self-discipline on the recipients. Because of emphasis on loans, Japan's performance is internationally ranked low, as seen in the ranking list of DAC of OECD in terms of quality of aid (measured by grant share and grant element, see Tables 2.1 and 2.2). Because of the focus on economic infrastructure and loans, Tokyo is placed at the

Table 2.2 Grant element of DAC countries in 1995–1996

Country	Grant element (%)
Australia	100.0
New Zealand	100.0
Ireland	100.0
Switzerland	100.0
Luxembourg	100.0
Portugal	100.0
Sweden	100.0
The Netherlands	100.0
Canada	99.6
Norway	99.4
Belgium	99.3
United States	99.3
Italy	98.5
Finland	97.9
United Kingdom	96.7
Denmark	96.6
Austria	93.5
France	91.9
Germany	91.5
Spain	90.8
Japan	80.5
DAC Average	91.8

(Ministry of Foreign Affairs, 1999b)
Note: The grant element indicates the leniency of the terms and conditions of aid. The higher the figure, the more lenient the aid.

bottom of the list (Ministry of Foreign Affairs, 1999b). According to a DAC peer review on Japan, Tokyo's development model cannot be easily replicated in other developing countries:

> Japan's ODA is largely based on the country's own experience. To rebuild its economy after World War II, Japan obtained loans from the World Bank to develop its economic infrastructure and industry, which it punctually repaid. However, at that stage, Japan already had a capacity to use external aid effectively, with a highly literate population, a burgeoning private sector, and a solid national planning system with an effective revenue collection capacity. Unfortunately, these assets are often lacking in today's developing countries, and thus the parallels with Japan's own development after World War II do not apply well in many cases. (Development Assistance Committee of the Organization for Economic Cooperation and Development, 1999)

Japanese officials initially responded to international criticism by claiming that loan aid for building economic infrastructure was valuable as a stimulant for lasting economic growth. They also cited the successes of economic development of Asia, the primary concentration area of Japanese loans for economic infrastructure projects (Hankes, 1993). But gradually, the government's—especially MOFA's—response to foreign criticisms have become more positive.

MOFA, the key player of the aid administration, has undergone the process of learning since the end of the 1980s. It is experiencing a "trial-and-error learning" (P. Haas, 1990), which has resulted not in a radical, fundamental shift in policy but in gradual, incremental changes. The learning process involves the development of new perspectives on aid and the reevaluation of existing ODA policy. MOFA has thus reexamined traditional Japanese aid programs and supplemented them with new types of aid that stress citizens' participation in grassroots projects. The source of MOFA's new knowledge is external: from the international aid regime that emphasizes sustainable human development.

According to E. Haas (1990), "no body of knowledge is ever final and complete" (p. 130); rather, knowledge constantly evolves and changes. In the case of development and aid, the knowledge shared by the international aid regime has constantly changed over the past four decades. For example, in the 1950s, donor governments and international organizations embraced a growth-centered, trickle-down modernization model promoted by Keynesian economists. This model contended that development should be promoted by a government to increase the country's level of industrialization, capital formation, and economic growth. The benefits of economic development were thought to trickle down eventually to the poor in the process of development. In the late 1960s, however, this model was replaced by a basic human needs (BHN) approach. This new approach stressed the importance of the equal distribution of benefits of development, rather than the trickle-down effects (World Bank, 1981). In the 1980s, the BHN approach was itself replaced by a market-led development model proposed by neoliberalists who emphasized the importance of structural adjustments of the economies of developing countries. Under the market-led economic model, massive amounts of structural adjustment loans (SALs) were disbursed by the World Bank and other donor institutions. Finally, the 1990s witnessed the emergence of the sustainable human development model, which emphasizes a holistic approach to development, with a focus on poverty reduction, human resource development, and sustainable economic growth (World Bank, 1992).

An increasing number of MOFA policy makers now genuinely believe that small-scale, labor-intensive aid effectively alleviates poverty in the developing world and that it is the responsibility of Japan, the world's second-largest economy, to provide such aid (Saotome, 1999).[11] These officials acknowledge (unofficially) that the modernization paradigm based on trickle-down economic effects failed to benefit the poor in many developing countries and that it is necessary to provide safety nets for them. The failure of the modernization approach was made clear by the Asian economic crisis of 1997. Despite Japan's provision of massive investment and ODA in some Asian countries that achieved remarkably high GNP growth rates in the 1980s and early 1990s, some of these countries plummeted into poverty following the crisis. Japanese officials seem to have lost some confidence in the applicability of Japan's economic development model. As other donor governments urge Japan to implement more soft aid, MOFA has begun to realize both the limitation of relying solely on hard aid and the increasing necessity to launch a new aid policy based on grassroots perspectives and citizens' participation in ODA. For example, a career MOFA diplomat specializing in African development stressed the importance of grassroots aid to Africa and argued that Japanese NGOs are able to reach local communities more readily than the Japanese government Plent and that they are better suited to offer grassroots aid to the target population (*Nikkei Weekly*, 1999a). His sentiments are widely shared by MOFA officials who have come to realize that grassroots aid through the participation of NGOs is necessary to effectively bring benefits to the poor in recipient countries.

A high-ranking official of the Economic Cooperation Bureau in MOFA states in an interview with a Japanese reporter that:

> The way of thinking of development has been definitely changing throughout the world. ... I think it is very important for Japan to change its aid system and methods to keep abreast of the new mainstream trend in the international aid community. ... In terms of aid philosophy, I also think that Japan should join in the world's main trend of development and take the lead (in the international aid community). (*International Development Journal,* 1991, p. 75; parenthesis added; translation mine)

The change in ideational thinking among some MOFA officials indicates that they have gone through a learning process of acquiring new ideas and values of development. As Japan has become the world's largest aid donor, they have become more aware of what other governments expect of them, have begun to heed the norms and values of the aid regime, and have become more willing to adopt new ways of thinking. In particular, MOFA has increased contact with development specialists in the epistemic community through international conferences and fora on aid and development. Since the early 1990s, MOFA has hosted numerous conferences and fora on aid together with the Foundation for Advanced Studies on International Development (FASID), a MOFA-sponsored think tank established in 1990. Through these conferences MOFA officials have become more exposed to the thinking of the epistemic community.[12]

For MOFA, however, knowledge and norm do not exist in a vacuum, and knowledge or norm by itself cannot be transformed into new policies. Knowledge and norm are used by policy makers to advance their own interests within particular political and social contexts. ODA policy develops within particular sociopolitical contexts, reflecting various perceptions, values, beliefs, and the interests of actors in the aid administration. MOFA tries to utilize new ideas and norms that it finds congruent with its own organizational interests and with its own views of Japan's national interest. Thus, it is necessary to examine how the new knowledge and norm of sustainable human development fit in the contexts surrounding MOFA.

Several points deserve special attention. First, MOFA's acceptance of sustainable human development is linked to the ministry's realization that soft aid can offer new opportunities for the ministry in domestic bureaucratic turf battles. Soft aid is either grant or technical assistance aid[13] under the auspices of MOFA. This means that increases in soft aid can strengthen the ministry's jurisdiction vis-à-vis other ministries, particularly MOF, the main ministry in charge of loan aid, and MITI, the ministry that has strong interest in large-scale capital projects. Also, soft aid also helps MOFA resist ODA budget cuts planned by MOF. Soft aid is labor-intensive and requires much less capital than physical infrastructure aid. Soft aid is thus advantageous for MOFA at a time of aid funding cutbacks determined by MOF. In addition, soft aid with NGO participation in ODA has popular appeal and can thus boost public support for MOFA, rather than other ministries. The demise of the Cold War system has led the public and government officials to view more positively the roles of Japanese NGOs: with the Soviet Union disbanded, Japanese NGOs no longer appear as communist agencies. Instead, they appear as conduits of global norms and justice.[14] Thus, it is advantageous for MOFA to make NGOs an ally and to gain popularity among the public, vis-à-vis other ministries.

Second, the acceptance of sustainable human development is related to MOFA's international ambition. MOFA's ultimate goal in diplomacy is to make Japan an international leader in the areas of aid. Efforts in such arenas as poverty alleviation and human resource development would improve Japan's international image and elevate the country's international standing (see Araki, 1998a). As Schreurs (1996) claims, aid leadership requires a certain degree of conformity to the norms and rules of behavior of the international aid regime. The presence of a strong NGO community, for example, has increasingly become a norm for industrialized states in which NGO representatives are now expected to play an important role in agenda setting, policy formation, and policy evaluation in international development and aid. As a result, MOFA officials have begun to pay attention to the value of the new development paradigm and have been slowly changing Japanese policy to incorporate NGOs into ODA programs.

Third, another MOFA's diplomatic ambition related to the second helps explain why the ministry has accepted the value of sustainable human development. By promoting sustainable human development and exerting aid leadership, MOFA wants to achieve broader foreign policy objectives, including gaining a permanent seat on the UN Security Council. Since Japan does not have military means to exercise influence, ODA is one of the most effective ways to gain a UN permanent seat.

Another related reason for MOFA's acceptance of the sustainable human development paradigm is that the ministry attempts to strengthen Japan's external relations, particularly with the United States. MOFA lacks industry constituents at home and considers foreign governments its key constituents. Having good relations with those governments has a high priority.

Related to MOFA's ambition in international politics is the ministry's deep sense of vulnerability, which accounts for MOFA's willingness to accept international criticism of Japanese aid. Blaker (1993) points out that Japanese policy makers are hampered by "hypersensitivity to any form of anti-Japanese sentiment abroad" (pp. 2–3). As Islam (1991) observes, this sense of acute vulnerability is "totally at odds" (p. 233) with their country's global position and influence. The sense of vulnerability may result from the Japanese defeat in World War II, the subsequent U.S. occupation, and the postwar Japan that was "reduced to the status of pariah in the international community" (Pyle, 1989, p. 50), as well as from the country's heavy dependence on overseas natural resources. MOFA officials' sense of vulnerability is reflected in various official documents that repeatedly stress that Japan is highly dependent on the rest of the international community and has to gain the trust of other countries.[15] The underlying message is that it is important to appease the international community by adjusting aid programs to the standards of the international aid regime. MOFA's "go with the flow" approach to the aid regime derives from the ministry's concern about what other governments perceive the Japanese government's and the ministry's intention to avoid international isolation.

The impact of global norms on MOFA is significant. Based on the sustainable human development paradigm, MOFA has attempted to reform Japanese ODA programs by increasing grassroots aid and by working with NGOs (Ministry of Foreign Affairs, 1999b). MOFA has now begun to experiment with the holistic approach of sustainable human development. Efforts to achieve sustainable human development involve a wide range of policy issues, such as promotion of health and education, sound economic policy, good governance, and a people-centered, grassroots-based approach. MOFA has gradually shown interest in some of these issues.

In summary, MOFA reaches out to NGOs because of the beliefs, values, and goals of the ministry. As MOFA has begun to learn about and adapt the sustainable human development approach, it has wanted to reach out to its natural allies, NGOs, for implementing such an approach. Although mutual distrust still exists—MOFA fears that citizens' groups will erode the ministry's political power, and NGOs fear that the state will control their activities—there has been increasing cooperation and collaboration between the representatives of MOFA and NGOs. Their relationship is not necessarily confrontational or zero-sum in nature. Both sides see advantages in working together. More details on MOFA–NGO relations will be discussed in Chapter 5.

Conclusion

The forces of globalization have had significant impacts on the state, NGOs, and the corporate sector. Globalization has made it increasingly difficult for inefficient Japanese firms, such as those in the ODA industry, to survive in the international market. The state no longer provides protection to Japanese firms against their foreign competitors, and this indicates the erosion of the former state–business alliance.

Globalization has empowered Japanese NGOs. It has made people converge around similar values and norms, such as poverty alleviation, environmental protection, and democracy. More important, people have begun to act collectively based on these norms, believing individual action has aggregated impacts. They also have begun to challenge state authority in violation of these norms.

Globalization has also led to the shifting capabilities of citizens. In the process of globalization, individuals have gone through a skill revolution. Largely due to the advance of communications technology, people have become increasingly more competent in analyzing and evaluating new information and assessing how their behavior can be aggregated into collective outcomes. This means that individuals are not easily deceived by state propagandas and who can be readily mobilized on behalf of goals they fully comprehend. Put differently, civil society actors who have become skilled and learned when and how to engage in collective action, have begun to constrain state elites by demanding appropriate performances and accountability.

Globalization has also impacted the perspectives of state (i.e., MOFA) leaders. MOFA officials have learned a new paradigm of sustainable human development. The ministry's learning has led to change in orientation of aid policy, although the ministry was spurred to adopt and apply new knowledge by its own interest in domestic and international politics.

CHAPTER THREE

Domestic Crises and Pluralism

This chapter examines how the changes brought by globalization—the retreat of the corporate sector, the weakening of the developmental state, and the empowerment of civil society—have been reinforced by the recent crises in Japan. We will examine in detail how these crises have been brought about by Japan's rapid industrialization.

The main argument of this chapter is that Japanese state authority has been seriously weakened due to ill-conceived economic policies and a series of corruption scandals involving state officials and the corporate sector in the late 1980s–2000s. As it has become increasingly clear to the public that the developmental state's economic strategies and practices, established and consolidated during the high growth period of the 1950s–1970s, have outlived their usefulness, people have begun to lose trust in the state. Similarly, due to economic slowdown, inefficiency, and corruption, people's trust in the corporate sector has weakened. As these changes have weakened the developmental alliance of the state and business, a new breed of citizens has emerged. Having grown up in affluence, these citizens refuse the developmental ideology of self-sacrifice and devotion to the national goal of economic development. They have developed postmaterialist values of seeking happiness and meaning outside corporate life. Accordingly, some of these postmaterialists have begun to devote themselves to NGO activities so as to pursue their own vision independent of the nation's economic interests.

Economic Problems and the Erosion of the

Developmental State

Today it seems that the heads of governments may be the last to recognize that they and their ministers have lost the authority over national societies and economies that they used to have. Their command over outcomes is not what it used to be. ... Popular contempt for ministers and for the head of state has grown in most of the capitalist countries. (Strange, 1996, p. 3)

At the beginning of the new millennium, Japan faces profound economic crises. There are two major problems that the country faces: prolonged economic recession that started with the burst of the "bubble" economy and growing fiscal deficits that have aggravated since the early 1990s. Since state officials are incapable of solving these problems—the problems that they have actually created themselves in the process of industrialization—public frustration with the state, especially the bureaucracy, has mounted. By examining both the issues of recession and fiscal deficits, we will analyze how they have impacted state authority.

Recession after the Bubble Economy

According to Katz (1998), the Japanese developmental state is a "system that soured" (p. 21). In the past, many developmental state policies (e.g., a variety of so-called administrative guidance and massive subsidies to strategic industries) were indeed great successes. These policies worked brilliantly to bring prosperity to the Japanese people in just a few decades. Japan's rapid economic growth from the 1950s to the early 1970s was, indeed, a "miracle" (Johnson, 1982, p. 3). During the 1960s, for example, the expansion of the price-adjusted gross domestic product (GDP) averaged a gigantic 10.1 percent a year (Ostrom, 2000). This miracle, however, did not last. By the 1970s, the Japanese economy had fully matured, and Japan's developmental state strategies became counterproductive to future economic development. In the 1970s, real GDP increased at a 4.4 percent annually (Ostrom, 2000). Although Japan recovered from the oil crises relatively quickly, it no longer enjoyed two-digit growth rates after 1973, when the first oil crisis took place. In the 1980s, GDP rates further declined to an average of about 4 percent a year, a rate still higher than that of other industrial economies (Ostrom, 2000). But following the collapse of the bubble economy, which began in 1990 with the fall of stock and land prices, Japan's growth rate has hovered around zero. The Japanese economy became far more sluggish than those of other industrial countries, especially compared to the United States in the late 1990s. Today, Japan is facing the longest recession in the postwar era. Japanese financial institutions are burdened with bad loans totaling at least ¥32 trillion (US$266 billion; Schoppa, 2001). The Japanese stock market has sunk to its lowest since 1984. Analysts have started calling the 1990s "the lost decade" for Japan, a term first used to characterize the 1980s economic slowdown of Latin America. Without a doubt, the Japanese economy has turned in chronically ill, with no improvement in sight (Anchordoguy, 2001).

The economic recession that started in the 1990s has made evident that developmental state policies no longer serve their purpose. The recession has demonstrated the obsolete, increasingly irrelevant role of the state in guiding and protecting inefficient but well-connected corporate sectors. Tokyo's economic landscape has been dominated by legal and illegal cartels, import restrictions, easy bank loans and state subsidies to inefficient sectors, and other interventionist practices of the high-growth era of the 1950s and 1960s. But the positive role of these practices disappeared long ago, and, despite early signs of economic problems, the government, especially the Ministry of International Trade and Industry (MITI), has not fully reversed its protectionist policy, nor has it promoted deregulation. State protection of inefficient industries from foreign competition (through cartels and regulation of market entry) has debilitated Japan. Katz (1998) explains how MITI harbored cartels and excluded foreign competition:

> In industry after industry, MITI formed so-called recession cartels under a series of laws in the 1970s and 1980s. These cartels allowed MITI (or another Ministry depending upon the industry) and the relevant Industry Association to coordinate prices, production levels, capacity reduction, investment and modernization plans and, covertly, to limit imports. Thousands of these cartels in dozens of industries have come and gone—often several times within the same industry. (pp. 170–171)

One of the most serious problems of these cartels was the reinforcement of inefficiency. Cartels established certain minimum prices that all member firms needed to adhere to so that they could maintain their profits. However, overcapacity—caused by insufficient demands due to high prices maintained by cartels—exerted downward pressure on prices, and therefore cartels were often obliged to come up with a plan to reduce output and capacity. Thus, they planned a reduction in production or capacity aimed at stopping prices falling below the level at which member firms could maintain profits. In the name of egalitarianism, or the so-called convoy system (*gosōsendan-shiki*), all cartel member companies were obliged to make cuts according to their share of the market or their share of capacity. To help out the weakest, however, the stronger companies were forced to take an extra-large cut by MITI and/or industry associations. The result of the cartel system was the protection of weak firms at the expense of strong firms. The weak expected a government bailout at times of economic downturn and thus did not attempt to improve (Katz, 1998).

One may wonder why some firms did not resist cartels and pursue maximum profits without restrictions. Japanese cartels existed across industry lines, which restricted an individual firm's freedom to act not only within its own cartel but also in dealing with a business partner in another cartel. For example, why did a construction company continue to buy expensive Japanese cement if it could get the same product from abroad at a much cheaper rate (below the cartel price)? This is because MITI and interlinked trade or industry associations representing the construction and cement businesses kept their association members in line by threatening to restrict supplies from other sources. For instance, steel companies would refuse to sell their products to a construction company that bought foreign cement. Similarly, an automobile firm would not buy cheap foreign steel or glass because of fear of retaliation from industry associations. This agreement of refusal to deal with "cheaters" was the main power that kept the cartels intact. In addition, firms faced not only punishment from other firms but also fines and other penalties imposed by MITI (or other relevant ministries; Katz, 1998; Tilton, 1996).

Indeed, the protection of inefficient firms was the fundamental problem of the Japanese economy. While MITI initially succeeded in selecting strategic industries (up until the early 1970s), it was never good at phasing out sunset industries. For example, many declining industries such as coal, agriculture, and cotton textiles resisted downsizing, and MITI was not able to force them to exit. The problem became more serious in the 1980s and 1990s, when MITI failed at both phasing out declining industries and phasing in the right industries. By assisting the wrong kinds of industries, the government wasted enormous amounts of money. For example, Callon (1997) argues that in the 1980s MITI poured resources down the drain by unsuccessfully promoting key high-tech projects, particularly fifth-generation computers, supercomputers, and artificial intelligence.

The failures of MITI to phase industries in and out are indicative of the ministry's growing inability to guide the Japanese economy.

As discussed in Chapter 2, the Japanese economy eventually turned into a dual economy as a result of the state-led industrialization: one of strong exporting industries and the other of weak, domestic sectors. While efficient exporters eventually got out of domestic cartels and other costly regulations, went offshore to cut costs, and "hollowed out" Japan, inefficient sectors remained in the country. During the time of Japan's high growth (until the first oil crisis of 1973), efficient exporters earned enough to prop up weak domestic industries. Although these successful exporting firms, such as automobile companies paid high prices to domestic suppliers for goods such as glass, rubber, and basic steel, they still remained in Japan while trying to cut costs. By the late 1980s, however, Japan's growth had slowed down and the exporting firms had found it increasingly difficult to bear the burden. They faced the high costs at home and the rising yen caused by the Plaza Accord, which made it harder to pass on the costs in export markets. As a result, efficient export sectors moved overseas, the productivity of the entire economy was dragged down, and the Japanese economy stagnated. The inefficient, domestic-oriented sectors that were long protected by the developmental state started clogging the arteries of the Japanese economy (Pempel, 1998; Katz, 1998; Ohmae, 1995; Schoppa, 2001).

Japan's economic problems confound not only the manufacturing sectors. Banking was also part of the "convoy" system in which state regulations of prices and products preserved the profitability of the weakest link. No bank was forced to fold during the developmental era. In fact, until the end of the 1990s, Japanese banks were under government protection from failure. Furthermore, banks were pressured by MOF and the ruling Liberal Democratic Party (LDP) to support weak but politically well-connected firms, such as construction firms and agricultural cooperatives.

Like MITI, MOF's failure in appropriately managing Japanese firms (i.e., financial institutions) has seriously affected the Japanese economy. It is generally agreed that MOF was responsible for managing monetary policy throughout Japan's postwar development via the Bank of Japan (BOJ) and that MOF pressured BOJ to keep interest rates too low for too long, contributing to the enormous asset overvaluation (bubble economy) of the late 1980s. Then when MOF/BOJ finally increased interest rates and the economy subsequently collapsed, MOF was responsible for not letting interest rates fall quickly enough to stimulate an economic recovery. MOF also blundered several years after the bursting of the bubble.

From 1992 to 1995, Japan's economy grew at an average of only 0.6 percent. The Japanese economy finally began to recover in 1996, due to temporary fiscal policies, such as a cut in income tax. Then, in April 1997, MOF's Budget Bureau, preoccupied with minimizing government spending and reducing the national debt, rushed to end the income tax cut, increased the nationwide sales tax from 3 to 5 percent, and raised other government fees. These ill-timed changes cut off an incipient recovery, further damaged the economy, and shrank Japan's GDP by 2.5 percent (Lincoln, 1998). Consumer demand dropped immediately as a result, and the economy stagnated again. Corporate bankruptcies increased, and the unemployment rate reached a record high of 5 percent (see *Nikkei Weekly*, 1999e). Worse, MOF temporarily nationalized and later recapitalized debt-burdened banks such as the failed Long Term Credit Bank of Japan and used tax payers' money (BOJ emergency loans) to keep credit flowing to failing small businesses. MOF also sought to protect a number of other financial institutions facing bankruptcy, even extremely weak ones, because it feared the consequences of large-scale bankruptcy. MOF found itself under public attack for pursuing a convoy system or "financial socialism" (Stockwin, 1999, p. 188) by which it protected weak institutions along with the strong.

The decline of bureaucratic authority has paralleled the downfall of the Japanese economy. The bureaucracy has lost people's confidence by badly mismanaging the economy for more than a decade. The public has targeted its anger at the bureaucracy, especially at MOF, for its failure to effectively manage the economy and its attempt to shield failing banks from the ill effects of the nation's soured economy. MITI has also come under strong criticism for pursuing a convoy formula to keep weak institutions that retarded efficiency in the Japanese market, a problem that the ministry was well aware of but that it hardly has done anything to remedy. Popular contempt for the bureaucracy has grown. The economic recession has raised public demands for effective governance.

Fiscal Crisis

Related to the economic slowdown is mounting fiscal deficits in Tokyo. In the late 1990s–2000s, the Japanese government recorded its worst fiscal deficit in history. In 1996, Japan's deficit spending (by central and local governments) stood at 7.4 percent of the country's gross domestic product (GDP), a level that the Organization for Economic Cooperation and Development (OECD) describes as unsustainable. Debt-servicing costs accounted for 21.8 percent of the initial fiscal year 1996 budget, which was more than the government's allocation for education, science, and defense combined (*Economist,* 1997; *Japan Times Weekly International,* 1996). Even more noteworthy, Japan's gross debt-to-GDP ratio reached nearly 100 percent in 1997 (*Forbes Global,* 1998) and reached almost 130 percent in 1999 (Katz, 1999). These figures were by far the worst of any of the countries in the G-7 nations.

Japan's fiscal predicament of the 1990s–2000s stemmed from state policies of the 1970s. The developmental state at that time had to deal with political discontent arising from declining economic growth in the wake of the first oil crisis and changing demographic trends. Due to the oil crisis and subsequent economic slowdown, traditional strong supporters of the developmental state such as small shopkeepers, small businesses, and farmers began to oppose the state, especially the LDP, and to support opposition parties. Similarly, as a result of industrialization and urbanization, more people became detached from traditional LDP links (concentrated in the countryside) and began to support opposition parties. The response by the state to these changes was to extend subsidies and other financial assistance to people. The state, under the guidance of MOF and the LDP, provided cheap credit for small businesses, special taxation in favor of small businesses, increased public works for construction firms, and financial subsidies to farmers. For urban dwellers, the state gave improved health insurance, social security, education, and new infrastructure such as bullet trains (Katz, 1998; Pempel, 1998).

In the 1990s, the fiscal problems were further aggravated by a prolonged economic recession. There were two main overlapping sources of the fiscal problems: increasing social welfare-related expenditures due to the economic downturn, and declining revenues from personal and corporate income taxes as a result of the negative impact of the recession on personal incomes and business profits (Alexander, 1998). The fiscal balance worsened further following 1998, when the government expanded its budget with massive spending on public works while cutting taxes to stimulate the ailing economy.

Due to the prolonged recession and worsening deficits, the Japanese people have become pessimistic about their future. According to an *Asahi Shimbun* survey at the end of 1998, 63 percent of respondents feared they could not rely on government services and pensions after retirement. Seventy percent said that they did not trust the Japanese political system, and 90 percent said that their country would need some sort of political and economic reforms (*Asahi Shimbun Online,* 1999).

The budget deficit crisis has had a significant impact on Japanese ODA. With the public increasingly pessimistic about government solvency, calls

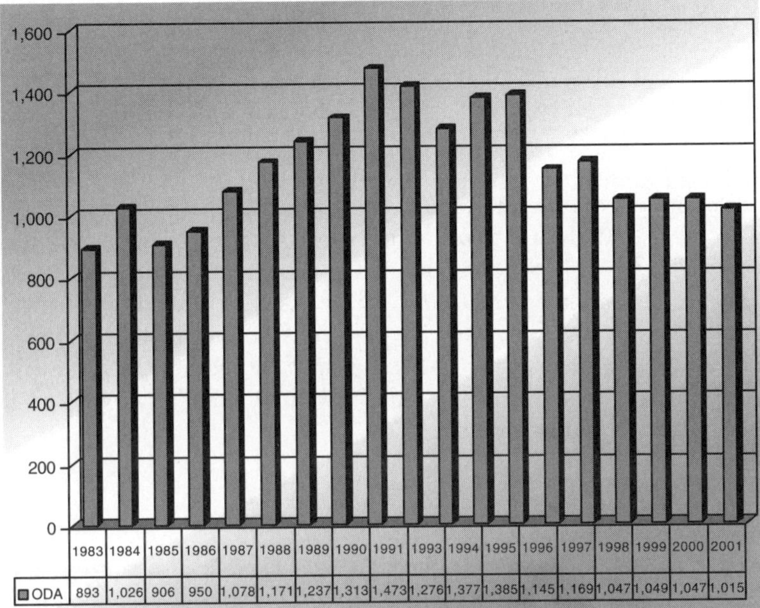

ODA	893	1,026	906	950	1,078	1,171	1,237	1,313	1,473	1,276	1,377	1,385	1,145	1,169	1,047	1,049	1,047	1,015
	1983	1984	1985	1986	1987	1988	1989	1990	1991	1993	1994	1995	1996	1997	1998	1999	2000	2001

Figure 3.1   ODA budget in Yen – 1983 to 2001 (¥ billion)
(Ministry of Foreign Affairs, 1995b; Ministry of Foreign Affairs, 1996c; Ministry of Foreign Affairs, 1997; Ministry of Foreign Affairs, 1998; Ministry of Foreign Affairs, 1999b; Ministry of Foreign Affairs, 2000c; Ministry of Finance, 2001).

from MOF and politicians for aid budget reductions have begun to gain support in the public (see *Nikkei Weekly,* 1997b; see Figure 3.1). Politicians joined MOF in efforts to cut down on ODA budgets, because aid does not lead to votes (*International Development Journal,* 1998e; *International Development Journal,* 1999g; see *International Development Journal,* 1999i). The Ministry of Foreign Affairs (MOFA), in particular, has been criticized for allegedly wasteful aid projects that are not benefiting the people in aid recipient countries. With disclosure of ODA corruption cases by the media (see below), public confidence in MOFA and traditional ODA practices (e.g., *dangō* or rigging, cartel, state-corporate collusion, exclusion of foreign competition) has waned. At the same time, the public has begun to ask the government to cut down on the number of expensive, large-scale infrastructure projects and increase the number of small-scale, cost-effective grassroots projects that would involve NGOs (*Nikkei Weekly,* 1997a; *Nikkei Weekly,* 1997c; see *Nikkei Weekly,* 1996; *International Development Journal,* 1998a; *International Development Journal,*

1998i; *International Development Journal,* 1999j; *International Development Journal,* 1999f).

Corruption and the Erosion of the

Developmental State

Public confidence in the developmental state was further undermined in the late 1980s–2000s due to widespread corruption among political and economic leaders. In particular, a series of recent corruption scandals has had a serious impact on the authority of the developmental alliance of the LDP, the bureaucracy, and the corporate sector. In this section we will examine the involvement of these actors in corruption scandals in general and specifically in ODA, and how these scandals have impacted Japanese politics and aid policy.

Corruption and the Fall of the LDP

The problem of corruption in Japan is closely linked to the extraordinary level of cooperation between business and the developmental state in pursuing the shared goals of economic development and prosperity. As mentioned in Chapter 1, three-way ties have developed among the corporate sector, the bureaucracy that regulates business, and the LDP that represents business interests. Politicians and civil servants regarded corporate Japan as the engine of the economy and worked closely with firms to ensure their strength and protect their interests over those of workers, consumers, or other stakeholders in the system (Farrell, 1999). Until recently the government not only offered protection from foreign competitors but also provided subsidies, tax breaks, and other forms of assistance, particularly to industries that the state, especially MITI, had decided would be "winners" in world trade. Thus, in Japan, business and the state became allies rather than adversaries, and corruption became an integral part of the iron triangle relationships of the politicians, bureaucrats, and business (Wanner, 2000). In the iron triangle, corporate bribery went in two directions: to probusiness politicians, especially those in the LDP, and to ministry officials who dominated decision-making processes. I will focus on corruption cases involving LDP politicians here and will discuss cases involving bureaucrats in the following section in the chapter.

Bribery (campaign contributions and other benefits such as golf outings and entertainment fees) from business to LDP members worked for both parties. First, Japanese politicians needed large sums of campaign money because of a competitive electoral system. Up until 1994, the Japanese House of Representatives was based on medium-sized multi-member districts. In this system, voters could cast their ballots for only one candidate, but there were multiple winners in each district. Thus, the LDP often had several candidates running against each another in the same districts, which intensified competition among the factions. This candidate-centered election campaign required great sums of political funds for each faction, whose leaders often resorted to illegal fundraising with the assistance of the corporate sector. Second, business has needed political help to reflect corporate interests in economic policies. Business representatives have used politicians, especially probusiness LDP *zoku-giin* (policy "tribes") who have developed a specialized knowledge of the affairs of a particular ministry, to press their case with the ministry. With Japanese bureaucrats controlling the economy, business representatives have enlisted the *zoku-giin* to lobby the bureaucracy by providing the *zoku-giin* with cash gifts and other amenities (e.g., costs related to weddings and funerals). In these cases, the *zoku-giin* has served as a go-between (Wanner, 2000).

The cozy relationship between the LDP and business has bred corruption, as evidenced by a series of political scandals in the late 1980s–1990s. The first scandal case that deeply affected the Japanese political environments of the 1990s was the 1988 Recruit scandal, in which Recruit Corporation, an information-industry company, bribed dozens of politicians and bureaucrats in the ruling LDP, opposition parties, and high-ranking bureaucrats. These cases exposed unethical and illegal behavior of business leaders, politicians, and elite bureaucrats, deepening public discontent with the present politico-economic system in Japan. Eventually, the Recruit scandal so enraged the public that voters retaliated against the LDP in the 1989 upper house elections. As a result, the scandal directly terminated LDP Noboru Takeshita's prime ministership and forced his finance minister Kiichi Miyazawa (of the LDP) to accept responsibility for the debacle and resign.

Wrongdoings by Japan's political and economic leaders undoubtedly existed prior to the 1990s. "Money politics" had developed in Japan in the 1970s under the rule of Prime Minister Kakuei Tanaka of the LDP, who was arrested after his term of prime ministership (1972–1974) with a charge of receiving bribes from the Lockheed Aircraft Corp in the United States. The Japanese public has previously been aware of illegal money-raising activities of politicians who kept close ties with big businesses.

Yet, what distinguishes new scandals from the old is the aggravation of money politics and the impact of such scandals on the domestic political scene. The 1992 Sagawa Kyubin (trucking firm) scandal is a case in point. This scandal became the catalyst for the LDP's devastating losses in the 1993 lower house elections, the subsequent step-down of the LDP as a ruling party, and the demise of Japan's so-called '55 system (*gojūgo-nen taisei*), which had lasted without interruption for 38 years from 1955. The '55 system was dominated by the LDP, which held political power at the national level continuously from the founding of the party in 1955 until 1993. In the Sagawa scandal, Shin Kanemaru, LDP vice president and a powerful *zoku-giin* with strong ties to the corporate sector, was arrested in 1993 and charged with receiving a payoff of some ¥500 million from a trucking firm that was seeking special treatment from transport regulators.

Japanese voters lashed out at the LDP following the Sagawa scandal. With the economy showing signs of serious problems in the early 1990s, the Sagawa case reinforced the growing perception that the LDP was out of touch with the economic realities of the average Japanese. The corporate sector was trying to fill the pockets of key political figures to secure certain benefits, and politicians were hoping to accumulate money to increase power, even at the cost of the economy. Not surprisingly, worried Japanese people began to see the iron triangle as an unfair arrangement that hurt the economy (Wanner, 2000).

Since the collapse of the '55 system in 1993, Japanese politics has been in flux, with the creation of many new parties and constant alignment of politicians. In 1993, Morihito Hosokawa of the Japan New Party, in a coalition of seven parties, became Japan's first non-LDP prime minister since 1955. Although the LDP returned to power shortly thereafter in coalition with the Socialists (their Cold War foe) and the small conservative party Sakigake, the LDP's influence had declined, ending the era of stable one-party rule in Japan.

The end of the '55 system also had significant implications for the developmental state, since it weakened the relationship between the state and the corporate sector. With the weakening of the LDP power base, the corporate sector no longer has a strong political ally to pressure the bureaucracy as it used to, and business contributions to the political world have sagged (Wanner, 2000).

Furthermore, the collapse of the '55 system showed how people had lost confidence in the infallibility of the iron triangle. In the past, the Japanese people tolerated corrupt behavior by politicians and business leaders as an unavoidable side effect of Japan's rapid economic growth.

Politicians received bribes from private firms in exchange for political assistance to increase profits. Thus, people tended to think that political bribes were a necessary element of corporate prosperity. However, with the worsening economy, people have come to realize that overly close state–business relations can in fact harm the long-term interests of their country.

Bureaucratic Corruption

A series of corruption scandals in the 1980s–2000s involving bureaucrats—including the 1988 Recruit scandal, the 1995 *jūsen* (housing loan firms) bailout, the 1996 HIV-tainted blood scandal, and the 2001 diplomatic funds scandal (see below)—infuriated the public and triggered bureaucracy bashing in Japan. These cases revealed the pervasiveness of "structural corruption," involving not only politicians and big businesses but also bureaucrats in powerful ministries (*Nikkei Weekly*, 1998f). In the past, the public distinguished bureaucrats from politicians and big businesses, with the former considered untainted by corruption. Civil servants' long-held reputation for selfless devotion to Japan's economic development brought them power and prestige. However, the status of elite bureaucrats substantially declined in the 1990s. The Recruit scandal resulted in the arrests for corruption of two high-ranking civil servants, former vice minister of the Ministry of Labor Takashi Kato and former vice minister of Education Kunio Takaishi. The public began to take bureaucratic corruption seriously, witnessed by frequent citizens' letters to newspapers, media reports on public discontent, and seminars and conferences on corruption issues (Inoguchi, 1997).

Since the Recruit case, subsequent allegations of corruption have continued to taint the once highly respected bureaucracy, affecting virtually every bureaucratic agency and especially MOF, the Ministry of Health and Welfare (MOHW), and MOFA. MOF, the most powerful and prestigious ministry in Japan, became seriously mired in scandals. In the 1995 *jūsen* housing loan scandal, MOF and MAFF became the targets of intense public criticism due to the harmful impact of the business–bureaucracy collusion on Japan's ailing economy. During the bubble years of the late 1980s, *jūsen* (housing loan) institutions, all established in the 1970s by parent banks with MOF's backing to provide loans to home buyers, lent huge sums of loans not to home buyers but to shady real estate speculators, many of whom were linked to the *yakuza* (Japanese gangsters). After the real estate market crashed in 1990, these housing loan institutions were left holding bad loans of at least about US$80 billion.

MOF, supported by the Ministry of Agriculture, Forestry, and Fisheries (MAFF), spent approximately US$6.85 billion of tax money to save these bankrupt institutions, because, in the public's view, these institutions provided top posts (*amakudari*) to retired MOF and MAFF officials (Inoguchi, 1997). The housing loan institutions were only partially bailed out (with the US$6.85 billion public money) and there was broad agreement among economists that the government would have to spend billions of dollars more to write off loans to restore the system to health. The *jūsen* bailout enraged Japanese people who felt that they were being forced to take financial responsibility for the mismanagement of private firms with links to gangsters. The public criticized MOF for leaving the defunct institutions alone and merely hoping that eventual economic upturn would solve the problems.

On another occasion in 1998, two MOF officials were arrested for bribery in a scandal that eventually forced minister of Finance Hiroshi Mitsuzuka to resign. In the same year, MOF took action (e.g., forced resignations, reductions of salary, written or oral warnings) against 112 of its own bureaucrats for inappropriate behavior in dealing with financial institutions in Japan. Among those reprimanded was a MOF official heading the General Affairs Bureau within the Overseas Economic Cooperation Fund (OECF), the former Japanese ODA loan agency (*Asahi Shimbun*, 1998e).

As the public learned in 1996, bureaucratic corruption had also spread to MOHW in a serious and deadly manner. Citizens found that MOHW had permitted the sale and use of HIV-contaminated blood by pharmaceutical firms for blood transfusions for hemophiliac patients, even though these officials were aware of the potential danger. Fearing the impact on domestic pharmaceutical firms, with which it had close relations, MOHW chose not to import heated blood products in the 1980s, thereby exposing patients to potentially infected blood. The consequence was fatal. About two thousand people, mostly hemophiliacs, had been infected with HIV via blood products from domestic suppliers in the 1980s. More than four hundred of them have since died (Inoguchi, 1997). Following this scandal, public disgust with and mistrust of the bureaucracy have reached to an unprecedented level.

In 2000–2001, scandals involving officials in MOFA, a ministry that had not previously been seriously tainted by corruption scandals, came to the surface. Several MOFA officials were arrested or reprimanded on charges of fraud, embezzlement, or bill-padding. These incidents have seriously hurt the reputation of the ministry, once revered as a prestigious organization of elite diplomats. In one case, a MOFA official was arrested for embezzling discretionary diplomatic funds worth more than ¥500 millions (*Mainichi Daily News,* 2001b). Another case involved a Japanese consul in Denver who embezzled several millions of yen to lead an extravagant life in the United States (*Mainichi Daily News,* 2001a). In other cases, MOFA officials embezzled tens of millions of yen from state coffers by padding bills for hired cars or hotel accommodations in Japan. To the embarrassment of the ministry, some of these officials allegedly entertained their mistresses in hotels at the taxpayers' expense (*Japan Times Online,* 2001b; *Japan Times Online,* 2001c). When the first scandal case involving secret diplomatic funds was revealed, MOFA denied organizational complicity, asserting that it had been caused by a single individual. However, when several other fraud cases were disclosed, the ministry was forced to admit that corruption was endemic, involving approximately 30 divisions within the ministry (Johnson, 2001; *Japan Times Online,* 2001a; *Japan Times Online,* 2001c; *Asahi Shimbun,* 2001b). Media reports revealed the depth and breadth of corruption in MOFA, indicating that ministry officials think nothing of using official funds for purposes that have little to do with their work. According to some report, MOFA diplomats proficiency at embezzlement of public funds leads to career success, especially for noncareer officials (who did not take the diplomatic I-class exam and are thus treated as the second–class diplomats within MOFA). As one diplomat explained, "(t)he more a non-career official can squeeze cash through unofficial channels for high-ranking officials to spend freely … the more likely it is for that person to be promoted" (quoted in Johnson, 2001, p. 1). These revelations of fraud stunned the public and gravely tarnished MOFA, which has become the subject of media and public mockery.

In the field of ODA, numerous corruption and mismanagement cases have been disclosed. While the majority of them have involved Japanese corporations and recipient government officials, some have also involved Japanese bureaucrats. Although these are usually small-scale, seemingly trivial cases (e.g., an official of the Japan International Cooperation Agency, JICA, arrested in 1986 for receiving a bribe from a Japanese consultant), the fact that the bureaucracy fails to properly use taxpayers' money for foreign aid has raised public suspicion toward the bureaucracy. Also, many cases of bureaucratic mismanagement of ODA involve intraministerial wrangling for power, leading the public to believe that aid is used by officials merely to increase their own power within the bureaucracy and that these officials care little about assisting people in developing countries. An incident involving the World Bank's Japan Special Fund (JSF) scholarship is a case in point. The JSF was established by the Japanese government in 1987 to provide scholarships to people in the developing world for overseas study and training. Although the main recipients designated of this MOF-managed fund were officials in developing countries, a small quota was allocated for Japanese individuals to become qualified to work at international institutions upon the completion of their study or training. It was revealed in 1998 that MOF dominated the Japanese quota without adequately sharing it with other ministries and agencies. From 1987 to 1998, of 94 Japanese fund recipients, 56 were MOF officials, and all of the remainder were from institutions closely linked to the ministry, such as OECF and the Ex-Im Bank (*International Development Journal*, 1998j; *Mainichi Shimbun*, 1998). As criticism of the JSF management mounted among other ministries and in the media, Japan's "special funds" at other multilateral development banks (MDBs), such as the Asian Development Bank (ADB) and Inter-American Development Bank, were also scrutinized (see *International Development Journal*, 1999h) and found to have been used exclusively by MOF officials for their overseas study (*Asahi Shimbun Online*, 1999).

ODA corruption cases (e.g., corporate bribes and price rigging) are often caused not by self-serving motives of the aid bureaucrats themselves but, rather, by structural problems that prevent the bureaucracy from conducting proper project supervision, effective project implementation, and proper training for aid personnel. MOFA and the Japan International Cooperation Agency (JICA) are overburdened with large amounts of work and have insufficient personnel, especially in recipient countries, to supervise the process properly. Due to budgetary and personnel shortages, JICA does not even have offices in many aid recipient countries, thus further hindering aid supervision. Though these problems are to some extent beyond MOFA and JICA's control, the agencies still bear the brunt of criticism for the resulting corruption.

Petty fraud cases, especially those of small-scale embezzlement or an agency's bending the rules to increase its power base within the government, or lack of proper oversight by the government over corporate behavior, may be ubiquitous in industrial countries. The fact that some of these cases were revealed to the Japanese public may simply indicate that information on official misconduct or mismanagement of public funds is relatively transparent in Japan. Yet, the revelation has had a serious impact on the public's view of the bureaucracy. Public confidence in the bureaucracy has plummeted. Pharr (2000) argues that the public crisis of confidence in the Japanese government is best explained by public perceptions of misconduct by state officials. Public discontent with the bureaucracy is fueled by Japan's moribund economy and the bureaucratic failure to rectify it. Within this context, revelations of pervasive scandals, have seriously undermined people's faith in the once-respected, highly prestigious ministries.

Corruption and the Corporate Sector: Declining
Corporate Authority

State–corporate collusions, as seen in the aforementioned cases involving the LDP, ministry officials, and corporate representatives, have seriously eroded public trust in the integrity of the state as well as that of the corporate sector. In the field of ODA, corporate authority has declined since the media disclosed corruption cases involving Japanese businesses (see, for example, *Mainichi Shimbun Shakai-bu ODA Shuzai-han,* 1990). The public has learned that fraud cases are numerous in ODA and that the main culprits in aid corruption are Japanese firms.

There are two main practices that corrupt Japanese firms commit: bribery and *dangō* (bid-rigging). Bribery cases involve Japanese firms that provide lucrative monetary offers to local officials and cronies in recipient countries. The most notorious bribery case was undoubtedly the "Marcos Scandal" of 1986. When Filipino President Ferdinand Marcos fled to Hawaii after the "People's Revolution," the U.S. Customs office confiscated his secret documents on entry into the United States. These documents were later made available to the U.S. House Foreign Affairs Subcommittee on East Asia and Pacific and to the public. The documents revealed systematic corruption in Japan's ODA loan projects in the Philippines, involving a number of Japanese trading firms such as Sutmitomo Shoji and Toyo Tsusho (later renamed Toyo Technica) as aid contractors. It was revealed that these firms had paid kickbacks (estimated about 10 to 15 percent of ODA loans) on a regular basis to the Marcos family and to Marcos's cronies via Filipino firms (Yokoyama, 1994). The revelation of the scandal galvanized public attention in Japan to the issue of corporate corruption in ODA.

Another bribery case involved a Japanese consulting firm, which was found in 1998 to have given a bribe to Bhutanese government officials. This fraud occurred in a grant aid telecommunications project in Bhutan, in which the consulting firm diverted about ¥200 million in ODA funds in 1991 to purchase vehicles for Bhutan government officials' personal use (*Asahi Shimbun,* 1998a; *Nikkei Weekly,* 1998a). In 1999, another bribery case was made public, this time involving several Japanese general construction firms (e.g., Kashima, Taisei, Obayashi, and

Tokai Kogyo) that had paid kickbacks to Indonesian officials in charge of Japanese ODA in that country. The Tokyo National Tax Bureau charged that these Japanese firms had masked the kickbacks as ODA "agency fees" and demanded that the firms pay tax on the amounts of the kickbacks. These types of kickbacks are considered common, especially because Japanese firms have difficulty winning competitive international bids for untied loan aid because of high labor costs in Japan (*International Development Journal,* 1999j; *Yomiuri Shimbun,* 1999a; *Yomiuri Shimbun,* 1999b; *Yomiuri Shimbun,* 1999c; *Yomiuri Shimbun,* 1999d). Although relatively small amounts of aid funds were diverted to the officials, *Yomiuri Shimbun* reported the case as headline news because of the anticipation that they could lead to a "Suharto scandal," similar to the 1986 Marcos case (*International Development Journal,* 1999a).

According to some analysts, many Japanese firms give bribes to officials in aid recipient countries because these firms are forced by Japan's single-year budgeting system to finish their aid projects on time. These firms are especially vulnerable to bribery demands after the conclusion of the exchange of notes (E/N) between the Japanese and recipient governments. After the signing of E/N, Japanese consultants have to negotiate directly with recipient governments and sign contracts. This causes many problems for Japanese consulting firms, which often find their counterparts intentionally delaying the planned schedule unless they receive financial contributions (Araki, 1998b; *Asahi Shimbun,* 1998a; *Asahi Shimbun,* 1998b; *International Development Journal,* 1998b; *Nikkei Weekly,* 1998b; *Asahi Shimbun,* 1998d; *International Development Journal,* 1999k). However, no matter how unfairly the ODA system works for Japanese firms (by imposing a serious time limit and forcing them to directly deal with corrupt recipient officials), the public does not approve of corporate corrupt behavior such as giving bribes using taxpayers' money. A public outcry has demanded structural reform in ODA to eliminate such corruption (*Japan Times Weekly International,* 1999).

In addition to bribery, another practice that has caught public attention is *dangō* (bid-rigging). *Dangō* aims at maintaining high costs and at eliminating market competition. This practice is widespread in Japan's domestic public works, and thus it is not surprising that *dangō* is prevalent in overseas aid projects that involve Japanese firms. This practice in ODA is costly for taxpayers, resulting in inflated design fees, exaggerated cost estimates, and selection of inappropriate equipment by consulting firms to benefit the anticipated contractors. In 1994, Japanese newspapers published a Fair Trade Commission (FTC) investigation of an alleged *dangō* practice committed by nearly forty Japanese firms (including major trading firms such as Itoh Chu, Mitsui, Marubeni, Mitsubishi, Nisshō Iwai, Tōmen, and Nichimen) for machinery procurement on technical cooperation aid. The press speculated that these firms had been engaged in *dangō* for many years in the area of technical cooperation aid and that some of them even formed an ODA *dangō* network called Heisei-kai (*Nihon Keizai Shimbun,* 1994; *Tokyo Shimbun,* 1994). According to Sophia University professor Yoshinori Murai, the firms inspected by FTC were not willing to compete in an open bidding process, which would require more time and money, given the fact that machinery used for technical cooperation was usually relatively low cost (around ¥10–100 million). Murai concluded that if these firms had participated in open bidding, preparation for the bid would have ended up costing more than the actual profits expected from the machinery they were bidding for, because of the high labor costs required for bidding (*Asahi Shimbun Weekly AERA,* 1994). Other aid *dangō* cases were reported by the media, usually involving large Japanese general trading firms in infrastructure-based, tied grant aid projects. Though many of these ODA bid-rigging cases involve relatively small amounts of money, these cases have nevertheless attracted public attention (Asashi Shimbun Enjo Shuzai-han, 1985).

The revelations of corporate corruption have increased public mistrust of the Japanese business sector and diluted corporate authority. Many citizens now consider Japanese firms in the aid industry as corrupt and illegal. In addition, an increasing number of people have come to realize it is costly to hire Japanese firms to carry out ODA, because they overcharge due to their bribery and *dangō* practices. In response, an increasing number of citizens have started demanding that more aid projects be carried out by NGOs, rather than by corporations.

Post-materialism

In addition to the political and economic crises occurring since the late 1980s, the Japanese have also undergone spiritual crises as a result of rapid industrialization. As the Japanese have become one of the wealthiest peoples in the world, they have begun to sense that they have achieved their nation's long-standing goal since the 1868 Meiji Restoration of catching up with the West. The single-minded pursuit of economic growth and the worship of an ideology of "GNPism" (Curtis, 1999a, p. 3) after World War II had unified Japan and helped it to become a rich country. A national consensus considered attainment of rapid economic growth and catching up with the West the country's mission in the postwar era. The quest to catch up with the West economically became an important common national goal, particularly during the Cold War, when security matters such as defense and the constitutional order were sensitive issues that divided people into right and left camps. The bureaucracy–LDP leadership emphasized the unifying theme of economic development and won a strong national consensus to concentrate the country's energies on fostering a rapid increase in GNP (Curtis, 1999b).

The state ideology of GNPism created a corporate culture of hard work and self-sacrifice, often characterized by phrases like *kaisha-shijō-shugi* (company-firstism), *kigyō senshi* (corporate warrior), and *mōretsu shain* (fierce company employees). To pursue high GNP growth, the Japanese endured poor work conditions, including extremely long work hours (usually without extra pay), limited vacation days, and compulsory excessive drinking (called "entertainment") with superiors or customers after work (Koiso, 1991). GNPism also meant distorted development that neglected the welfare of family and community. Fathers stayed away from home most of the time, thus leaving their family *chichioya fuzai* ("with absent father"); women had few job opportunities and thus stayed home to take care of family; children underwent "examination hell" to pass an entrance exam to go to a prestigious university and later become a *kigyō senshi* (corporate warrior) at a high-status corporation; and there was insufficient investment in public amenities such as urban parks and sports facilities. The Japanese made great sacrifices for their nation's economic development. During the 1950s–1970s, the developmental state and the Japanese people concentrated on improving the competitiveness of the nation's industries, rather than improving their living standards or welfare of their communities.

However, as Japan has become a wealthy country, the pursuit of national economic growth by means of aggregated corporate prosperity is no longer the sole goal of the Japanese people, especially of the younger generation. Many young people today reject the lifestyle that accompanied the economy-first policy when people sacrificed their lives for their nation's and companies' welfare by working 70 to 80 hours a week or even by dying from overwork (i.e., *karōshi*). Given a choice, many young people would rather work less and perhaps earn less, but have a more comfortable, relaxing life that allows them to spend more time with their family and friends. They would prefer not to join in the corporate rat race or have their own children become a *kigyō senshi* (*Economist,* 2001). Of course, short-term economic downturns can elicit attention to material or economic needs, and people may become ambivalent during times of economic recession, because they still want their country to prosper and do not want to experience economic hardship. Since the early 1990s, when the bubble economy burst, some segments of the population—especially those who have lost or in danger of losing jobs due to corporate restructuring—may have been greatly concerned about their economic welfare. However, the people have been merely reacting to a postindustrial economic slump, but they have not overturned the direction of the overall trend moving away from the state ideology of GNPism. Economic issues remain important, but they no longer dominate people's lives in the same way as they did in the past, when Japan was still poor and trying to catch up with the West. Over the long haul, Japanese people are predominantly losing belief in GNPism or developmentalism.

While people have lost a clear sense of direction in life, traditional aspects of Japanese society have also eroded in the process of economic development and urbanization, resulting in the weakening of the patriarchal family and of traditionally closeknit community systems. The erosion of traditional values has created many new social problems, demonstrated by an increase in youth violence and the spread of destructive cult groups, such as the Aum Shinrikyo cult that killed 12 people and injured thousands with a sarin gas attack in 1995. Many problems can be explained by the alienation of youth that grew up in material affluence but lacked a spiritual or moral compass. Metraux (1999) and Castells (1997) describe many Aum followers as young people in their twenties and thirties who could not find meaning in the stratified, hierarchical structure of schools, administrations, and corporations, and who were revolting against traditional family and social structures. Other unlawful or destructive religious cult groups also grew rapidly in the 1980s–1990s. Ho-no-Hana Sampogyo (Flower of Law and Three Law Practice), for example, attracted people searching for alternative ways to attain good health and spiritual meaning in the 1990s. It was later revealed that the group was swindling billions of yen from its followers by examining the soles of their feet and telling them that they would die of AIDS or cancer if they did not pay for the "treatment" (Chang, 1999; *Mainichi Interactive,* 2001). Another group called Life Space was charged in the late 1990s with mummifying the body of a former follower whose family let him die in front of them, believing he was alive and receiving "medical treatment" from the cult leader (*Mainichi Interactive,* 1999). These bizarre crimes show many Japanese people became gullible and vulnerable as they searched for happiness and spiritual meaning.

During the developmental state era, people had concentrated all their energies on economic recovery from the devastating war and creating rapid GNP growth, which in a sense gave them spiritual satisfaction, feelings of accomplishment, and pride in themselves. In contrast, in the postdevelopmental era, many people find themselves in an existential void. As Castells (1998) observed:

> An increasingly confused society, particularly in its younger sections, having grown up in affluence, becomes deprived of meaningful values, as the traditional structures of familial patriarchalism and bureaucratic indoctrination lose their grip in a culture filled with information flows from diverse sources. A mixture of ritualistic Japanese traditions, American icons, and high-tech consumption fills the vacuum in social dynamics, cultural challenges, or personal dreams of a society that has finished its assigned task: to make Japan secure, rich, and respected within 50 years. Now, after their strenuous effort, the Japanese find the tunnel at the end of the light, as increasingly abstract, new technocratic challenges are proposed by a developmental state that has outlived the state of emergency. (pp. 235–236)

While some Japanese have turned to cults, many more have been drawn to citizen activism. As Japan has become a wealthy country, many individuals, especially the young and educated middle class, are shifting from an emphasis on economic well-being to postmaterial values such as the quality of life, self-expression, freedom, and democracy. According to Inglehart (1990), postmaterial values spread in an industrial society where most of the population does not live under conditions of poverty, hunger, and economic insecurity. In Inglehart's view, people in Western Europe and the United States, especially the educated youth, tended in the 1970s–1980s to look beyond their own financial self-interest and to place morality, rights, and other nonmaterial political goals above the pursuit of personal economic gain. What Inglehart observed in Western Europe and the United States in the 1970s–1980s has been occurring in Japan since the late 1980s. Japan's economic boom began in the late 1950s; by the mid-1980s Japan had risen to one of the world's richest economies and had surpassed many European countries in GNP, thus providing enough material comfort to allow people to pursue noneconomic goals. Individuals now have the luxury of devoting their time and energy to humankind rather than to their own material needs.

Young individuals tend to support postmaterial priorities more readily than older people whose life experiences are dramatically different. The older generations underwent war and poverty; the younger generation grew up in affluence. At the same time, some older individuals have also joined the youth in trying to address postindustrial concerns. Now that they have attained affluence, they feel it is their turn to help those in need outside Japan, just as the international community assisted the Japanese by providing food and other necessities after World War II.[1] Overall the Japanese are moving away from an emphasis on economic growth at any price toward increasing concern for world affairs.

An important political ramification of the value change toward postmaterialism is the emergence of a new political culture characterized by the rise of grassroots activism (Inglehart, 1990; Inglehart, 1997). The rise of citizen activism is seen in the proliferation of NGOs and nonprofit organizations (NPOs) in Japan since the late 1980s, as discussed in Chapter 1. Some analysts of Japan disagree with Inglehart's hypothesis that postmaterialist values lead to citizen activism. Umemori (1997), for example, argues that Japanese citizens instead become more apathetic, as evidenced by his research on people's declining political participation. However, Umemori's study was mainly concerned with people's attitudes toward formal political processes including elections and political parties in the 1970s–1980s, rather than toward non-partisan, informal grassroots activism in the 1990s–2000s. As discussed earlier, people in Japan have become disenchanted with the formal political systems due to the incompetence and corruption of state officials. Without relying on conventional political processes, Japanese people are now searching for alternative avenues (e.g., NGOs, NPOs) to express themselves on issues related to quality of life. Thus, Umemori's study does not accurately reflect the emergence of civic activism in Japan, which takes place largely *outside,* rather than *via,* established political channels.

As Inglehart (1997) asserts, postmaterialists are more likely to act in autonomous, elite-challenging fashion. This is seen in Japan, where many individuals no longer find their personal goals to be subordinated to the goal of the developmental state. During the period of economic catchup, people willingly sacrificed their personal lives for the sake of the country's broader economic goals. But they are not willing to do so any more. In other words, the shift toward postmaterialism is linked with a weakening of Confucianist hierarchy, declining deference to state authority, and the decentralization of power. Japanese people are less respectful of state elites and more ready to challenge them.

In summary, Japan's economic development has had major social consequences. The Japan of the late 1980s–2000s differs sharply from the Japan of the 1950s–1970s. Material needs have been met and new issues and concerns that were almost invisible prior to the 1980s—such as humanitarian assistance to developing countries, promotion of democracy and human rights—are becoming as important as economic issues. Postmaterialist values are expressed in the pursuit of political autonomy and self-expression through participation in grassroots movements. Mistrusting the state and established political mechanisms, people have turned to NGOs and other nonstate organizations to make changes within Japan and the world. In short, people's confidence in the established political system has been declining, but citizens' grassroots participation has been increasing. Thus, Japan has two related trends: the erosion of state authority and the rise of citizen participation in grassroots politics.

Conclusion

Due to the recent government authority crises of the 1990s—including a prolonged economic recession, the worsening balance in Japan's fiscal budget, and corruption scandals—public confidence in the integrity of the bureaucracy–corporate alliance has plummeted. The public has learned that their civil servants, the nation's elite, wield enormous discretionary power in an environment in which information is confidential and in which the bureaucracy–private sector relationship is often based on collusion and favoritism.

People in Japan have begun to realize that they cannot depend solely on the state for guidance and assistance. The new awareness of the state's limited capacities and of citizens' own responsibility for social welfare has started moving the public away from the traditional dependence on a formal state system. Many citizens have come to realize that they must be directly involved in looking after the public interest through their own support and involvement in grassroots groups. This has spurred people to become more active citizens, rather than relying on the state to solve problems. In the end, this shift has strengthened the growth of a wide range of grassroots organizations, not only those specifically related to Japan's domestic problems but also NGOs working on a range of international issues.

The weakening of the state and corporate sector during the economic downturn has created openings for broader involvement of NGOs, both because the fiscal crisis creates a demand for deployment of cost-effective grassroots organizations in aid and because NGOs are seen as less corrupt and more capable of implementing community-based projects. In addition, Japanese individuals have developed postmaterialist values due to their country's past economic success. People have become less concerned with material affairs, but more concerned with non-material affairs and spiritual meanings in life. These individuals have become the engine of Japanese NGOs.

NGO Advocacy

There is little understanding about the way Japanese nongovernmental organizations (NGOs) carry out their work of lobbying and pressuring the Japanese state. How do NGOs advance their aims? How successful are they? How does the state respond to their campaigns?

Japanese NGOs try to promote change on a wide range of aid issues, from sustainable development to the environment to human rights. They exert their pressure primarily on the bureaucracy because it dominates the process of aid decision making. Although limited in size and finance, NGOs have a growing influence over policies. They have started challenging the conventional developmental state system of bureaucratic dominance and citizens' noninvolvement in policy making. By protesting the government's policies and pressuring the government to embrace global norms of sustainable human development, NGOs have become an integral part of Japanese official development assistance (ODA).

This chapter introduces a general overview of the history of NGO campaigns for ODA reform, followed by an analysis of three specific cases of NGO campaigns in the 1990s. These cases illustrate how Japanese NGOs, working in conjunction with NGOs of other countries, have become a conduit of global norms and a successful advocate for change in Japan's ODA and foreign policy. Each case, unique in its own way, became an important precedent in Japan's aid history. The first case addresses issues of sustainable development, involving Japanese loan aid to India. The aid, started in 1987, was designed to build a power plant in India's Narmada Valley to supplement the World Bank's Sardar Sarovar Dam project in the area. In 1990, Japanese environmental NGOs, in coalition with NGOs of other countries and local grassroots groups, succeeded in terminating the aid on the ground that large numbers of indigenous people would be forced to relocate. The second case also involves environmental NGOs concerned about the impact of Japanese aid on the local environment. NGOs campaigned against Japan's ODA project in Cambodia, a grant aid project began in 1992 to provide pesticides to the country. Again, Japanese environmental NGOs, in collaboration with NGOs of other countries, succeeded in canceling an aid project that they viewed as harmful to the local people and environment. The last case is an antilandmine campaign that led the Japanese government to sign and ratify the Mine Ban Treaty in Canada in 1997 and 1998 respectively and to increase ODA funds for landmine eradication and victim assistance.

Each of these cases made officials in the Ministry of Foreign Affairs (MOFA) reconsider Japanese ODA and foreign policy and forced the ministry to change preexisting policies. These are the first three major NGOs campaigns against government foreign policies and also the first three major successes Japanese NGOs have had vis-à-vis MOFA. They represent significant milestones in Japan's civil society–state relations and ODA history. Before examining these three cases, I will first provide a brief overview of NGO advocacy campaigns.

NGO Aid Reform Campaigns

The ODA reform movement by NGOs began in the mid-1980s, following the sharp increase in media coverage of ODA discussed in Chapter 3. After the media revelation of the Marcos scandal, some Japanese citizens started grassroots groups to investigate how the Japanese government manages its rapidly expanding ODA program in collaboration with Japanese businesses and recipient governments.

One such group is the Reconsider Aid Citizens' League (REAL), established in 1986 by aforementioned Sophia University professor Yoshinori Murai. REAL is Japan's first NGO dedicated to changing Japanese aid. To further promote investigation on aid, Murai and others established another group called the ODA Investigation Study Group in 1988. This group, consisting of about 30 Japanese people from its sub-groups in Japan, the Philippines, Indonesia, and Thailand, published a booklet of onsite reports on ODA projects. The booklet pointed to business and political interference in ODA and claimed that many Japanese aid projects do more harm than good to the poor in developing countries (Murai, 1991). This claim shocked many Japanese, who had assumed that their tax money was being used for humanitarian purposes.

In the late 1980s, many more NGOs began campaigning for aid reform. Operating aid projects in developing countries, these groups tried to present perspectives from the developing world and look beyond the official rhetoric of Japan's aid. To pressure the aid programs to change, they held seminars and meetings and frequently appeared in the media, exposing cases of ODA failures and corruption.[1] Like-minded NGOs also established networks to promote their cause. One such group is the Japan Tropical Network (JATAN), established in 1987 as a coalition of 12 Japanese NGOs. On its establishment, JATAN immediately launched a campaign against a Japanese grant aid project (US$1.5 million) for construction of a logging road in Sarawak, Malaysia. This project stirred strong opposition from the indigenous Penan tribe and local and international environmental NGOs, because the road cut into lands where the Penan people lived. JATAN sided with the Penan, who claimed title to the land, and demanded that the Japanese government terminate the aid project. Although the Japanese government refused to back down—the road was eventually built and logging firms succeeded in establishing operations there (Hosmer, 1988)—JATAN achieved a partial success in forcing Itoh Chu, Co., one of the firms that won the aid bid, out of the project by revealing its financial mismanagement.

Spurred by growing public interest in Japanese aid, some Japanese academics joined in the NGO efforts to tackle ODA issues, individually as well as via NGOs. Active debates have been under way among academics regarding the effectiveness of Japan's aid. On the one hand, some academics, such as Sophia University's Murai, Niigata University/ Yokohama Shiritsu University professor Kazuo Sumi, Waseda University professor Jun Nishikawa, and Daito Bunka University professor Yosuke Fuke, criticized Japan's current aid program, especially large-scale infrastructure projects, as harmful to the poor in the developing world. These scholars maintained that all forms of Japanese aid should be beneficial to the poor and humanitarian in nature (Sumi, 1989; Sumi, 1990; Murai, 1992; Nishikawa, 1991; Fuke & Fujibayashi, 1999). Unlike previous academic works on ODA published prior to the mid–1980s, which were read only by other academicians, these new publications were read widely and had a significant impact on the public's view of aid. The primary goal of these activities, especially in the 1980s and early 1990s, was to bring about pressure for change in Japan's aid programs by exposing corruption, mismanagement, and misuse of funds, and by mobilizing public support for aid reform. The central point made was that many ODA funds recycle to the coffers of Japanese firms and that Japanese officials tacitly approve acts of corruption and injustice, harming the interests of the local people who should be the primary beneficiaries of aid.

On the other hand, other academics pointed out that NGOs, mainly interested in publicizing the ill effects of aid on people in recipient countries, paid little attention to apparently successful programs or the well-designed projects that *do* benefit the poor. These critics accuse NGOs of overgeneralizing from a small number of bad aid projects, such as ill-planned cultural centers and environmentally harmful dams, in order to promote their own version of aid reform (Kusano, 1993).

In the 1990s, NGOs further increased their level of coordination through the establishment of networks. For example, an environmental coalition group, Mekong Watch, was established by 12 Japanese NGOs engaged in environmental or development work in Indochina. The group directed its criticism at the proposal for the development of the Mekong River Basin, submitted in 1996 by the Greater Mekong Task Force consisting of MOFA officials and Japanese consulting and construction firms. This proposal, entitled "Strategies for the Development of the Greater Mekong Area," emphasized large-scale infrastructure development in the Mekong River region, especially hydroelectric development and irrigation projects. Mekong Watch blasted the report, charging that the development plan attempts to maximize short-term economic benefits to Japan while hindering efforts to promote sustainability in the region. In the group's view, the plan fails to take local people's needs into consideration. Critical of the role that Tokyo previously played in the construction of the controversial Nam Ngum Dam along the Mekong River in Laos, Mekong Watch urged the government not to repeat the same mistake and to instead completely withdraw from the hydropower development plans in the region.

Similarly, another NGO coalition, the Citizen-NGO Liaison Council for ODA Reform (renamed as ODA Reform Network in 2000), was established by more than 50 Japanese NGOs and some individual academics, to press the Japanese government for ODA reform. In June 1997, the group submitted a proposal for aid reform to MOFA. The proposal contained seven key demands: (1) clarification of ODA doctrine (i.e., ODA should be used to improve the livelihood and self-reliance of the poorest); (2) prioritization of expenditures in the field of social development (i.e., shift from infrastructure-based hard aid to grassroots-based soft aid); (3) unification of the aid administration (i.e., establishment of an ODA agency); (4) establishment of aid guidelines and an ODA law; (5) promotion of citizens' participation in ODA; (6) establishment of an ODA committee in the Diet, in which the bureaucracy would be required to provide detailed information on aid; and (7) promotion of education on aid and development to increase public awareness. The coalition emphasized that Japan is obliged to make efforts to contribute to sustainable human development. Referring to several UN conferences in the 1990s as reference points (e.g., the 1992 Earth Summit in Rio De Janeiro, the Cairo Population Conference, and the 1995 Copenhagen Social Development Summit), the group argued that because Japan signed declarations and plans of action at these conferences, the government is obliged to ensure that Japan's ODA policy is in line with these international agreements (Citizen-NGO Liaison Council for ODA Reform, 1997).

As Japanese NGOs matured, NGO criticisms of Japanese ODA have become more balanced. While the NGOs engaged in advocacy do not hesitate to express themselves, articulating their agendas in public, they are not *abolitionists* who advocate eliminating Japanese ODA or deny the value of giving aid. Increasingly, members of these NGOs have become *reformists* who by and large accept the continued existence of ODA programs. An increasing number of independent NGOs have begun to evaluate the effectiveness of confrontational advocacy and explore alternative methods in dealing with government officials. In particular, they are searching for common ground with reform-oriented MOFA officials to bring about increased changes, starting from situations in which MOFA can comply with NGOs' demands.

Case Studies

The following three cases illustrate how Japanese NGOs campaigned against the bureaucracy, namely the Ministry of Foreign Affairs (MOFA), to successfully bring about change in Japan's aid and foreign policies. In each case, Japanese NGOs worked closed with NGOs of other countries and the press. The first two cases deal with NGO campaigns against ODA projects in India and Cambodia, while the third case involves a campaign not against a specific aid project per se but, rather, on behalf of a treaty that the Japanese government had not originally supported. Also in contrast to the first two cases, the third case does not directly involve environmental NGOs but instead human rights and development NGOs concerned with the use of landmines in wartorn countries. Also, the third case, as well as the first, illustrate that NGOs worked closely with legislators who provided them with access to information and the policy-making process.

Narmada Dam

The case of the Narmada valley project represented the first time the Japanese government yielded to pressure from Japanese NGOs to cancel an ODA program. Due to a campaign led by environmental NGOs such as Friends of the Earth Japan, MOFA and the other ministries in the four-ministry cooperation system abandoned in 1990 a Japanese ODA loan project for the construction of a large-scale hydroelectric plant for the Sardar Sarovar Dam (informally known as the Narmada Dam) on India's Narmada River. Carried out from 1987 by Japan's ODA loan agency, the Overseas Economic Cooperation Fund (OECF), this ¥2.85 billion hydroelectric project was to support the World Bank's effort in the construction of the Sardar Sarovar Dam that had started in 1985 (US$450 million) (Sumi, 1990).

The Sardar Sarovar Dam was part of the Narmada Valley Project planned by the Indian government to construct a great number of dams (30 large dams, 135 medium-size dams, and more than three thousand small dams), irrigation canals, and power plants on the Narmada River over several decades (Sumi, 1990). The Narmada Valley Project raised a furor among environmental groups all over the world as it was expected to submerge 350,000 hectares of forest and force the relocation of more than a million indigenous people living in the river basin (Heyzer, 1995; Sumi, 1990).

A global anti-Narmada campaign opposed the project. Prompted by Indian grassroots activists who formed Narmada Bachao Andolan (NBA or Save the Narmada Movement), NGOs throughout the world began pressuring their home governments, including legislators and bureaucrats, not to support the World Bank's Sardar Sarovar Dam project and Japan's power plant project. NGOs demanded that people in the dam area be given control over their own lives and resources and be permitted to make decisions about development projects that directly affect their lives. It was estimated that the Sardar Sarovar Dam alone would cause the resettlement of some 100,000 people living in 230 villages (Sumi, 1990). Japanese NGOs were particularly angry at their government's role, not only in supporting the dam project as the second largest shareholder in the World Bank but also in OECF's hydropower plant project that was supposed to complement the dam. Within the Japanese government, all four ministries in charge of loan decisions were in favor of the project. The Economic Planning Agency (EPA) and MOF oversaw OECF, thus promoting the loan deal. MITI was eager to push for the aid project, as three Japanese firms (Sumitomo Shoji, Hitachi Seisakujo, and Toshiba) won the bid for the hydroelectric plant. MOFA also promoted the project as the chief coordinator of the four-ministry system. The major task for Japanese NGOs was to reverse the support of the decision makers in these ministries for the dam construction and the Narmada Valley project.

Friends of the Earth Japan and other Japanese NGOs worked in close cooperation with the local communities in the river basin and with other environmental groups in India and the West. Japanese NGOs mounted public campaigns in Japan to protest the construction of the dam and the power plant, holding symposia and informing the media of the likelihood of environmental destruction. They also lobbied both the Japanese government and the World Bank, the main sponsor for the Sandar Sarovar Dam project, to reconsider their funding (Sumi, 1990). The central figures in the NGO campaign in Japan were Yukio Tanaka of Friends of the Earth Japan and Professor Kazuo Sumi of Yokohama City University (later moving to Niigata University). As a key member of the Narmada Action Committee, a coalition of International NGOs for the protection of Narmada Valley, Tanaka represented the Japanese NGOs in public campaigns and became a bridge between the international coalition and Japanese NGOs. He organized a symposium on Narmada in Tokyo in April 1990, as discussed later. Meanwhile, Sumi worked closely with the Japanese press. As a frequent contributor to Japanese monthly and weekly journals such as *Ekonomisuto* and *Shukan Asahi,* he released information on Narmada to the media. With his engineering background, Sumi had technical knowledge of dam construction and could argue persuasively that the dam construction would be unsustainable. His two books critical of Japanese ODA became so popular that they were reprinted several times (Sumi, 1989; Sumi, 1990).[2]

From late 1989, there was a growing concern among NGOs and legislators throughout the world about the Narmada issue. One important turning point was when the Narmada campaign became the subject of a Congressional special hearing in Washington, DC. The fact that the Narmada issue was discussed at the Congressional hearing gave more credibility to Japanese campaigners. This hearing had an impact on not only Japanese NGOs but also on Japanese legislators interested in environmental issues. In October 1989, congressman James Scheuer (D-NY), Chairman of the House Subcommittee on Natural Resources, Agricultural Research, and Environment, chaired a special hearing to investigate the World Bank's environmental and social performance in the Sardar Sarovar Dam project. The hearing involved testimony by Indian antidam activists, Medha Patkar of the Narmada Bachao Andolan, Grish Patel of

Lpk Adikar Sangh, and Vijay Paranjpye, an Indian economist, as well as American grassroots activists such as Peter Miller and Lori Udall of the Environmental Defense Fund. At the hearing, various problems of the project were identified, including issues related to resettlement and rehabilitation, environmental damages, economic hardship for minority people, and human rights violations. Following the hearing, a series of letters from members of Congress were sent to President Barber Conable of the World Bank, calling for a suspension or cancellation of the project.[3] In addition, Sheuer organized in Washington, DC, a meeting of Global Legislators for a Balanced Environment (GLOBE), an international organization established in 1989 to enhance international cooperation between parliamentarians on global environmental issues. The meeting brought together U.S.-based environmentalists and legislators from Japan and European countries to discuss the Narmada project and problems related to it. This meeting increased interest in Narmada among Japanese legislators such as Akiko Domoto, then a member of the Socialist Party. After the GLOBE meeting, Sheuer wrote a letter to all GLOBE members arguing them to take up the issue in their own countries. His letter, the GLOBE meeting, and the previous Congressional hearing pleased NGOs working toward the cancellation of the dam construction in the Narmada region. Also, these U.S. Congressional initiatives sparked the interest of Japanese Diet members in the Narmada issue (Udall, 1995; Udall, 1998; Sumi, 1990).

Reflecting the heightened interest of Japanese NGOs and politicians in Japan's aid involvement in the Narmada Valley, Friends of the Earth Japan hosted in April 1990 the first International Narmada Dam Symposium, which brought together Indian, Japanese, and international activists, as well as Japanese Diet members, journalists, and academics. The representatives from India included three antidam activists from Narmada Bachao Andolan and an official from the Indian Embassy in Japan, S. C. Tripathi. From the United States, Udall of the Environmental Defense Fund attended the symposium. Japanese NGOs were represented by aforementioned Yukio Tanaka of Friends of the Earth Japan, Professor Kazuo Sumi of Yokohama City University, and Yoichi Kuroda of the Japan Tropical Forest Action Network (JATAN) (Sumi, 1990).

In defense of the Indian government, Tripathi asserted that the benefits from the dam construction would outweigh its drawbacks and that the poor would be the greatest beneficiaries of the project. In response to this statement, Kisan Mehta, one of the Indian activists, replied that the Narmada project would not bring about progress to the people but would instead drive the poor to infertile lands and deprive them of the land, water, and forest that they had inherited from their ancestors. Another activist, Ramesh Billorey, emphasized the potential environmental damage from the construction of a large number of dams and the lack of clear resettlement plans (Sumi, 1990).

The Tokyo symposium was a significant success for the anti-Narmada Dam campaigners. The Japanese ODA project received major attention from the press (see, for example, *Asahi Shimbun,* 1990a, p. 30). The symposium attracted more than five hundred people, including journalists from major Japanese daily newspapers (Sumi, 1990). The exchange of information at the Tokyo Symposium sparked a rapid proliferation of news regarding the Sardar Sarovar Dam, and Japan's role in it, throughout the country. The symposium was the first kind in Japan that publicly exposed the adverse impacts of a project funded by Japan.

Japanese NGOs also organized a special press conference a few days prior to the Tokyo symposium for the Indian antidam conference participants. Through the conference, these Indian activists appealed to the Japanese public to pressure the Japanese government to cancel the project (*Asahi Shimbun,* 1990a; *Asahi Shimbun,* 1990c).

Meanwhile, Japanese legislators joined the NGOs in taking on the Narmada issue. In April–June 1990, some Diet members asked MOFA and OECF officials to verify Japan's assessment research that led Tokyo to approve the aid. For example, at the Foreign Affairs Committee of the House of Councilors, Domoto and Eiichi Nakamura (Rengo Party) asked what kind of preliminary assessment had been conducted. At the Budget Committee of the House of Representatives, Hisashi Miura (Communist Party) asked about research on the possible condition of the people who would be forced to relocate prior to the implementation of the project. Similarly, Kentaro Koniwa (Komei Party) at the Budget Committee of the House of Councilors asked about the preliminary assessment for the dam construction. It was revealed that although the Director of the Economic Cooperation Bureau at MOFA, Akishichi Kinohata, repeatedly claimed that the Japanese government had sent many missions to the construction site to do preliminary studies, Tokyo in fact sent only one mission that had conducted flimsy research and that had not produced even a single report. Worse, while the president and vice president of OECF (Akio Kodaku and Shoichi Tanimura) insisted that the government's decision on the aid was based on the World Bank's meticulous studies regarding the environment and relocation of the people in the area, it was found that such studies did not exist. To deflect domestic criticism, these aid officials lied to the Diet, claiming that the government had used the World Bank's studies, assuming incorrectly that the World Bank had done such assessments (Sumi, 1990). The hearings revealed how arbitrarily Japanese ODA assessments were conducted and how ignorant Japanese aid officials were of potential negative consequences of Japanese aid projects. The hearings also showed how badly Japanese bureaucrats wanted to support any decisions that were already made in order to protect their own jurisdiction in ODA. These hearings attracted further media attention to ODA and raised public uproar against the Narmada aid project.

In the face of NGO and political pressure, Tokyo finally rescinded its involvement in the loan project in June 1990, only two months after the NGO symposium in Tokyo. MOFA announced that it would not provide further financing because of local opposition to the project, lack of resettlement planning, and absence of an environmental assessment (*Asahi Shimbun*, 1990b). It was extremely unusual for the Japanese government to cancel a project that had already begun three years previously and was already half built.

Sumi attributes the government's decision to cancel the aid project to the efforts of Japanese NGOs, which tirelessly appealed to the public to respect the rights of the indigenous people in the Narmada region. He also believes that Japanese NGOs succeeded in persuading Azusa Hayashi, then the Head of the Loan Aid Division within MOFA, to withdraw the aid project. Sumi notes Hayashi listened carefully to Sumi's and other activists' claim of how badly the project was designed and then took the initiative in canceling the funding for the project. According to Sumi, Hayashi persuaded MITI officials who strongly opposed the cancellation.[4] In addition, the government's decision to cancel the aid project is due to NGOs' success in attracting media attention. In the media, the Narmada conflict was frequently portrayed as a struggle between a powerful development apparatus (i.e., the Japanese government and the World Bank) and a powerless indigenous people.

The Narmada case illustrates how NGOs, in cooperation with some politicians, succeeded in revealing to the public how incomplete the government's preparatory research for ODA projects is, how poorly informed Kasumigaseki (i.e., the bureaucracy) was of the negative consequences of Japanese aid, and how dominant so-called approval culture (pressure to lend money) was in the government, overwhelming other considerations such as the welfare of the people in the affected area. Tokyo's decision to cancel the project ultimately affected World Bank support of the Sarsar Sarovar Dam, with the Bank ceasing its own funding in 1993.[5]

Pesticide Aid

In contrast to the Narmada campaign in which NGOs targeted their criticism at both the Japanese government and the World Bank (the cosponsor of the Sarsar Sarovar Dam) the case involving Japanese pesticide aid to Cambodia solely targeted at the Japanese government. The specific targets of criticism were MOFA, which overseas the Japanese Embassy in Phnom Penh, and the Japan International Cooperation Agency (JICA), grant aid implementing agency. The anti-Japanese pesticide aid campaign was carried out by Japanese and non-Japanese environmental NGOs in Tokyo and Phnom Penh. The lead NGOs in the campaign were the Japan International Volunteer Center (JVC) and the Cooperation Committee for Cambodia (CCC), an NGO network in Cambodia to which JVC belonged.

Japanese pesticide aid to Cambodia was agreed on by the two countries in 1992. The aid was to be provided, together with chemical fertilizer and agricultural machines, as part of the Second Kennedy Round ("2KR") of the General Agreement on Tariffs and Trade (GATT). 2KR aid, formally known as "Aid for Increased Food Production," is a unique form of Japanese grant aid that began in 1977. During international trade negotiations under the auspices of the GATT (informally known as the Kennedy Round) in 1967, 16 developed countries, including Japan, established a Food Aid Convention to ensure that grain exports would not have a negative impact on agricultural production or on the international trade of developing countries. Under this convention, the developed countries were assigned to provide certain minimum amounts of grains to developing countries as part of foreign aid. Since Japan was not an exporter of food, it introduced in 1977 2KR aid to provide agricultural inputs as fertilizers, agricultural chemicals, and farm machinery to developing countries (Tobin, 1996).

Pesticide aid to Cambodia was intended to promote agricultural productivity in the country's countryside. It cost ¥500 million (about US$3.8 million) in total, of which ¥350 million was allocated for three tons of agricultural chemicals for use on rice. The controversy surrounding this aid package was that the aid consisted of three types of insecticides—diazinon, fenvalerate (or sumicidin), and fenitrothion (or sumithion)—which environmental and development NGOs and international organizations considered harmful to the local environment and the people. According to Peter Kenmore, an expert on pests in Asian rice at the Food and Agricultural Organization (FAO), diazinon and fenitrothion are organphosphates that could disrupt people's nervous system if protective clothing is not worn; in Cambodia's tropical climate, farmers would find such clothing uncomfortable, and thus the pesticides "cannot be applied safely by small farmers" (Mallet, 1993, p. 17). Opponents of the Japanese aid argued that even in the United States, the use of these chemicals was strictly restricted (and in fact they were banned on golf courses and certain farms). They also maintain that fenvalerate, a synthetic pyrethroid insecticide, was toxic to fish and aquatic invertebrates (Japan International Volunteer Center, 1993; Kuroda, 1993; Tobin, 1996). NGOs claimed that Cambodia was ill-suited for these chemicals because the country had neither legislation controlling pesticides nor any other means of insuring their safe use (Tobin, 1996).

Japan's decision to provide the pesticide aid came rather suddenly. In February 1992, the Japanese government received a request for 2KR aid from the Cambodian government. In March and April 1993, a team consisting of JICA staff and a Japanese engineering and consulting company conducted a study to determine whether this request could be the legitimate basis for a Japanese aid program. The study, however, did not involve consideration of potential environmental effects or appropriateness of the pesticides for Cambodia's ecosystem. Two months later, the Japanese government sent a mission to Phnom Penh to instruct the Cambodian government on how to write documents for aid contracts. Sumitomo Chemical, Co. was alleged to have been part of this mission, advising the Cambodian government on which pesticides to order (Kuroda, 1993; Tobin, 1996).

The issue of the Japanese pesticide aid was first criticized by CCC and international organizations located in Cambodia, such as the International Rice Research Institute (IRRI) and FAO, all of whom questioned the environmental safety of the Japanese pesticide aid. In particular, the agricultural subdivision within CCC focused on the issue and submitted a letter of protest to the Japanese Embassy in Phnom Penh and to the Cambodian Ministry of Agriculture in December 1992. In the letter, the group expressed several points of concern over the pesticide aid. First, they claimed that pesticide spraying would pose a major threat to rice crops by destroying beneficial insects, leading to resurgence of insect pests. Evidence from Indonesia, Thailand, and other Southeast Asian countries shows that broad spectrum insecticides such as the three scheduled to be donated by Japan actually worsen pest infestation in tropical rice. Second, they said that pesticides would pose threats to the health of Cambodian farmers who were unaware about the hazards associated with pesticide use. Third, they charged that heavy use of agricultural chemicals would destroy the ecological balance in Cambodia. This included destruction of aquatic life, which forms a significant portion of Cambodians diet. In short, the criticism of the CCC subcommittee was clear: Japanese aid presented immediate threats to human safety and the environment in Cambodia. The letter went on to propose specific policy recommendations: (1) Japan should postpone the aid until the public (including NGOs) receive adequate information about the exact kinds and amount of the pesticides Tokyo was going to provide; (2) instead of bringing pesticides to Cambodia, Japan should promote Integrated Pest Management (IPM) in that country, an environmentally friendly method that does not rely on pesticides; and (3) in collaboration with FAO, IRRI and NGOs in Cambodia, the Japanese government assist the Cambodian Ministry of Agriculture in gathering information of adequate agrochemicals for the production of rice and vegetables (Japan International Volunteer Center, 1993). Then, in January 1993, CCC sent another letter of petition to the Japanese Embassy and the Cambodian Ministry of Agriculture. This was a follow-up letter to express NGOs' concerns over the Japanese aid. The Japanese Embassy responded to neither of the letters (Japan International Volunteer Center, 1993).

Taking up CCC's agenda, JVC campaigned with other NGOs in Japan. In December 1992, Japanese NGOs such as the Japan Tropical Forest Action Network (JATAN) and the Pacific-Asia Resource Center (PARC) visited MOFA to urge re-appraisal of the pesticide aid (Pesticide Action Network North America, 1992). In February 1993, JVC held a symposium entitled, "To think about the problem of Japanese pesticides and Cambodia." This symposium included Masaya Fujiwara, the head of the Grant Division in the Economic Cooperation Bureau at MOFA. In response to NGOs' criticism of the aid, Fujiwara insisted on the validity of the pesticide aid, claiming that: (1) The Japanese aid responded to a request made by the Cambodian government to try to increase rice production; (2) Japan's pesticides are safe, meeting Japanese safety standards; and (3) the Japanese government would train Cambodian officials in the Ministry of Agriculture so that proper use of the pesticides would be practiced. Fujiwara said that the government would neither release any internal reports on the pesticides nor publicly announce where the pesticides would be provided. He made it clear that the government had no intention of stopping the aid. Refuting the claim of the Japanese NGOs at the symposium that Cambodia should adopt IPM, Fujiwara contended that IPM was inappropriate for Cambodia, an impoverished country in desperate need of rapid increase in rice production (Japan International Volunteer Center, 1993). After the symposium NGOs and individual citizens submitted a statement to MOFA, demanding that the aid package be immediately terminated and that the entire 2KR aid be reevaluated (Kuroda, 1993; Japan International Volunteer Center, 1993).

From the very beginning of the controversy over Japanese aid, NGOs questioned the involvement of Japanese agrochemical firms in the aid and their ties to the Japanese government. Two major Japanese chemical corporations were involved in the aid: Sumitomo Chemical Co. (which sold two of the three insecticides, fenvalerate and fenitrothion, to the Japanese government for the aid package) and Nippon Kayaku Co. (which sold diazinon to the government). These firms had been aggressively tying to make their products the object of Japan's aid. Given that Japanese aid is request based, they had allegedly asked the Cambodian government to make a request to MOFA for the pesticides as part of Japan's ODA programs (Japan International Volunteer Center, 1993; *Mainichi Daily News,* 1994).[6]

These Japanese firms and Japan's Society of Agricultural Chemicals Industry (SACI), to which they belonged, lobbied hard on behalf of the Japanese pesticide aid programs, even holding a public seminar in February 1993, just a month after the FAO held a seminar critical of agricultural chemicals. The seminar, cosponsored by the Japanese and Cambodian governments, invited propesticide scholars from Japan and representatives from the Japanese Pesticide Association. At the seminar, the Japanese speakers emphasized how safe and effective Japanese pesticides were. Since NGOs were not allowed to make any statements at the seminar, they refused official attendance but participated as observers (Japan International Volunteer Center, 1993; Kuroda, 1993). Later, these firms sent propesticide agrochemical specialists from Japan to the Cambodian Ministry of Agriculture for seminars, mainly to advertise Japanese pesticides (Japan International Volunteer Center, 1993).

Japanese NGOs were critical of Japanese chemical firms and SACI. In their view, SACI wanted to expand the overseas market for Japanese pesticides, since it expected domestic demands would dwindle following the liberalization of the rice market in Japan based on at the 1993 Uruguay Round; due to the liberalization Japan would import foreign rice and thus make less rice domestically, thereby requiring less pesticide used for rice cultivation at home. Japanese NGOs maintained that the agrochemical industry was one of the most depressed industries (*fukyō sangyō*) in Japan, but that grant aid, usually tied to Japanese procurement and services, was a great opportunity for the industry to expand its market shares overseas. From NGOs' perspective, 2KR aid was optimal for the industry because it was Less Developed Country (LDC) untied aid, meaning that the bidding was only open to Japanese and LDC firms, thus excluding competition from Western firms (which made it easier for Japanese firms to win the bid) (Japan International Volunteer Center, 1995). NGO critics argued that 2KR programs were de facto subsidy programs for the export of Japanese agrochemicals (Kuroda, 1993).

In defiance of the criticisms, the Japanese government took the initiative to advocate for pesticide aid. JICA, for example, invited three officials from the Cambodian Ministry of Agriculture to Japan for "training," but in fact the agency mainly showed them pesticide factories and labs to advertise Japanese pesticides. JICA also held training workshops for Cambodian officials, but these workshops were co-sponsored by SACI, with most speakers from Japanese pesticide firms. Toru Imamura, the first secretary responsible for overseeing the pesticide aid at the Japanese Embassy in Phnom Penh, argued that the protest campaign was politically motivated and that the protestors were overreacting (Mallet, 1993).

MOFA was neither accustomed to protest campaigns against small-scale grant aid such as the one in Cambodia, nor well equipped to deal with protestors. MOFA kept the aid program unnecessarily veiled in secrecy, refusing to release to NGOs any information on the aid package, including very basic information such as plans on how the chemicals would be used in Cambodia. Also, MOFA was reluctant to admit that it conducted no environmental impact assessment or feasibility study on the aid project (Kuroda, 1993). Furthermore, MOFA angered NGOs by arguing that the distribution and safe handling of the pesticides was the responsibility of the Cambodian government, a stand that, in NGOs' view, took no consideration of the local situation, that is, how dysfunctional the Cambodian Ministry of Agriculture was. NGOs maintained that, after decades of civil war, the Cambodian ministry was extremely corrupt and seriously lacking both financial and human resources and that it was irresponsible for the Japanese government to say that the Cambodian government would provide education to Cambodian farmers on the proper use of the chemicals (Hadfield, 1993; Mallet, 1993; Japan International Volunteer Center, 1993). Yet despite international and domestic criticism, the government went ahead and shipped Japanese pesticides to Cambodia in March 1993.

JVC and other NGOs kept up the pressure on MOFA. In July 1993, JVC in Phnom Penh brought Professor Koua Tasaka of International Christian University, a member of an International NGO Pesticide Action Network North America, to do research on Cambodia's agricultural conditions and to meet Cambodian officials in the Ministries of Agriculture, Environment, and Health, as well as Japanese Ambassador Yuko Imagawa. While Tasaka was able to explain to the Cambodian officials the danger of pesticides, his meeting with Imagawa proved to be most successful. Tasaka explained to the ambassador the dangers of the pesticides and elaborated on how Cambodian farmers were handling pesticides in general. Tasaka went on to discuss harmful practices that he either witnessed or heard about: farmers do not wear protective gear when they use pesticides; they drink water near the rice fields where pesticides were used; and they eat fish floating in rivers killed by pesticides. Ambassador Imagawa's response to Tasaka was positive. Even though Imagawa initially said that NGOs should not overemphasize the danger of pesticides, by the end of the meeting he seemed genuinely concerned about Cambodian people who came in contact with agricultural chemicals. He eventually stated that he personally didn't think Cambodia needed pesticides and that he would not endorse pesticide aid starting the following year. As for the pesticides already shipped to Cambodia, he assured that they would not be used until Japan sent experts to Cambodia for training (Japan International Volunteer Center, 1993). Since Imagawa was then the most prominent, well-respected expert on Cambodia within MOFA, his tacit recognition of the danger of Japanese pesticide aid was greatly encouraging to NGOs.

In October 1993, CCC submitted a petition to the Japanese Embassy and the Cambodian Ministry of Agriculture, stipulating that there should be a law to regulate and monitor the use of pesticides. Meanwhile, JVC published a booklet to inform the public of the danger of the Japanese pesticide aid (Japan International Volunteer Center, 1993; Japan International Volunteer Center, 1995). The NGOs' efforts caught the attention of the mass media, and several prominent newspapers covered the issue. Most media articles pointed out the involvement of Japanese firms in the aid. For example, the British newspaper *the Financial Times* bluntly reported the business factor of the aid package:

> The Japanese government is … suspected of donating the pesticide not to help Cambodian farmers but to help the Japanese chemical industry secure a new market for its products. These suspicions are fuelled by the knowledge that Japan may eventually be forced by world trade negotiations to open its rice market to foreign suppliers. Japanese farmers account for only 2.5 percent of world rice production, but they are heavy buyers of pesticides. (Mallet, 1993, p. 17)

JVC further stepped up the pressure on MOFA. JVC initiated a memorandum among expatriate agronomists in Cambodia, expressing concerns about the health of Cambodian farmers, destruction of aquatic life, likelihood of pest resurgence, and pollution of wells and ponds that were

the main source of drinking water. In late 1993, after the JVC's memorandum was presented to the Japanese Embassy and Cambodian government, the Japanese Embassy set up a meeting with representatives of
MOFA, IRRI, JVC, and Church World Service. The NGOs expressed
their concerns about the pesticide aid shipment (Loring, 1995).

During most of 1993, MOFA and JICA vehemently defended their
position, but international and domestic criticism of the aid eventually
forced them to reconsider. After conducting field research in Cambodia
in November–December 1993, JICA finally acknowledged in an internal report that sending pesticides to Cambodia was a mistake, based on
the fact that the country lacked safety regulations. The report further
stated that it would be appropriate to suspend the aid because there was
no need for pesticides in Cambodia. By saying that Cambodia did not
need pesticides, the report accepted the view of NGOs that the Japanese
aid was ill-suited in Cambodia (*Mainichi Daily News*, 1994). It is interesting that JICA admitted the government's "mistake" in late 1993, because
the agency knew from the beginning of the controversy that Cambodia
lacked any legal regulations for pesticide use. Clearly it was pressure from
NGOs that led the agency to conclude that the Japanese government
should stop the pesticide aid in Cambodia. Immediately after the JICA
report, MOFA finally announced the termination of the pesticide aid
program in December 1993. Citing the absence of domestic laws controlling pesticide use in Cambodia, MOFA decided to suspend further
shipments, thus making an about-face on the ministry's claim that the
pesticides were environmentally safe.[7]

The decision to withdraw the pesticide program was an especially
important victory for JVC, and for the broader NGO community. It gave
an important signal that influence over ODA policy had ceased to be
the exclusive domain of the government and Japanese corporations and
that Japanese civil society could have its say in aid decision making.
Furthermore, unlike in the Narmada campaign, Japanese NGOs in the
pesticide case did not have any significant support from Japanese politicians. The pesticide case illustrates that Japanese NGOs were able to pressure MOFA to cancel the project without relying on Japanese legislators.

Landmine Campaign

Of the three cases discussed in this chapter, the antilandmine campaign
was the largest global movement, involving more than 120 governments
and hundreds of human rights and development NGOs. In this movement, NGOs were the primary movers in generating worldwide concern

for antipersonnel (AP) landmines, in particular, the International Campaign to Ban Landmines (ICBL), established in 1992 by six NGOs involved in antilandmine campaigns.[8] The ICBL and other NGOs made a major contribution to the establishment of an anti-AP mine treaty in Ottawa in December 1997 (the Convention on the Prohibition of the Use, Stockpiling, Production, and Transfer of Anti-Personnel Mines and on their Destruction, or so-called Mine Ban Treaty).

While the ICBL mobilized international public opinion for the promotion of the ban treaty, it was local NGOs that campaigned for their governments to sign and ratify the ban treaty. In the case of Japan, the role of the Japan Campaign to Ban Landmines (JCBL), a local branch of the ICBL, was significant in educating the public and policymakers about the indiscriminate nature of the weapon and eventually creating a network with pro-Ottawa Diet members to generate support for normative change within the government. JCBL became a catalyst for politicizing the issue of AP mines in Japan, interacting with state actors (politicians, MOFA officials, Defense Agency officials) in the Ottawa process and bringing about increasing collaboration between NGOs and MOFA.

The so-called Ottawa process consists of two stages: the first with the signing and the second with the ratifying the treaty. Japan signed the Mine Ban Treaty in December 1997 and ratified it in September 1998. The first stage (July to December 1997) was characterized by the establishment of JCBL, its lobbying of MOFA to sign the Mine Ban Treaty, and the domestic and international incidents that culminated Japanese public support for a ban of landmines. The second stage (December 1997 to September 1998) was marked by collaboration between JCBL and some Diet members in pressuring MOFA and the Defense Agency to ratify the treaty. At each stage, JBCL focused on pressuring MOFA and late Foreign Minister/Prime Minister Keizo Obuchi, who was sympathetic with antilandmine causes, to move forward in the process.

Although Obuchi is often recognized as the de facto leader of Japan's international antilandmine efforts, it is misleading to assume that he alone brought about policy change. It is more accurate to say that he came under strong pressure from JCBL and pro-Ottawa, pro-JCBL politicians, especially in the second stage, to move forward in the Ottawa process. It is not an exaggeration to say that NGOs and these politicians led the Obuchi administration to ratify the treaty. In fact, while Obuchi was relatively quick to lead the government to sign the treaty after he became Foreign Minister in September 1997 (during the first stage), he was slow to move the government to ratify it after he became Prime Minister in July 1998 (second stage). Indeed, although Japanese NGOs found the domestic political context of fall 1997 to be favorable to their advocacy, they ran into brick wall of the bureaucratic establishment during the second stage. Thus Japanese NGOs, together with pro-Ottawa politicians, stepped up their pressure during the second stage (Mekata, 2000).

The Ottawa process began with a Canada-sponsored international strategy conference in Ottawa in October 1996 ("Towards a Global Ban on Anti-Personnel Mines"), when 50 governments, the United Nations, the International Committee of the Red Cross (ICRC), and ICBL members met to discuss a legally binding international agreement to ban antipersonnel (AP) mines. The Canadian government, together with a small number of other governments, decided to hold this conference, apart from the Geneva-based Conference on Disarmament (CD), to try to end landmine casualties. The CD is a traditional UN body to discuss arms issues, but since it moved extremely slowly on a landmine ban due to disagreements among major powers, the Canadian government and its supporters decided to hold a meeting separately from the CD. This 1996 meeting resulted in the Ottawa Declaration, which committed the participants to working to ensure that a ban treaty would be concluded at the earliest possible date and to carrying out a plan of action to increase resources for mine clearance and victim assistance (Canadian Department of Foreign Affairs and International Trade, 1996). On the last day of the conference, the Canadian government, led by its foreign minister Lloyd Axworthy, seized the initiative by inviting all governments to come back to Ottawa at the end of the following year to sign a ban on the export, production, transfer, and use of AP mines. Axworthy's statement indicated abandonment of the CD as an arena for negotiations on a ban treaty and marked the beginning of the so-called Ottawa process (English, 1998).

In the first stage of the Ottawa process, several preparatory meetings were held in Europe. The first meeting was held in February 1997 in Vienna, where discussion on the draft text began. The second was held in April 1997 in Bonn to discuss possible verification measures to be included in a total ban treaty. But more important were the more formal subsequent follow-up meetings to the 1996 Ottawa conference. In June 1997, a conference was held in Brussels ("The Brussels International Conference for a Global Ban on Anti-Personnel Mines") and another session was held in August 1997 in Oslo ("Oslo Diplomatic Conference on an International Total Ban on Anti-Personnel Land Mines). The Brussels conference launched formal negotiations on a comprehensive ban treaty and announced a declaration to affirm the commitment of the participating states to the signing of a ban treaty by December 1997. The Oslo conference adopted the Convention on the Prohibition of the Use,

Stockpiling, Production and Transfer of AP Mines. It also set up time-tables for demining activities (Mekata, 1998; Mekata, 2000).

At each session, it was clear that the Japanese government was reluctant to take part in the Ottawa process. This was ironic because Japan had hosted a conference on demining technology, the "Tokyo Conference on Antipersonnel Landmines," in March 1997, following Prime Minister Ryutaro Hashimoto's well-publicized announcement at the 1996 Lyon summit that Japan would host an international conference on AP mines. Japan had also expressed its support of a global ban of AP mines during UN General Assembly meetings in 1996 (International Campaign to Ban Landmines, 1999). In addition, Japan was providing ODA to assist land-mine victims in Cambodia in 1997. But the signing of a ban treaty that was opposed by the U.S. government was a different matter. Washington opposed a total ban on AP landmines and insisted that the Korean Peninsula be exempted from the treaty to ensure the security of U.S. troops stationed in South Korea. The U.S. government also demanded that certain types of AP mines be exempted and that the enforcement period of the ban be delayed as long as nine years. Constrained by the U.S.–Japan Security Treaty, the Japanese government supported all of the U.S. demands. In addition, the Japanese Defense Agency insisted that Japan not sign the treaty, arguing that the circumstances surrounding Japan differed greatly from those of pro-Ottawa countries. In the agency's view, Japan had a long coastline but limited military personnel and thus landmines were a crucial frontline defense against invasion, for example by North Korea. Japan's reluctance in the Ottawa process was reflected in its behavior at both the Brussels and Oslo conferences. Japan participated in the 1997 Brussels conference as a mere observer and did not sign the Brussels Declaration until August 1997, when it decided to attend the Oslo conference. Japan's decision to participate in the Oslo conference came only after the U.S. government announced its intention to partici-pate in that conference. In Oslo, 121 governments agreed to the ban treaty, but Tokyo supported various proposals Washington put forth that would have seriously undermined the ban treaty. Japan made no formal statement concerning a total ban and it continued to favor negotiations in the CD over the Ottawa process until the last minute (Mekata, 2000).[9]

In the midst of uncertainty over Japan's future position on the ban treaty, JCBL was established in July 1997 to pressure the Japanese govern-ment to fully support the Mine Ban Treaty and contribute to the elimi-nation of landmines throughout the world. However, the establishment of JCBL was relatively late. The local branches of ICBL had been already established elsewhere, such as in Spain, the Philippines, Kenya, Cambodia,

South Africa, and New Zealand. JCBL was established only several months before the Ottawa conference in December 1997, by about 40 Japanese NGOs engaged in demining and/or victims assistance efforts in Southeast Asia, especially in Cambodia.[10] The reluctance of the Japanese government in the Ottawa process prompted these NGOs to take action.

Individual leaders of JCBL were aid workers with expertise on Cambodia, the world's "capital" of landmine casualties. The network was officially represented by Yasuhiro Kitagawa, who had worked in Cambodia in the 1960s as an electrician and had maintained interest in that country since then. In the 1990s, he established an NGO called the Association on Phnom Penh to send Japanese artificial limb makers and materials to make prosthetics in Cambodia. He also initiated the Citizens' Forum on Cambodia, a Japanese network NGO that collects and provides information on Cambodia and makes policy recommendations on the country's development. The steering committee of JCBL was headed by Toshihiro Shimizu, a member of Japan International Volunteer Center (JVC) who had previously worked at a Cambodian refugee camp on the Thai–Cambodian border as a vocational trainer and later at JVC's Phnom Penh office as a regional officer. During his development work on the border camp and within Cambodia, Shimizu came across many landmine victims and became interested in demining and elimination efforts (Metaka, 1998).

As soon as JCBL was established, it wasted no time in pressuring the Japanese government to join in the Ottawa process. It launched a public awareness campaign to highlight the tragedy of landmine victims and lobbied officials and politicians to participate in the Ottawa process. In mid-August 1997, JCBL submitted a petition to Prime Minister Ryutaro Hashimoto, urging the Japanese government to sign the ban treaty. Later that month, JCBL wrote another petition letter to Hashimoto to support the Ottawa efforts. In the letter, JCBL responded positively to the government's sudden decision to take part in the Oslo conference, but at the same time the group criticized the head of the Defense Agency, Akio Kuma, a key opponent of the Ottawa Mine Ban Treaty. JCBL complained that he had retracted his opposition to Japan's participation in the Oslo conference only after the U.S. government announced that it would send delegates to the conference. JCBL pointed out in the letter that Japan (as reflected in Kuma's decision) did not have any principles on the issue but wanted to merely follow the U.S. lead. Later after the conference, JCBL critiqued that Japan's position at the Oslo conference as quite passive in that the government, having no clear policy on the issue, wanted to see how the negotiations at the conference would go and how the

United States would act (and only then would decide what Japan should do). Due to the U.S. withdrawal from the Oslo declaration as its demands were rejected, Japan followed the United States and made no commitment to the Oslo proposal for a total ban treaty (Metaka, 1998).

However, the domestic environment surrounding JCBL suddenly changed after the Oslo conference. A series of international and domestic events between the Oslo conference (August 1997) and Ottawa conference (December 1997) heightened domestic public opinion in support of the treaty and made JCBL a legitimate player in Japanese politics and thus increased its influence in the decision making process. In particular, three incidents deserve special attention as they sparked public support for the treaty. First, in August 1997, the Princess of Wales Diana died from an auto accident. Her previous work to ban landmines and her memory became a powerful force raising both public awareness of inhumanity of AP mines and public support for a ban throughout the world. Her tragic death also influenced the Japanese public mood in regard to AP mines. Previously, Princess Diana had supported the publication of an anti–AP mine picture book ("Not Mines, But Flowers,") by the Association to Aid Refugees (AAR), a Japanese NGO engaged in assistance to landmine victims. She gave her signature to the AAR, and in Japan the book was sold with her signature on it. After her sudden death, many Japanese learned of the picture book in association with Diana and became sympathetic with AAR's efforts of victim assistance.

The second incident came in September 1997, when Obuchi became Foreign Minister and decided to review Japanese policy on landmines. Obuchi made a well-known statement that month that "it would not make sense for Japan to oppose the Treaty while cooperating in demining activities in Cambodia" (Mekata, 1998). Obuchi's statement surprised officials in the Defense Agency and MOFA, as it was completely unexpected for such a high-ranking politician to publicly express support for the treaty in spite of U.S. opposition. Although it was unclear why Obuchi expressed his support for the ban treaty, JCBL overwhelmingly welcomed his statement.

Last, in October 1997, the Nobel Peace Prize was awarded to ICBL and Jody Williams, ICBL Coordinator. The award raised not only the credibility of ICBL but also that of JCBL. JCBL, an organization created only a few months prior to the awarding of the Nobel Prize, all of a sudden began to receive public attention in Japan. The public realized that being part of ICBL, JCBL itself was indirectly awarded the Nobel Prize. This boosted the moral of JCBL members and helped the group gain public respect and trust. These three incidents—Princess Diana's death,

Obuchi's becoming Foreign Minister and his statement of support for the Ottawa efforts, and the Nobel Peace Prize given to ICBL—boosted public support for the treaty and JCBL. After internal discussions among relevant ministries in late October 1997, the government informally decided to break ranks with the United States and sign the treaty. Prime Minister Hashimoto reportedly summoned officials in MOFA and the Defense Agency to participate in the Ottawa Process as soon as possible.

However, the government was still slow in proceeding with signing the treaty and did not announce its intention to join in the Ottawa conference until the last minute. While MOFA, the ministry attempting to gain permanent membership on the UN Security Council for Japan, sensed the growing international and domestic support for the Mine Ban Treaty and changed its position from opposition to support,[11] the Defense Agency continued to resist NGO pressure to sign the treaty. The agency lobbied Japanese politicians in both the House of Representatives and the House of Councilors to oppose the Mine Ban Treaty.[12] The agency officials were especially concerned about the possibility of further cuts in the defense budget due to the ban of mines, which might accelerate the trend of streamlining defense expenditures. In addition, they may have been offended by NGOs that "intervened" in national security matters—the bureaucratic turf of the Defense Agency—in the name of humanitarianism (Osa, 1997).

JCBL further stepped up its efforts to pressure the government by taking advantage of the media and working on petitions. In mid-November 1997, JCBL submitted another petition to Foreign Minister Obuchi, with about 35,300 signatures. This time, the signatures were not submitted by a JCBL member via Obuchi's secretary, but were handed directly to Obuchi by Tun Channareth, landmine survivor and one of the founders of the Cambodia Campaign to Ban Landmines, who had been visiting Japan at that time at the invitation of JCBL. The meeting was a great success for Japanese antilandmine NGOs. First, it confirmed Obuchi's commitment to the ban treaty; in response to Channareth, who said he wanted to see Obuchi at the 1997 treaty-signing conference in Ottawa, Obuchi replied he was making a last-minute effort to sign the treaty. In addition, the meeting was widely publicized in Japanese major daily newspapers such as the *Mainichi Shimbun,* reflecting increased media interest in the ban treaty and JCBL (Maruyama, 1997b; Nakabori, 1997).

About ten days after the Channareth meeting with Obuchi, and just a week before the treaty-signing meeting in Ottawa, the Japanese government finally announced its decision to sign the treaty. Foreign Minister Obuchi himself flew to Ottawa to take part in the signing ceremony.

Japan joined some 120 other countries to become signatories to the Ottawa Convention. At the conference Obuchi announced that the Japanese government would contribute ¥10 billion for mine clearance and victim assistance in 1998–2003 (*Tokyo Shimbun,* 1997b).

It is clear the NGO pressure and international and domestic public opinion in support of the ban treaty prompted the Japanese government to sign the treaty. It reached the point where high-ranking politicians such as Obuchi could not ignore growing public support for the treaty. It is important to note, however, that Japan's signing the treaty was not based on government–NGO partnership as seen in the relationship between the Canadian government and NGOs. Motoko Metaka, an NGO representative of AAR explains, "Japan and Canada are at the opposite ends of the spectrum when it comes to partnerships between government and NGOs—no such partnership exists in Japan" (quoted in English, 1998, p. 128). In the first stage of the Ottawa process, there was almost no collaboration between the government and Japanese NGOs. (During the second stage, NGOs and politicians collaborated more frequently and closely.) While Foreign Minister Obuchi was sympathetic toward the causes of antilandmine campaigns, he was not an ally of JCBL but was subject to NGO pressure. Furthermore, the Japanese bureaucracy was slow to act. The bureaucrats in Obuchi's ministry, MOFA, were too cautious to take any initiative to sign the treaty. In addition, the Defense Agency adamantly opposed the treaty and delayed the government's decision to join in the Ottawa signatory conference. NGOs tried to appeal to Obuchi so that he would silence the opposition from the Defense Agency.

To NGOs' dismay, there was virtually no sign that the Japanese government would rapidly ratify the treaty at the beginning of the second stage of the Ottawa process. One reason for the delay in ratification was the nuclear test explosions conducted by India and Pakistan in May 1998. Since the same section (the Division of Arms Control and Scientific Affairs) within MOFA took charge of both landmines and nuclear arms control issues, the ministry officials focused on nuclear nonproliferation efforts and thus were unable to spend enough time on landmine issues (Ministry of Foreign Affairs, 1998a; International Campaign to Ban Landmines, 1999). Yet, more important, the major obstacle to the ratification was related to the U.S. troops in Japan under the U.S.–Japan Security Treaty. The U.S. troops stockpiled landmines on their bases in Japan. According to a MOFA official, three questions became central to the ratification: Once Japan ratifies the treaty, (1) would it be necessary for Tokyo to remove AP mines at U.S. bases in Japan?; (2) would U.S. forces in Japan be allowed to use these mines in its military activities in Japan?; and (3) would Japanese personnel be allowed to transport mines from U.S. bases in Japan, for example, to the Korean Peninsula? (International Campaign to Ban Landmines, 1999). In particular, the last question was an important one, because the task of transporting landmines is usually carried out by Japanese private firms or the nation's Self Defense Forces. MOFA maintained that the U.S. base issue had to be discussed with the U.S. government.

Furthermore, the Defense Agency became concerned with development of alternatives to AP mines. The agency was conducting research to find alternatives and wanted to delay the ratification until the completion of the research. Defense officials were uneasy about ratifying a total ban of landmines when they did not have any alternatives.

Given the reluctance of the government during the second stage towards ratification, JCBL worked closely with some pro-Ottawa Japanese politicians. These politicians had earlier formed a League of Diet Members to Promote a Comprehensive Ban on Antipersonnel Landmines (hereafter called the League), chaired by Kenji Kosaka of former Shinshinto (House of Representatives; as of 2001, a member of the LDP). This organization was unique in that its vice chair was Gen Nakatani of the LDP (House of Representative), a defense *zoku* and former personnel of the Self Defense Forces (who became the Chief of the Defense Agency in 2001). Nakatani stated that not ratifying the treaty was against the international trends and that Japan should contribute to a total ban on AP mines. As unique as Nakatani was the League's steering committee chair Toshihisa Fujita of Democratic Party (House of Representative up until 2000, when he lost an reelection), who previously worked for Japanese NGOs for nearly 20 years. For many years, Fujita worked as a representative of the aforementioned AAR, a Japanese NGO member of JCBL and one of the forerunners in the landmine campaign in Japan. Fujita became an important bridge between Japanese NGOs and politicians. He had earlier called on other Diet members to sign the AP mine ban treaty and successfully collected petition signatures of 387 Diet members of various political parties and submitted them to Prime Minister Hashimoto in June 1997. These signatures included those of seven former prime ministers, such as that of hawkish Yasuhiro Nakasone of the LDP (*Tokyo Shimbun,* 1997a; *Mainichi Shimbun,* 1997). Despite being a first-time Diet member (*ichinen-sei giin*), Fujita successfully appealed to senior politicians to join in the anti-AP mines campaign (Maruyama, 1997a).

Together with the League, JCBL worked hard to raise public awareness and pressure the government for ratification. For example, AAR invited Chris Moon, a landmine victim and a representative of the HALO Trust, a British NGO engaged in demining activities throughout the world, to run as a frame-bearer during the Nagano Winter Olympics in February 1998. With the backing up of the League (Fujita in particular), AAR was able to persuade the Nagano Olympic Peace Appeal Steering Committee to invite Moon. Moon's appearance at the Olympic opening Ceremony helped raise public awareness on the landmine issue not only in Japan but also around the world, through live coverage of the ceremony (Fujiura, Yanase, & Osa, 2000).

In June 1998 JCBL held a symposium on landmines in cooperation with the Canadian embassy in Japan. The symposium brought together officials from MOFA and the Defense Agency, the Canadian Ambassador to Japan, and Fujita of the League. NGOs lauded Japan's signing of the Mine Ban Treaty but expressed frustration at the low pace of developments since then. Similarly, Fujita argued that Japan should go ahead and ratify the treaty by setting aside the problem of interpreting the treaty (as to whether it is applicable to the U.S. bases in Japan), and he stated his hope that the Diet would ratify the treaty during the extraordinary session in the fall of 1998 and planned to submit a request for ratification by the current session. However, a MOFA representative reiterated that the landmines stocked in the U.S. bases in Japan were the major concern of the ministry and stated that the Japanese government needed to consult with Washington (*Japan Times,* 1998).

Both JCBL and the League submitted several petitions to Prime Minister Obuchi in the summer and early fall of 1998. Then, a turning point came in September 1998, when the League was able to arrange a meeting between Obuchi and JCBL. On September 11, 1998, Kitagawa and Shimizu of JCBL met Obuchi together with representatives of the League (Kosaka, Nakatani, and Fujita) and an official from MOFA's Division of Arm's Control and Scientific Affairs (Nobyasu Abe). JCBL handed in 201,500 signatures to Obuchi and urged the government to join and ratify the treaty before 40 other countries would ratify. At that point, 37 countries had already ratified. The JCBL representatives told Obuchi that, unless Japan hurried, it would not be among the first 40 ratifications needed for the treaty to enter into force. They emphasized that it would be an honor for the government to become one of the 40 ratifiers. Obuchi reportedly responded positively to JCBL's request and later encouraged the LDP and other parties to ratify within the same month.[13]

Less than a week after the Obuchi meeting, JCBL learned that 40 governments had already signed the treaty, thus leaving Japan out of the first 40-country group that would make the treaty take effect.

JCBL immediately released a statement of this news to the media. In the statement, the group urged the government to ratify before the end of September 1998, to join some 40 other countries to mark March 1, 1999, as the day when the treaty would enter into force.[14]

On September 30, 1998, the Diet finally passed a domestic law (the Law Concerning the Prohibition of the Production of Antipersonnel Landmines and the Regulation of their Possession) to ratify the ban treaty. The bill had been presented on September 24 to three Committees of the House of Representatives for hearings (Foreign Affairs Committee, National Security Affairs Committee, Commerce and Industry Committee). As soon as the House of Representatives passed the bill on September 29, it was presented to the House of Councilors for an approval on September 30. There had been only a week for the entire ratification process, which inevitably left fundamental questions unresolved from the viewpoint of NGOs. It was rushed through the Diet to be signed by the end of September 1998, in an effort for Japan to join some other 40 governments to make the treaty effective on March 1, 1999.[15]

JCBL had obtained the draft law a few days prior to the committee hearings and contacted Fujita of the League to ask and clarify key points at the hearings. One of the main concerns for JCBL was the landmines stockpiled in U.S. bases in Japan. The United States had earlier claimed that its bases were not on Japanese territory and thus that Japan could not handle these mines even it ratified the treaty. JCBL did not attempt to challenge the U.S. policy to maintain AP mines in U.S. bases in Japan due to the U.S. extraterritorial rights, but the group wanted to demand and/or clarify several points regarding the use and transportation of AP mines by U.S. troops in Japan. JCBL tried to confirm that (1) under the new law, Japan would not use AP mines on any occasions for its national defense, even in joint operations with the U.S. army; (2) neither the Self Defense Forces nor Japanese private firms would be allowed to transport AP mines for the U.S. troops under the law; (3) the U.S. government would be required to give Tokyo prior notification of transit of U.S. forces equipped with AP mines through Japanese territorial waters and land; and (4) the Japanese government would not take charge of financial responsibility for the transportation of AP mines by U.S. troops in Japan (Japan Campaign to Ban Landmines, 1998). Fujita asked for clarification on these points at the hearings as requested by JCBL. As it turned out, he was able to confirm all the points except for the third on the notification requirement of the United States. According to MOFA officials, the U.S. would not need to notify the Japanese government of the transportation of U.S. AP mines because Japan approved the possession of landmines by the U.S. forces stationed in Japan (House of Representatives, National Security Affairs Committee, 1998). Thus, the main limitation of the domestic law was clearly over the existence of AP mines on U.S. bases in Japan.

Other demands made by JCBL but unrelated to the issue of U.S. AP mines included a wording of a particular phrase and the Japanese government's plans of future eradication of AP mines. JCBL claimed that in the domestic bill direct and clear wording was needed to correspond with the Mine Ban Treaty and that the term "regulations to possess landmines" used in the Japanese draft bill should be replaced by "the regulation of use, storage, and possession" as expressed in the Mine Ban Treaty. On behalf of JCBL, Fujita asked these questions at the hearings and confirmed that the AP mines (estimated as many as one million) possessed by the SDF would be destroyed within the next four years. Yet, the first point regarding the issue of strict wording was not taken seriously at the Diet and Fujita's/JCBL's demand was rejected. Foreign Minister Masahiko Takemura and an official from the Ministry of International Trade and Industry (MITI) responded that the change would not needed since Japan's pre-existing Explosive Control Act prohibits the use of mines and the term "regulations to possess landmines" would cover the banning of acquisition, stockpiling, and retention. They insisted that there was no loophole in the proposed law regarding a total ban of AP mines (House of Representatives, National Security Affairs Committee, 1998).

Despite the shortcomings, the ratification of the Mine Ban Treaty was hailed by NGOs as a show of independent policy making against the United States and an important step toward the eradication of AP mines. "This is a clear illustration of the success of public awareness," stated Shimizu of JCBL (One World, 1998).

After the ratification of the Mine Ban Treaty, Japanese ODA was used to promote demining activities and victims' rehabilitation. The Japanese government committed ¥10 billion for 1998–2003 for the following: (1) machineries for eradication of mines, contribution to UN organizations for demining activities; (2) technical training for making prosthetics and rehabilitation of mine victims, and (3) assistance to NGOs involved in manufacturing prosthetics and rehabilitation of victims. In 1998, a study session was held among JICA officials and JCBL representatives on implementing demining policy in ODA. Tokyo further announced that it would provide US$2.1 million to the UN Voluntary Trust Fund for Assistance in Mine Action to promote mine-clearance, mine-awareness education, and victim assistance (Japan Economic Institute, 1999). In 1998–1999, Tokyo spent ¥1.5 billion, mainly contributing to UN agencies (e.g., the U.N. Development Programme, the UN International Children's Educational Fund or UNICEF), the Cambodian Mine Action Center (CMAC, a governmental organization in Cambodia established to conduct demining activities), and HALO Trust, a leading NGO from Britain in demining and assistance to mine victims. In 2000, the government established a new grant program specifically designed for assistance to mine victims and demining activities (¥2.2 billion). In addition, Tokyo expanded the preexisting Grassroots Grant Assistance Program to provide more assistance to NGOs involved in demining efforts. An NGO involved in this area could receive from MOFA a grant of as much as ¥100 million, ten times more than the maximum amount an NGO would otherwise get. As a result, ODA expenditures spent on NGOs through the Grassroots Grant Assistance Program jumped tenfold, from ¥23 million in 1997 to ¥294 million in 2000, even though the total amount of Japan's ODA was declining (Ministry of Foreign Affairs, 2000a).

JCBL became the prime mover in generating domestic concern about AP mines. It disseminated information about the scope of AP mine use and its effects, thereby helping to define the use of mines as a global problem. JCBL networked with sympathetic politicians, instigated political debates over the utility of mines, and put mine proponents in the Defense Agency on the defensive. It was extremely helpful for JCBL to have established a working relationship with the League, which opened access to the policy process. As seen in the Diet hearings on the domestic law, JCBL was able to deliver its demands through the League's Fujita.

JCBL also educated government officials who came to see the signing of a total ban treaty as a positive way to position Japan in global society. As the number of states supporting a ban reached a critical mass, increasing numbers of bureaucrats and politicians felt that Japan should get on the bandwagon. In a way, one can conclude that JCBL served as a catalyst for a change, focusing attention to the landmine issue and contributing to the emergence of a new norm in Japan.

The case of the antilandmine campaign demonstrates that Japanese NGOs, in collaboration with politicians and INGOs, could contribute to bringing about important change in Japan's foreign policy and aid programs.

Conclusion

What do the three NGO campaigns tell us about state–civil society and Japanese aid politics? First, the cases demonstrate how persistent NGOs were in demanding policy change, by holding seminars and symposiums, releasing information to the press, meeting government officials, and publishing books and articles to raise public awareness. Even though their goals initially seemed unrealistic, the NGOs did not give up and continued to pressure MOFA. At the same time, it was not Japanese NGOs alone that brought about change. They effectively worked with NGOs of other countries that backed their efforts. Japanese NGOs also made effective use of the media, making the press their ally.

Second, MOFA completely changed its previous positions when they yielded to the NGO pressures. MOFA's initial response to NGO criticism can be summarized in three behaviors: deny problems exist, hide information from the public, and deny any responsibility for harm afflicted. As seen in the pesticide case, for example, MOFA officials claimed that the local government had to take responsibility for any problems that might arise, because Japan's aid was request based. But MOFA was not able to continue to act in these ways in the face of NGO pressure. It was forced to behave in a more responsible manner, taking into consideration local conditions and people's needs. MOFA gave reasons for its policy changes, but these reasons coincided with what NGOs had claimed all along. In the Narmada case, MOFA stated that the ministry was going to cancel the loan aid due to a lack of environmental assessment studies. In the case of the pesticide aid to Cambodia, MOFA said that the aid would be terminated because of a lack of Cambodian domestic law regulating pesticides. In the last case, MOFA claimed that Japan would ratify the Mine Ban Treaty because Japan should be committed to landmine eradication. These reasons were actually originally given by NGOs when they were trying to influence the Japanese government.

Third, NGOs played an important role in representing the interests of the socially weak who were marginalized from political participation (in the first case, the indigenous tribes in the Narmada River basin; in the second case, Cambodian farmers; and in the third case, landmine victims). In the first two cases, Japanese NGOs campaigned against the state–business coalition that tried to protect its interests against the local people. In the last case, JCBL campaigned against the state's overreliance on U.S. sensitivities.

Fourth, by yielding to NGO pressure, MOFA has crossed a rubicon. Once it made precedents in incorporating NGO claims, it cannot easily go back to the old decision-making pattern. NGOs now demand that their voices be heard and reflected in government policy. Indeed, the cases demonstrate the defeat of an outdated, top–down decision-making model of the developmental state.

As these cases demonstrate, it is not an exaggeration to say that NGO activism has changed the relationship between the state and civil society. NGOs have been fashioning a new type of politics in Japan, and NGO activities have created a challenge for domestic governance. The state has had to incorporate their demands in the domestic political process by establishing new procedures of political participation.

CHAPTER FIVE

NGO–MOFA Cooperation and Contention in Aid

The previous chapters examined how globalization and industrialization have changed Japan, contributing to the weakening of the developmental state, the erosion of the state–business alliance, the empowerment of civil society, and a changing relationship between the state and civil society. We have also examined in Chapter 4 this changing state–civil society relationship through case studies of nongovernmental organizations' (NGOs) campaigns against official developmental assistance (ODA) policies. Through advocacy campaigns at home and abroad, NGOs not only demand state accountability for Japanese ODA but also challenge state authority.

In contrast to Chapter 4, which focused on confrontational aspects of NGOs' relations with the government, this chapter focuses on cooperative aspects. The chapter discusses patterns of interaction between the Ministry of Foreign Affairs (MOFA) and NGOs, and the political participation of NGOs in aid decision making.

The chapter first analyzes what factors promote MOFA–NGO cooperation. Next, it examines how MOFA and NGOs have come to work together since the early 1990s. Then it analyzes the diversity within the NGO community; while some NGOs try to maintain critical distance from the ministry, others are co-opted by the state with lucrative funding and contract opportunities. The chapter ends with comparative case studies of two Japanese NGOs, an independent NGO trying to maintain a critical distance from MOFA and an apolitical NGO working uncritically on MOFA-funded projects.

Why Cooperate?

The relationship between Japanese NGOs and the state changed in the 1990s, moving toward more collaboration and dialogue. Previously, government officials viewed NGOs with suspicion and preferred to take direction from business groups. Now, state officials have begun to view Japanese NGOs in a more positive light and listen to their opinions. Increasingly, they have begun to realize the importance of Japanese NGOs in development. How did their attitude change? In Chapter 2, we discussed MOFA's adoption of the sustainable human development approach, which highly values the role of NGOs in aid. At the international level, development paradigms have changed over the last four decades, moving from the modernization approach to the sustainable human development approach. As Japan has become one of the most prominent donors in the international community, other donors have demanded that Japan promote the sustainable human development approach and take a leadership role in international aid. As a result of international pressure, MOFA accepted the new paradigm.

But at the same time, it is important to point out that organizational learning took place at the ministry. Today, many MOFA officials genuinely believe that the sustainable human development approach works better than the traditional, infrastructure-based development approach. MOFA has come to acknowledge the growing capacity of NGOs to address a wide range of transnational issues that the state itself cannot to cope with. In particular, the ministry values NGOs' strengths in aid implementation. NGOs can implement grassroots aid projects that the state is ill-equipped to carry out. The Japanese aid administration lacks either the skills or personnel to implement small-scale grassroots aid. In contrast, NGOs can reach people at a grassroots level better than state officials and can provide small scale, labor-intensive aid.

Another factor contributing to the change in state officials' attitudes toward NGOs is the budget pressure caused by Japan's fiscal restructuring. NGOs' activities are usually small in scale, labor-intensive, and less expensive than government programs. Thus, government officials believe that the incorporation of NGOs into Japanese ODA can improve the efficiency and cost-effectiveness of aid, thus helping aid agencies overcome fiscal constraints.

In addition, bureaucratic sectarianism plays a role in increased state interest in the strengthening relations with NGOs. MOFA officials have begun to see NGOs as their own domestic constituency. They assume that NGOs can potentially become strong supporters of MOFA and proponents for the ministry's ODA policies, which could give MOFA increased leverage over other ministries in today's administrative restructuring processes. MOFA lacks a strong domestic constituency and thus the current "NGO boom" provides an opportunity for the ministry to strengthen its domestic standing. MOFA's relationship with NGOs is comparable to MITI's relationship with the Japanese business sector. As MITI represents the interests of Japanese business, MOFA has become the main contact ministry for the NGO community and the window through which Japanese NGOs channel their participation in ODA projects and decision-making.

For NGOs, cooperation with MOFA can mean a steady flow of financial assistance, desperately needed by the majority of Japanese NGOs. Many NGOs are cash starved and governmental financial assistance is invaluable. NGOs also hope to influence ODA policy by cooperating or collaborating with MOFA officials. They welcome opportunities to discuss development issues with MOFA officials whenever they can. In fact, NGOs have initiated regular meetings with MOFA (see below) to have their views reflected in ODA policy.

In short, increasing cooperation between NGOs and MOFA is valued by both sides. On the one hand, MOFA needs the support and skills provided by NGOs to bolster ministerial policy goals. On the other hand, NGOs want to interact with MOFA for financial and political reasons. There is, though, some disagreement within the NGO community as to how and to what extent to work with the bureaucracy, a point discussed further later in the chapter.

NGO–State Partnership

With the changing attitude of officials toward NGOs, Japanese NGO–state relations have been gradually shifting from confrontation to cooperation. The interaction between NGOs and MOFA occurs mainly in three forms: *financial assistance, policy dialogue,* and *operational collaboration.* The Japanese government's first gesture was financial assistance: simple, one-way transfers of money from the government to NGOs. It did not involve engagement between NGOs and the government to improve ODA. Policy dialogue refers to "an attempt to influence policy through information exchange and debate that explores both differences and areas of agreement" (Covey, 1998, p. 82) between NGOs and the state. Policy dialogue takes place formally through committees and study groups involving government officials and NGO members, and informally through casual interactions at conferences and seminars. Policy dialogue is "insider" advocacy (Covey, 1998, p. 82), the seeking of incremental reform rather than a radical fundamental shift. Policy dialogue does not employ high-pressure "street protest" tactics but could contribute to building up trust and partnership between NGOs and state officials. But for NGOs to impact state policy, they have to be seen as legitimate. Thus they must conform to the rules of the game and behave accordingly or concede to the particular views and values of state officials. Finally, operational collaboration is project-based NGO engagement. It refers to NGOs' direct involvement in any phase of aid projects. By such collaboration, NGOs participate in project-based policy making at the microlevel.

Financial Assistance to NGOs

Since the end of the 1980s, the Japanese government has established several mechanisms to assist NGOs involved in aid activities in the developing world. Several sources of funds are now available to Japanese NGOs from various ministries (e.g., MOFA, MOPS, the Environmental Agency, the Ministry of Forestry and Fishery, the Ministry of Health and Welfare) and local governments (e.g., Tokyo, Kanagawa, Toyama, Niigata). The most significant are two funds initiated by MOFA in 1989 (the Subsidy Funds for NGO Projects and Grant Assistance for Grassroots Projects) and one launched in 1991 by the Ministry of Posts and Telecommunications (MOPT; the Volunteer Postal Savings International Aid). MOFA's funding is now provided by the Nongovernmental Organizations Assistance Office in the Economic Cooperation Bureau (hereafter the NGO Assistance Office), established in 1994 within the Economic Cooperation Bureau (Ministry of Foreign Affairs, 1996a). MOFA's funding for NGOs has rapidly increased since 1989 despite Japan's economic recession of the 1990s. By 1998, the Subsidy Funds for NGO Projects had grown to ten times that of 1989 (from approximately ¥112 million to ¥1.15 billion) and the Grant Assistance for Grassroots Projects had expanded approximately 19-fold (from about ¥300 million to ¥5.7 billion) (Saotome, 1999, see Figure 5.1). In contrast to the Subsidy Funds for NGO Projects, which is available only to Japanese NGOs, the Grant Assistance for Grassroots Projects provides funding to both Japanese and non-Japanese NGOs for development projects outside Japan. MOPT's Volunteer Postal Savings International Aid is not subject to the yearly budgetary system.[1] Holders of this ordinary postal savings account designate that 20 percent of their after-tax interest will go to NGOs via MOPS. Reflecting the tax advantage of postal savings to the Japanese, this fund attracted some 24 million members. Due to falling interest rates in Japan, however,

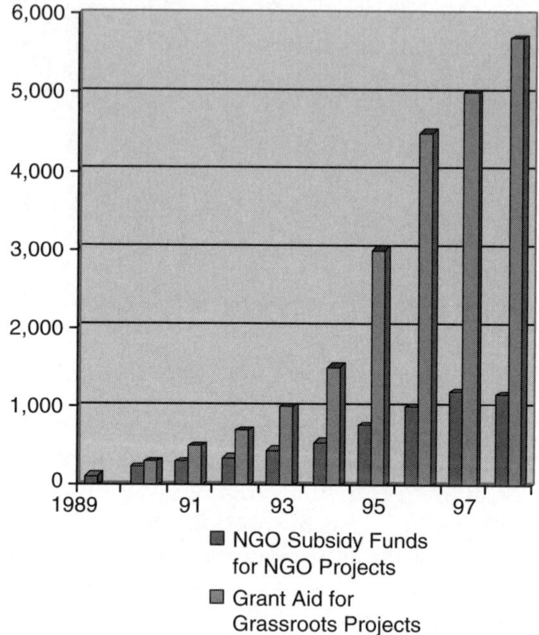

Figure 5.1   Growth of government funds to NGOs, 1989–1998 (¥ billion) (Saotome, 1999).

the fund fell from a high of ¥2.8 billion in 1995 to ¥1.2 billion in 1999 (Ministry of Posts and Telecommunications, 1999).

The decision making behind distribution of these funds is opaque to all but ministry insiders. However, a review of recipients indicates that a wide range of NGOs receive funding from these sources, including NGOs that have been critical of Japanese ODA policy.

In addition, the government has adopted policies that facilitate indirect financial assistance to NGOs. In 1990, the Japanese Diet passed a law permitting corporations to deduct charitable contributions (Salamon, 1994), a law which, for the first time, created tax incentives for Japanese firms to donate funds to incorporated NGOs. In 1994, MOFA established an Assistance System for International Volunteer Compensation that partially covers the insurance fees for volunteers working overseas and/or entering areas of war risks (Ministry of Foreign Affairs, 1995b). Finally, in FY2000, MOFA launched three funding schemes to support NGO personnel (*International Development Journal,* 1999c). First, the ministry set up an Overseas Training System as part of the Subsidy Funds for NGO Projects. This system funds NGO members to intern at overseas NGOs where they can learn about methods and management of development aid, improve their language skills, and network with foreign NGOs. Second, MOFA established an NGO Consultation System to provide information and advice to NGOs all over Japan. Leading NGOs are contracted to give counseling to other NGOs. For FY2000, 14 NGOs were contracted by MOFA as lead NGOs. Third, MOFA financed two new NGO research groups: the NGO Management Council and the NGO Research Group on Evaluation of International Cooperation. Consisting of NGO representatives, these groups conduct research on NGO management and evaluation of NGO activities.

Accelerating Policy Dialogue

The success of NGOs in influencing aid policy largely depends on their ability to engage state officials. While easy access to officials does not guarantee policy impact, accelerating mutual understanding through dialogue is one of the most important steps of NGOs to change aid policy.

Until the 1990s, MOFA and NGOs had very few channels to exchange views and information. Even in 1989, when the government began NGO financial assistance, NGOs had no opportunity to engage in policy dialogue with MOFA. In the mid-1990s, however, the government began to invite NGO leaders to participate in a variety of policy forums.[2] For example, complying with an NGO request, the Japanese government appointed three NGO representatives as official delegates to the 1994 Cairo International Conference on Population and Development. For the first time, NGO members were selected as part of a Japanese government delegation, and their participation in the international conference at the invitation of the Japanese government was a significant step for the Japanese NGO community toward more international visibility and influence. Their presence at the Cairo conference marked a sharp contrast to the previous International Population Conference in Mexico in 1984 at which Japanese Diet members "represented" Japanese NGOs (Ikegami, 1996).

In the 1990s, MOFA and NGOs began to hold numerous seminars, symposia, and conferences to promote dialogue. In these meetings, NGO members tried to establish themselves as equal partners with MOFA officials. In January 1997, for example, JVC and Mekong Watch organized a conference to exchange government and NGO views of Japan's ODA policy in the Mekong River region, promote dialogue between the government and NGOs, and discuss issues of sustainable development and citizens' participation in ODA. Officials from MOFA, JICA, and OECF participated, representing one of the first occasions when government officials joined an NGO-initiated dialogue, something that would have been unthinkable in the 1980s. The conference boosted the JVC's morale because, with the participation of government officials, the group realized that the government agencies took Japanese NGOs and the issues of sustainable development seriously.[3]

NGOs and government officials, especially those in MOFA and JICA, also exchange views through other conferences and seminars sponsored by development organizations such as the Japan Society for International Development (JSID), an academic association established in 1990, and the Foundation for Advanced Studies on International Development (FASID), a quasi-governmental research and training institution (*zaidan hōjin*) established in the early 1990s under the auspices of MOFA. JSID and FASID conferences include government officials, NGO representatives, academics, and corporate representatives involved in aid and development. In particular, FASID's research director, Kazuo Takahashi, encourages NGO participation in development and tries to create opportunities for NGOs to express their views.[4] In these fora, NGOs stress the importance of grassroots aid and try to elevate their status to that of equal partners with government officials and corporate representatives.

In addition, Japanese NGOs and government officials have formed councils that hold regular meetings to discuss issues related to humanitarian assistance to developing countries and state funding of NGOs. Several sets of regular meetings are held. The most important ongoing meeting between NGOs and government officials is the NGO–MOFA Regular Council Meeting (NGO–MOFA *teiki kyōgi-kai*). The council, started in 1996, usually meets quarterly and involves about ten representatives from the NGO community and another ten from different divisions within MOFA. JANIC is in charge of the NGO side and MOFA's Policy Division of the Economic Cooperation Bureau is in charge of the ministry's representation. This NGO–MOFA council originated from a JANIC–MOFA symposium in 1995, which analyzed how other donor countries (such as the United States) were funding and involving NGOs in international aid projects and discussed possibilities for adopting similar strategies in Japan.[5] At the NGO–MOFA Council meetings, NGO representatives and MOFA officials discuss how Japanese NGOs can be strengthened by public funding and how MOFA's NGO funding systems (i.e., Subsidy Funds for NGO Projects and Grand Aid for Grassroots Projects) can be improved by removing obstacles to the involvement of Japanese NGOs. According to the minutes and reports of these NGO–MOFA Council, NGOs have raised a number of constructive criticisms regarding MOFA's handling of NGO assistance funds (see Table 5.1).

MOFA officials have responded to NGO criticisms raised in these council meetings, attempting to meet NGO concerns. For example, per NGOs' request, MOFA approved research fellowship funds for NGOs starting in FY2000. At the same time, MOFA officials countered that on some issues they either disagreed with NGOs (e.g., the desirability of distributing aid to human rights groups) or they were constrained by broader government policy (e.g., changing from single to multiyear budgeting or increasing embassy staff in charge of NGO grants).

Originally, the council's main purpose was to discuss issues related to MOFA's funding schemes. Yet the council has gradually evolved to

Table 5.1   Issues raised by NGO representatives at NGO–MOFA Council Meetings*

Emphasis on hardware/lack of qualified officials. There is a serious shortage of qualified officials at Japanese embassies and consulates overseas who understand the importance of soft aid and the role of NGOs in development. Many overseas officials in charge of Grant Aid for Grassroots Projects mistrust NGOs' management ability and therefore prefer to give NGOs funds for of purchase equipment rather than for training programs. Many overseas Japanese officials are seconded (*shukkō*) from various ministries for a two to three year assignment to supervise MOFA's NGO funding and lack adequate understanding of issues of sustainable development. (from July 10, 1996; October 18, 1996; January 28, 1997; and September 30, 1997 meetings)

Lack of transparency of criteria for selecting grantees. MOFA lacks consistency in selecting grantees. The ministry appears to favor NGOs that are already well-established. (April 25, 1996; September 30, 1997)

Lack of funds for daily administrative costs. All the grants are project-based and do not cover daily management costs. (April 28, 1996)

Single-year budgeting. NGOs cannot make plans for multiple year projects under the current one-year grant system. In addition, the grant application procedure takes several months and many NGOs usually end up spending less than a year, often only about six months, on actual implementation of their projects funded by MOFA. (July 10, 1996; September 30, 1997)

Late payment of funds. MOFA usually pays funds after the project is finished. Many NGOs, especially unincorporated NGOs, lack sufficient funds to launch projects. (July 10, 1996; June 29, 1998)

Reluctance to hire foreign NGOs. MOFA prefers Japanese NGOs to NGOs of other countries because the ministry wants to help Japanese NGOs build capacity to play a professional role in aid and to improve the image of Japanese aid by enhancing *kao no mieru enjo* (aid with Japanese faces). However, Japanese NGOs should not be overly protected; they should compete with NGOs of other countries to win contracts for Japanese aid. Such open competition will improve the quality of Japanese NGOs as well as that of Japan's ODA programs. (November 6, 1998; May 12, 1999)

---

* *Summarized from NGO representative statements published in Council minutes, available at JANIC office in Tokyo.*

address broader topics at the macro level, including untied aid policy, debt relief, and grant aid policy. NGOs are given an opportunity to express their views of Japan's ODA policy. MOFA officials indicate some understanding of NGOs' claims but stress that, at a time of budget crisis, the ministry has to make policy based on "national interest" to maintain support from the public and the corporate sector.

One positive note of NGO–MOFA Regular Council Meetings is that they are not packed, as might be expected, with progovernment NGOs. On the contrary, independent NGOs represent the whole NGO community. This is because MOFA selected JANIC, the largest NGO network in Japan, as the ministry's counterpart for the meetings. Many of JANIC's active members are representatives of independent NGOs.

The NGO–MOFA Regular Council Meeting has led to another important forum of NGO–MOFA interaction. Following the release of the final report by the Council on ODA Reforms for the 21st Century, MOFA established a Subcommittee to Achieve the Objectives of the ODA Reform Council's Final Report (*ODA kaikaku kondan-kai saishū hōkoku-tō jitsugen ni muketa shō-iinkai*) in 1999, at the request of NGOs. This subcommittee, commonly called the Subcommittee to Follow up the Proposal by the Council on ODA Reforms for the 21st Century (*21-seiki ni mukete no ODA kaikaku kondan-kai teigen forō appu shō-iinkai*), is accountable to the NGO–MOFA Council Meeting and meets six times a year. As the name indicates, the subcommittee discusses concrete

Table 5.2 Composition of the NGO–MOFA Regular Council Meeting, 1996–1999★

MOFA (Economic Cooperation Bureau)★★	*NGOs*★★★
Policy Division	JANIC
NGO Assistance Office	SIV
Research and Planning Division	Shapla Neer
International Organization Division	Nagoya NGO Center
Technical Cooperation Division	JVC
Grant Aid Cooperation Division	CARE Japan
Development Cooperation Division	Kansai NGO Council
United Nations Administrative Division	
International Emergency Aid Office	
Evaluation Office	

★Based on the NGO–MOFA Regular Council Meeting Minutes, from April 25, 1996, to May 12, 1999.
★★In addition to MOFA officials, a JICA representative usually participates as an observer.
★★★One to two additional NGOs sometimes participate as observers.

Table 5.3 Composition of the NGO–MOFA subcommittee to achieve objectives of the ODA Reform Council's Final Report, 1999[6]

MOFA (Economic Cooperation Bureau)	NGOs*
Policy Division	JANIC
NGO Assistance Office	JVC
Research and Planning Division	Shapla Neer
Technical Cooperation Division	Asia-Pacific Information Center
Grant Aid Cooperation Division	Institute for Alternative Community Development
	Africa Japan Forum

*In addition, some NGOs (e.g., OISCA, Development Education Council) participate as observers.

ways to achieve the goals specified in the final report (Kanda, 1999a). The establishment of the subcommittee seems to signal MOFA's interest in working seriously with NGOs.

Another example of state—NGO cooperation is the NGO–JICA Council Meeting (*NGO–JICA Kyōgi-kai*), which began in 1998. The NGO–JICA meeting was initiated by the participants in the NGO–MOFA Regular Council Meeting and is designed to promote information exchange and cooperation between NGOs and JICA based on equal partnership (*International Development Journal,* 1998g; Kanda, 1999a; Kanda, 1999b). The council held its first workshop for junior NGO and JICA staff in 1998 to promote mutual understanding and partnership in aid. The workshop was sponsored by JANIC and JICA and recognized as a success by both parties. In particular, NGOs found it significant that many young JICA officials share similar views of sustainable development with NGOs and try to reform ODA. Many JICA officials overcame their stereotype of NGOs as radical groups with extreme views of development. By the end of the workshop, both NGOs and JICA confirmed the possibility of collaboration in aid. At the same time, they recognized challenges to collaboration, such as legal obstacles that make it difficult for the Japanese government to fund NGO personnel costs for implementing joint aid projects. One NGO participant in the workshop pointed out that unless NGO workers are financially supported by the government, the gap in benefits and salaries between NGO members and JICA officials working on the same projects will be large, creating an unequal relationship between NGO and JICA project participants (Japan International Cooperation Agency and Japanese NGO Center for International Cooperation, 1999).

The policy dialogues between NGOs and MOFA/JICA staff have created an environment where both parties listen to each other and learn

Table 5.4   Composition of the NGO–JICA Council Meeting, 1998–1999[7]

JICA*	NGOs**
Evaluation and Management Office	JANIC
Public Relations Division	JVC
Planning Division (Planning Bureau)	Shapla Neer
Coordination and Cooperation Division (Planning Bureau)	SVA
	CARE Japan
Planning Division (Dispatching Experts Project Bureau)	Nagoya NGO Center
	Kansai NGO Council
Planning Division (Social Development Cooperation Bureau)	Education Center for Global Citizens
Agricultural Development Research Division (Agricultural, Forestry, and Fishery Development Research Bureau)	
Clerical Division (International Cooperation Training Center)	
Technical Information Division (International Cooperation Training Center)	

*MOFA (NGO Assistance Office and Technical Cooperation Division of Economic Cooperation Bureau) and OECF (Environmental and Social Development Office) send representatives to the NGO–JICA meeting as observers.
**In addition, there are NGO observers.

about their differences. The dialogues have offered an opportunity for mutual discussion about the relative strengths and weaknesses of NGOs and the government in promoting development and implementing aid projects. While MOFA and JICA have learned about problems faced by Japanese NGOs, NGOs have also learned from MOFA and JICA about the ins and outs of the ODA system. Over time, these policy dialogues are providing an opportunity for increased input by NGOs in ODA policy making.

Operational Collaboration

Another important area of NGO–MOFA relations is in operational collaboration. This collaboration has in fact grown out of the policy dialogues mentioned above. During the NGO–MOFA Regular Council Meetings, NGOs and MOFA decided to start joint evaluation of ODA projects, through a program called "NGO–MOFA Mutual Learning and Joint Evaluation." Thus far, two NGO–MOFA teams have conducted ODA and NGO project evaluations in Bangladesh and Cambodia. The Bangladesh team, for example, was formed in 1997 and consisted of representatives from MOFA (The Policy Division of the Economic

Cooperation Bureau) and NGOs such as JVC, Save the Children Japan, and Shapla Neer. The team evaluated Shapla Neer's community development project and two ODA projects for agricultural development in Bangladesh (Nongovernmental Organization—Ministry of Foreign Affairs Regular Council Meeting, 1999c). The successful joint evaluation process was assessed as a significant step to accelerate state-NGO collaboration in aid (Nongovernmental Organization—Ministry of Foreign Affairs Regular Council Meeting, 1999a). A MOFA representative, speaking at the NGO-MOFA Regular Council Meeting, expressed the ministry's positive view of joint evaluation:

> About a year ago, NGOs proposed [to MOFA] to conduct joint learning projects. … Hearing the reports from the NGO participants, I am truly glad that we conducted the evaluation project together. The report will be soon published and I think it will be a very important document for us. I think the quality of ODA will improve by responding to problems pointed out in the report, complying with the suggestions proposed, and cooperating with NGOs. … It will be valuable for us to have NGOs point out our shortages and coordinate with NGO activities. (Nongovernmental Organization—Ministry of Foreign Affairs Regular Council Meeting, 1999a; translated by the author)

At the same time, it should be pointed out that this type of field-based assessment of project implementation covers specific projects rather than entire sectors or country profiles. Thus, the utility of such assessments is limited. For example, they do not address the linkage between microprojects and sector or country policies, or the comparative merit of using funds for these projects as opposed to other priorities.

As a result of the increased interaction between NGOs and MOFA/JICA, MOFA decided for the first time in 1999 to contract out ODA grassroots projects to NGOs (as well as to universities and local governments) on a regular basis. Unlike USAID, which heavily relies on NGOs for aid project implementation, the Japanese government did not previously have a regular system of subcontracting projects to unincorporated NGOs and universities. Although in the 1970s and 1980s JICA had, on an irregular basis, contracted the staff of several NGOs for research and training, these NGOs were all incorporated organizations (Japan International Cooperation Agency, 1996). In fall 1998, a JICA–NGO taskforce was established to develop a contracting system, which was completed after five taskforce meetings. JICA then began soliciting project proposals from NGOs in mid-1999. Based on the proposals, JICA awarded contracts to NGOs in late 1999 to be implemented starting January 2000. One of the motivations for MOFA to start the contract system in the end of the 1990s was the expectation of subsidy cutbacks. Since MOFA anticipated that MOF would demand cuts in the Subsidy Funds for NGO Projects, MOFA decided to allocate JICA funds to hire NGOs as contractors (Nongovernmental Organization—Ministry of Foreign Affairs Regular Council Meeting, 1998; see Ministry of Foreign Affairs, 1999a).

Government financial assistance to NGOs, state–NGO policy dialogue, and operational collaboration of NGOs and the state, all of which started in the late 1980s–1990s, have been positive steps in enhancing the role of NGOs in development. With more access to funding and greater opportunity to voice their views, NGOs have started to influence MOFA policy. Although NGOs' influence is still limited to the project level, through cooperation and collaboration with MOFA they can channel their grassroots views and offer perspectives that can improve ODA projects and policies. In this sense, the role of NGOs is incremental. They may not directly influence overall ODA policy immediately but they can influence MOFA's views of development and aid and help the ministry gradually bring about change in ODA.

At the same time, sharp differences in perspectives still remain between MOFA and NGOs. MOFA officials put diplomatic interests first and regard ODA as a diplomatic tool to achieve "national interests." In contrast, NGOs usually have little interest in foreign policy as such and tend to argue that aid should first benefit people in the recipient countries rather than Japanese interest groups or government agencies. In addition, MOFA does not want to antagonize interministerial relations and Japanese business interests. MOFA officials want to maintain and increase support for ODA from other ministries and the corporate sector, which would strengthen their own domestic standing. MOFA officials strive to maintain their position and create and consolidate their own power within the government, an interest which sometimes puts the ministry at odds with the views of NGOs. For example, NGO representatives at NGO–MOFA Council meetings claimed that the Japanese government should adopt untied policy not only for loan aid but also grant aid. However, MOFA rejected such an idea in consideration of domestic interests (Nongovernmental Organization—Ministry of Foreign Affairs Regular Council Meeting, 1999b). In addition, while MOFA claims that it wants to work with NGOs as equal partners, many NGOs still perceive that MOFA, and even JICA, treat NGOs as a tool to win public support for ODA and to facilitate project implementation at a low cost.[8]

Frustrated by MOFA's slow pace in aid reform, some NGO leaders have begun to seek ways to cooperate with politicians interested in NGO issues to pressure MOFA. Following the 1999 establishment of a Parliamentarian Coalition for the Promotion of International Cooperation and NGO Activities, a nonpartisan group headed by the LDP's Takashi Kosugi (president), and the Democratic Party's Yukio Hatoyama and Yukihisa Fujita (vice presidents), NGO representatives started contacting politicians in this group. While these politicians may be merely interested in NGO affairs rather than ODA per se,[9] NGOs nonetheless found them a potential ally. Representatives of the Japanese NGO Center for International Cooperation Center (JANIC) had an initial meeting with some members of the group in July 1999 to discuss a wide range of issues related to ODA and NGO development, including the possibility of passing an ODA Basic Law and creating a united aid agency. A second meeting was held in fall 1999 and further meetings are planned to coordinate efforts (*International Development Journal,* 1999m).[10] Although the long-term goal of these politicians is to increase their own power and authority over NGO affairs vis-à-vis the bureaucracy, NGOs are supportive of these politicians since they think that, with the support of politicians, they can provide an additional means of pressuring the bureaucracy for change.

Diversity in the NGO Community

As Japanese NGOs are increasing their visibility in international aid, the types of NGO—state relations become an increasingly important factor affecting the course of Japan's future aid policy. Four modes of interaction are relevant to NGO–MOFA relations: *conflict, co-optation, critical cooperation,* and *disengagement.* Although many observers of civil society tend to see NGO–state relationship in dichotomy—conflict or co-optation—a closer examination reveals that NGOs can be simultaneously highly critical and highly cooperative (critical cooperation). Critical cooperation allows NGOs to work willingly with the government while maintaining autonomy and critical distance. In contrast, disengagement involves low conflict and low cooperation (Covey, 1998).

Of the four modes of interaction, critical cooperation and co-optation best characterize the relationships that most large NGOs have with the ministry. NGOs engaged in critical cooperation challenge the government's ODA policy while simultaneously cooperating with MOFA

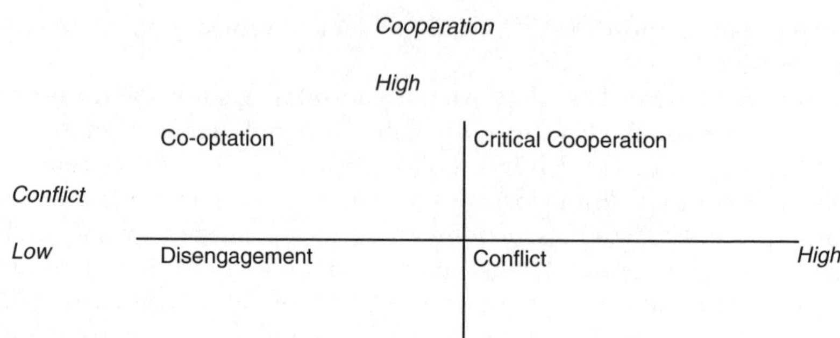

Figure 5.2   NGO–state relations
(Covey, 1998).

officials via policy dialogues and operational collaboration. These NGOs may occasionally use protest and advocacy as reform strategies, but they apply "soft" advocacy through policy dialogue more frequently than confrontational strategies. Since MOFA has begun to open its door to constructive dialogue, NGOs feel they no longer have to shout antigovernment slogans to gain attention. In contrast, NGOs considered to be "co-opted" are usually pragmatic groups that try to benefit as much as possible from working with government officials, without trying to publicly critique policy at all.

The differences between critical cooperation and co-optation can be seen more clearly through the following examples of Japanese NGOs engaged in international aid. Japan International Volunteer Center (JVC) centers its activities on advocacy for sustainable development. It places a high priority on autonomy but also cooperates with the government to try to change aid policy. In contrast, the Association of Medical Doctors of Asia (AMDA) is apolitical and interested mainly in expanding its own projects all over the world. JVC and AMDA represent important segments of Japanese NGOs. As we examine these two examples, we can see how NGO relations with the state have begun to affect Japan's aid and can potentially impact Japan's future aid policy.

Japan International Volunteer Center (JVC)

JVC was established in 1980 in Bangkok under the leadership of Masako Hoshino, who had lived in Indochina since 1965 as a member of the Japan Overseas Cooperation Volunteers (JOCV, the Japanese version of the U.S. Peace Corps). Hoshino moved from Laos to Bangkok in the late 1970s and organized an NGO of Japanese residents in Thailand and Japanese youth who came to Thailand to give assistance to Cambodian refugees on the Thai-Cambodian border. Although JVC's initial activities were limited to emergency relief in the border camps, over the years its operation has expanded into the areas of development, education, health, and environmental protection. At the same time, JVC has become more globalized, extending its activities outside Indochina to North Asia (North Korea), Latin America (e.g., Bolivia), Africa (e.g., Somalia), and the Middle East (Palestine). JVC moved its headquarters from Bangkok to Tokyo in the 1980s and by late 1999 had overseas offices in eight countries and territories.

JVC is a pioneer among Japanese NGOs in many respects. Established in 1980, it is one of the oldest unincorporated NGOs in Japan. Also, JVC was the only Japanese NGO to maintain a regional office inside Cambodia in the 1980s under the Vietnam-backed People's Republic of Kampuchea (PRK) government that the Western bloc, including the Japanese government, refused to recognize. In 1986, JVC followed Western NGOs that had moved to Cambodia in the early 1980s (e.g., the American Friends Service Committee, Oxfam, World Vision) and established an office and technical training center (Japan International Volunteer Center, 1995) in Phnom Penh.[11] MOFA did not welcome JVC's activities in Cambodia in the 1980s, as Tokyo did not have diplomatic relations with the Phnom Penh government. However, JVC's work was greatly appreciated by Cambodian recipients who desperately needed basic assistance to survive the economic isolation imposed on their country by the West (Kumaoka, 1993). Today, JVC's work is well respected and has begun to gain greater recognition in Japan. JVC has received awards from MOFA, the Prime Minister's Office, and two Japanese major newspaper companies, *Asahi Shimbun* and *Mainichii Shimbun* (Japan International Volunteer Center, 1997b).

JVC networks with other NGOs in a selective manner. JVC has close working relations only with like-minded independent Japanese NGOs such as the Services for the Health in Asian and African Regions (SHARE), a medical NGO with similar views on development and aid. JVC has assisted SHARE in Cambodia, for example, by contributing seeds for SHARE's agricultural project. Also, JVC is a leading member of Mekong Watch, the NGO network promoting sustainable development in the Mekong River region. In terms of non-Japanese NGOs, JVC has worked with Oxfam UK in both Indochina and Rwanda (Japan International Volunteer Center, 1997a) and some JVC members are interested in further strengthening the group's relationship with Oxfam, UK. These members established in the mid-1990s a study group on the British NGO to learn about its policies, activities, and campaign strategies.[12] JVC also cooperates with other non-Japanese NGOs in particular countries. In Cambodia, for example, JVC works closely with Western NGOs, Cambodian NGOs, and other Asian NGOs in a NGO network called the Cooperation Committee for Cambodia (CCC).

JVC is mainly interested in finding long-term structural solutions to poverty in the developing world and, to this end, advocates just and sustainable development. JVC is one of the leading NGOs in Japan that pressures the Japanese government to adopt aid policies that promote sustainable development rather than policies that focus only on economic infrastructure.

As a leading NGO in JANIC, JVC often represents the Japanese NGO community in government–NGO negotiations. Many, if not all, MOFA–NGO conferences and councils include JVC members as participants. Even though JVC is outspoken about its opposition to Japanese infrastructure-based aid, MOFA has thus far been willing to work with the group, partly because of the influence of the group over other NGOs in Japan.

Although JVC advocates sustainable development in the developing world, it does not take an extreme stance regarding ODA programs like some leftist activists who see all current Japanese aid projects as unnecessary and harmful. In contrast, JVC's view on ODA is based on realism and optimism. JVC understands that ODA will continue to play an important role in Japanese foreign policy, and the group thus works with the government to try to improve the current system for the future. This view is based on the acceptance of co-existence of ODA and NGO-led development activities and the hope that, by cooperating with MOFA, JVC will be able to exert more influence over government aid policies.

JVC's advocacy has targeted not only MOFA but also politicians. While most Japanese NGOs lack connections to Diet members, JVC has succeeded in winning support from some individual politicians interested in social welfare, women's rights, environmental protection, and development. One such politician is Akiko Dōmoto, governor of Chiba Prefecture and a former member of the New Party Sakigake in the Upper House) who has participated in a number of UN conferences such as the 1992 Earth Summit and the 1994 Cairo International Population and Development Conference, and who coordinated with JVC to press the antipesticide campaign within the Diet.[13] Dōmoto also took a leadership role in designing the NPO law that gave corporate status and tax breaks to Japanese NGOs (Nakano, 1998).

In addition, one of JVC's own representatives ran for the Upper House elections in 1998. Shunsuke Iwasaki, an advisor to JVC and a former Tsukuba University professor who had previously worked for the UNDP, received strong support for his candidacy from the independent Japanese NGO community and academicians engaged in issues of environment and development. Although he was not elected, partly due to the unpopularity of the party from which he ran (the Socialist Democratic Party), his candidacy indicated the increasing interaction between NGOs and the political system and the potential for greater participation of the NGO community in national politics.

Due in part to the JVC's persistent efforts, many ODA issues are now being debated more openly. It has become more acceptable to argue against Japan's aid policies in public debate involving state officials and politicians. In this sense, JVC has contributed to the expansion of the boundaries of acceptable political discourse between civil society and the state.

At the same time, critics say that JVC is too ideological about development (e.g., tending to view all state-led development aid projects in negative terms) and thus has difficulty finding common grounds with the government and with other NGOs interested in getting involved in Japanese aid projects.[14] JVC is also viewed as being highly idealistic but lacking tactical finesse to deal effectively with state officials. Critics claim that JVC is too confrontational and provocative in dealing with MOFA officials, and thus loses opportunities to exert greater influence over ODA policy. Instead of persuading MOFA officials to reform Japanese ODA, according to this view, JVC merely offends them.

The Association of Medical Doctors of Asia (AMDA)

AMDA is a "nonpolitical, nonsectarian"[15] medical NGO that originated as the Association of Medical Students of Asia (AMSA) in the 1970s. AMSA began networking with medical students in Southeast Asia in the early 1980s, and in 1984 the group transformed into AMDA. Its founder, Shigeru Suganami, M.D., was one of the Japanese youth who rushed to Thailand in the late 1970s to provide medical assistance to Cambodian refugees on the Thai–Cambodian border camps. However, since he was not on the staff of any official refugee operations organized by NGOs, the United Nations, or the Japanese government, he was unable to utilize his medical background to help the refugees. The border camps were controlled by the United Nations and its affiliates and there was little room for nonaffiliated individuals to take part in the operations. Based on his experience in Thailand, he realized that good will alone was not sufficient to help the needy and that some sort of organized effort was needed to provide humanitarian assistance (*Nikkei Weekly*, 1998c). Suganami also noticed that the doctors examining the Cambodian refugees on the border camps were primarily from the West and felt the urgent need to organize Asian doctors to take part in regional relief activities. The frustration and helplessness he felt in Thailand became the engine for the establishment of AMDA several years later.[16]

While initially designed to help Asian doctors conduct emergency relief activities within Asia, AMDA gradually expanded its activities to other regions. Accordingly, AMDA changed its original name, the Association of Medical Doctors *for* Asia, to the Association of Medical Doctors *of* Asia in 1994 (italics added). By 1998, AMDA established field project offices in 20 countries—including Cambodia, Burma, Lebanon, Zaire, Rwanda, Brazil, and Bolivia—which manage the group's activities in both development and humanitarian emergency relief. AMDA has a network of about seven hundred doctors (including approximately two hundred from Japan and five hundred from other Asian-Pacific countries) to provide emergency medical assistance throughout the world (*Nikkei Weekly*, 1998c).

A strength of AMDA is its public relations work. AMDA promotes itself through national television advertising and is frequently cited in Japanese newspapers about the dispatch of its doctors abroad to provide emergency assistance. Media coverage of AMDA is usually favorable, describing the NGO as a philanthropic organization with devoted doctors working in the developing world (*Asahi Shimbun*, 1996; *Sankei Shimbun*, 1996a; *Sankei Shimbun*, 1996b; *Sanyō Shimbun*, 1996). Due to its successful public relations efforts, AMDA has become well known in the Japanese aid scene, and in the 1990s it received several awards for its contributions to international cooperation, such as the UN Boutros Ghali Award and the Mainichi Shimbun and Yomiuri Shimbun Awards from two respected Japanese newspaper companies.[17]

While AMDA receives more recognition and respect domestically and internationally than do other Japanese NGOs, what most separates AMDA from the rest of the Japanese NGO community is the extensive networks it has built. AMDA pursues a wide range of alliances beyond the NGO community, seeking to cooperate wherever possible with the bureaucracy, the UN, the private business sector, and the media. AMDA emphasizes the importance of collaborating with a wide array groups to bring about mutual benefits. It stresses win–win situations in which all of its associates—NGOs, the state, and even the private sector[18]—benefit from cooperation and collaboration.

Of all the sectors that AMDA works with, its relationship with the bureaucracy, particularly MOFA, is of foremost importance. MOFA not only provides financial assistance to AMDA through its Grant Aid Division and the NGO Assistance Office, but also helps the group gain access to diplomatic channels for its relief activities. For example, when AMDA wanted to send its staff and medical supplies to Indonesia in the mid-1990s to help earthquake victims, the NGO first asked the Indonesian Embassy in Japan for discounted use of an Indonesian Garuda Airline flight for the transportation of medical goods. The embassy staff flatly rejected the request, so AMDA then consulted the NGO Assistance Office. On behalf of AMDA, this office asked another division in a different MOFA bureau, the Southeast Asia Division in the Asia Bureau, to make a request on AMDA's behalf to the Indonesian Ambassador to Japan. Contacting the Indonesian Embassy via MOFA's two bureaus worked well for AMDA. At the request of MOFA's Southeast Asia Bureau, the Embassy swiftly agreed to help AMDA by granting use of the airplane. This process confirmed to AMDA the importance of having a close working relationship with MOFA.[19]

In addition to utilizing MOFA's bilateral channel, AMDA also takes advantage of the ministry's multilateral links. AMDA has asked the Multilateral Cooperation Division within the Economic Cooperation Bureau of MOFA to exert diplomatic pressure on UN agencies to give more contracts for relief work to Japanese NGOs. Japan is the second largest donor country to the United Nations after the United States, and thus MOFA has a basis for arguing that more Japanese NGOs should be involved in UN activities. MOFA encourages Japanese NGOs to get involved in the United Nations and the ministry's diplomatic assistance is valuable to AMDA, which finds it difficult to compete with larger, more experienced Western NGOs with informal ties to UN officials.[20]

The AMDA–MOFA relationship is not one-way but is mutually beneficial. MOFA benefits from AMDA's participation in ODA projects that highlight the presence of Japanese aid at a grassroots level. For example, AMDA and JICA have joint projects in the Philippines and Zambia that the ministry cites frequently as an example of the increased "human face" of Japanese ODA. Another potential benefit to MOFA is increased domestic support; since MOFA lacks a natural constituency, AMDA and other pro-MOFA NGOs help the ministry get support from NGO members and the public. Cooperation with high-profile NGOs such as AMDA also can strengthen the ministry's position in coping with administrative and financial reform. As MOFA's NGO-related offices expand their constituency, the ministry can argue that Japanese NGOs are indispensable for Japanese ODA and that MOFA's NGO budget and programs should thus not be subject to budget cuts.

AMDA's relationship with the bureaucracy is not limited to its relations with MOFA. AMDA has working relationships with other ministries, such as the Ministry of Health and Welfare and the Ministry of Transport, through which the group receives support for its emergency relief activities abroad (e.g., free medical supplies, approval to transport medicine at discounted costs). AMDA also works with JICA through joint health projects in the Philippines and Zambia.

According to Kondo, secretary general of AMDA, the NGO is a "frontier" Japanese NGO trying to bridge the gap between the government and NGOs. He notes a changing attitude among MOFA officials toward Japanese NGOs in the 1990s. In his view, MOFA has begun to take Japanese NGOs more seriously than before and has come to appreciate their activities. He suggests that Japanese NGOs should engage in constructive dialogue with state officials and find ways to increase the capacity of both the government and NGOs in mutually cooperative ways.

While Kondo acknowledges the concerns of many NGOs about cooperating with state officials, he claims that they should become more confident in their ability and that they should not worry too much about possible state intervention. From his perspective, NGOs are engaged in unique activities and neither the state nor the private sector can replace them. He is especially critical of some leftist NGOs that first denounced state funding in the 1980s, but now have decided to accept it, while still claiming complete independence from the state. To the AMDA secretary general, these groups ignore the contradiction between receiving state funding and claiming to be autonomous actors in development. At the same time, he believes that if these NGOs are truly changing their attitudes toward the state through the acceptance of state funding, they are moving in the right direction.[21]

Through its extensive networks with the Japanese bureaucracy, AMDA promotes wider participation of Japanese citizens in ODA (*kokumin sanka-gata* ODA or, literally, people's participation-style ODA) based on collaboration among the central government, local government, and NGOs (*sansha renkei* or three-party collaboration). According to AMDA, this type of collaboration has several advantages. First, NGOs and local governments have more contact with people at a community level than does the central government. Thus, they can more readily inject grassroots perspectives into Japanese ODA. Second, the incorporation of

NGOs and local governments can increase small-scale, community-based projects in Japanese ODA that reach the poor effectively and thus complement the traditional infrastructure-based Japanese ODA projects that tend to favor the rich. Third, such small-scale community-based aid can be cost effective, since it can be carried out at a cost of ¥50 million per project (Association of Medical Doctors of Asia, 1998). Although a project that costs ¥50 million may not seem very cost-effective, such a project is certainly less expensive than most ODA projects.

In addition to the bureaucracy, AMDA tries to maintain close relations with UN organizations. Recognized as an NGO of Special Category (former Category-II) by the UN's Economic and Social Council (ECOSOC), AMDA collaborates with UN agencies such as the United Nations High Commissioner for Refugees (UNHCR) and the United Nations Development Program (UNDP) through joint projects.[22] AMDA is particularly interested in participating in UNHCR relief activities. However, it is difficult to do so since UNHCR works closely with already established Western NGO networks on emergency relief. AMDA members feel that the Western networks dominate UNHCR projects, making it difficult for non-Western NGOs such as AMDA to participate. Thus, as mentioned earlier, AMDA has asked MOFA to pressure UNHCR to accept more Japanese NGOs for its relief work. AMDA is one of the leading Japanese NGOs engaged in relief activities, so if UNHCR decides to accept Japanese NGOs, AMDA will likely be one of the first Japanese NGOs selected. In addition to consulting with MOFA on UN matters, AMDA also contacts Japanese UN staff regularly and receives the latest information on UN activities, which helps the group develop strategies to win UN contracts. AMDA is also closely attuned to available funding sources and projects from the government and the United Nations. The organization thus differs from advocacy NGOs such as JVC in that AMDA is driven more by pragmatism than by ideology and thus has more in common with private business in the way it conducts its aid operations.

AMDA's businesslike approach to aid is criticized by some Japanese NGOs, particularly the more independent and ideological ones. Critics of AMDA say that the group is too close to the state and thus risks co-optation. Others contend that AMDA is more concerned with its media image than with results. Some of AMDA's relief operations are high-profile short-term operations lasting no more than a few days. According to one critic, AMDA skillfully takes advantage of Japanese media that may know little about the organization's overseas work. In his view, these media merely report, before AMDA doctors leave Japan, on where they will be sent and what they plan to do there, but they fail to follow up on what AMDA actually does and the effectiveness of its operations.[23] At the same time, however, critics admit that AMDA can appeal effectively to the Japanese public. Unlike the slogans of leftist organizations, AMDA's messages are simple, clear and, above all, free from ideology. They appeal to many Japanese who lack knowledge about development and aid but nonetheless want to assist the poor in the developing world. In contrast, many leftist organizations have difficulty in reaching the Japanese people. Because their messages are often complex, employing jargon such as capitalism or oppression, the groups are often considered dogmatic.[24]

JVC and AMDA are excellent examples of NGOs that have chosen to cooperate with MOFA, albeit from different perspectives. What about the groups that are not cooperating with the state? These fall into two categories, that of disengagement (i.e., low cooperation with the state and also low conflict) and conflict (i.e., low cooperation but high conflict) (Covey, 1998). In the disengagement category are mostly very small NGOs, such as organizations of two to three people working on narrow issues. These groups may not be ideologically opposed to cooperating with the government, but are too small either to be taken seriously by MOFA or to allocate personnel to work on cooperation. In the conflict category are a range of organizations that oppose government policies and are in principal against receiving funding from the government or collaborating with the state. These include a handful of small leftist groups as well a few mainstream organizations such as Amnesty International Japan.[25] Thus, while some organizations abstain for either practical or ideological reasons, the general trend among Japanese NGOs is toward greater cooperation and collaboration with the state. And these groups favoring engagement with the government are rewriting state–civil society relations in Japan today.

Conclusion

The rapid expansion of the NGO movement over the last two decades has been unprecedented in Japanese history. As Japanese NGOs have grown both in number and influence, they have found a role in the field of international aid that suit their goals. On the one hand, some NGOs such as JVC have become watchdogs of government aid projects and have critiqued the quality of Japanese aid. By doing so, they have brought pressure on the government, primarily on MOFA, to change the course of Japan's ODA policy. These NGOs are in general concerned with environmental protection, human rights, and people's participation in development, but oppose Japanese ODA infrastructure projects that they see as failing to help the poor. On the other hand, there are NGOs such as AMDA focusing on cooperating with the government and increasing their own capacity to provide aid.

While appearing to be at odds with each other, these two types of Japanese NGOs share some common ground: they want the Japanese government to expand ODA projects in the social sector and incorporate NGOs in policy planning and implementation. They may disagree on methods of achieving this goal—groups like JVC may insist that MOFA compromise and incorporate JVC's views into ODA programs, whereas organizations such as AMDA may accept MOFA's views as they are—but both stress that the Japanese government, particularly MOFA, should give priority to grassroots aid projects with NGO participation.

The growth of NGOs and their expanded relations with the state poses challenges both to the NGOs themselves and to MOFA. NGOs' increased access to state funding and support concomitantly increases the danger of the NGO movement losing its autonomy and identity. In the United States, for example, some of Private Voluntary Organizations (PVOs) receiving the most funding from the United States Agency for International Development (USAID) are huge, apolitical organizations, with no social base and resembling corporations in form and function more than grassroots advocates of change. Japanese NGOs have a particularly strong grassroots orientation—one of their strengths—but this orientation may be difficult to maintain if funding from government sources increases. First, reliance on state funding will decrease the needs of groups to seek funding from an activist base, thus potentially severing them from their roots. Second, opportunities for state funding may tempt organizations to moderate their politics in order to maintain a good relationship with the government and thus maintain access to its money. Third, as organizations become better funded and larger, they may become more moderate and bureaucratic due to their increased size as well as the higher salaries and better living conditions they can offer their leading staff. In other words, right now, NGOs, with few ties to the government and existing in relative poverty, have little to lose by their critical stance. NGOs drawn into a web of government-sponsored funding and support have more to lose by challenging the government. This applies to individual NGOs, to NGO networks, and to the overall NGO movement. Even if an individual NGO does not change its orientation, it may see its critical views overshadowed by NGO coalitions and an NGO movement that are becoming dominated by larger, more apolitical NGOs.

MOFA also faces challenges in navigating its future relations with NGOs. MOFA, to its credit, appears to be dealing impartially with

NGOs, whether they critique government policy or support it. Both types of NGOs receive MOFA funding, and those criticizing the government are well represented in NGO–MOFA policy fora. If MOFA continues to work closely with NGOs engaged in critical cooperation, the ministry may adopt their views and suggestions and accelerate aid reform. If the ministry starts working with "co-opted" NGOs more closely and frequently than NGOs in critical cooperation, aid policy change may be more difficult to achieve.

What kind of role MOFA is willing to grant NGOs? Thus far, MOFA has acceded to NGO demands principally at the project level (e.g., canceling aid projects due to NGO protests) rather than at the policy level. As MOFA gradually shifts toward a new aid paradigm, the ministry must decide how willing it is to accept NGO input on a broader range of overall policies. MOFA is currently trying to keep a balance between its support for NGOs, which it views as its constituency and ally, and its relations with other ministries and the private sector. MOFA wants enough NGO inclusion so as to strengthen its hand in dealing with other ministries and the private sector, but not so much that MOFA's relations with other ministries and the private sector might become polarized. If the NGO movement continues to increase in size and influence, maintaining that balance will be difficult.

Both MOFA and NGOs will have to consider their relations with partners in developing countries, especially local NGOs. Japanese NGOs have been able to forge especially close and fruitful relations with local NGOs in recipient countries, in part due to the common grassroots orientation on both sides. This may become more difficult if Japanese NGOs become better funded and more reliant on the state. At the same time, MOFA must consider to what extent it wants to channel its own funding into developing country NGOs to carry out projects. So far, MOFA has not been very interested in funding developing country NGOs, but the shifting of aid money from Japanese corporations to Japanese NGOs can be viewed as just another way of putting Japan's interests above those of recipient countries.

In summary, MOFA and NGOs have begun to forge an alliance to promote soft aid. Their relationship, however, is characterized by both cooperation and conflict. NGOs are in general willing to cooperate with the ministry for common goals. Yet, some independent NGOs do so while trying to maintain a critical distance.

The growth of the NGO movement in Japan, and the increased contact between NGOs and the government, indicates a potentially new era of state–civil society relations. MOFA is shifting resources to an important new ally, thus strengthening its own hand but potentially upsetting the delicate balance among government ministries and the private sector. Meanwhile, an emerging civil society has burst forth on the scene, but its newfound access to government support and funding could threaten the grassroots orientation that has given it so much dynamism. And both MOFA and NGOs must reassess their relationship to outside partners, including developing country NGOs, Western NGOs, and foreign governments that are pressuring Japan to continue aid reform. At stake in all these issues is not only the future direction of Japanese foreign aid but also the overall nature of state–civil society relations in the world's second-wealthiest country.

CHAPTER SIX

Conclusion

Japanese nongovernmental organizations (NGOs) have clearly come far during the past decades, growing in number and influence and in the capacity to act together. By focusing on NGOs' new involvement in Japanese official developmental assistance (ODA) policy, I have emphasized that there are more political openings for citizens' groups engaged in development and aid today than ever before. Advocacy groups can make their voices heard via mass media, public seminars, and conferences, and other means. Some NGOs have direct contact with bureaucrats through regular meetings where they can express their views. Also, some NGOs have begun implementing ODA projects under a new contracting program that started in 1999. NGOs have now entered the political arena, attempting to influence ODA policy.

Clearly, the milieu surrounding NGOs has dramatically changed. And this reflects changes in Japan's broader political economy since the late 1970s. By then, Japan's industrialization drive had reached its peak, allowing the Japanese to enjoy unprecedented wealth. Postmaterial values gained ground, as people's concerns began to shift from becoming richer to finding the quality of life. At the same time, as globalization advanced in the 1980s, the Japanese economy became more fully integrated into the world market. Some Japanese firms moved their production sites out of Japan, gaining autonomy from the Japanese state. Other firms failed to adjust to the new economic environment and tried to cling to the protection of the state from global competition. However, the state has lost its grips on the economy and is unable to prevent foreign firms from coming into the Japanese market. Globalization also has spread new norms and values, prompting Japanese to act on the global scale as a *chikyu-jin* (global person) for people's welfare, regardless of nationality. Thus, the Japanese sense of *uchi-soto* (insider–outsider) has weakened and people have turned to NGOs to assist the poor in the developing world. Meanwhile, the public has begun to see the Japanese developmental state as corrupt and ineffective in the midst of economic crises, and has become mistrustful of the policy-making elite. The end results of these economic and political changes are the weakening of the state, the emergence of more active citizens in the civil society, and increased level of pluralism on the political scene.

These changes in Japan's political economy have led to a changing relationship between the state and civil society. As seen in Chapter 5, the Ministry of Foreign Affairs (MOFA) and civil society have begun to explore a new work relationship with each other to reform Japan's official development assistance (ODA) programs. Yet, the impact of their relationship is unclear. It can be mutually beneficial or harmful; it can help both sides achieve their goals or force them to compromise these goals.

Further questions arise regarding the emergence of Japanese NGOs and the erosion of the developmental state. In a consolidated democracy, a strong civil society is crucial. Can NGOs promote democracy in Japan? If so, how? What are major obstacles to NGOs' efforts to promote democracy? Another question concerns the implications of the changes in the state–civil society relations for other East Asian countries. Since Japan achieved rapid industrialization, Tokyo's developmental state has attracted much attention from leaders in developing countries in the region. The erosion of the developmental state, however, casts new doubts on whether it should be a model for the developing world.

This chapter will first examine how the changing state–civil society relationship may affect MOFA and NGOs in the future. It will then analyze how the emergence of NGOs can contribute to democracy in Japan. Finally, the chapter will address the erosion of the developmental state and the implication of the emergence of civil society in Japan on other East Asian countries.

State–Civil Society Relations

As seen in Chapter 5, MOFA has steadily increased its support for NGOs since the end of the 1980s. Its financial support includes the Subsidy Funds for NGO Projects, the Grant Assistance for Grassroots Projects, and numerous funds to promote NGO training. Increasing MOFA support for NGOs has brought about both opportunities and dangers.

For MOFA, cooperation with NGOs creates many opportunities. MOFA can utilize the expertise of NGOs in grassroots aid implementation. NGOs can reach people at a grassroots level with small-scale, labor-intensive aid better than state officials can.

Cooperation with NGOs also strengthens the ministry's stance vis-à-vis foreign governments, other ministries, and Japanese citizens. As discussed in Chapter 3, development paradigms have shifted over the last four decades, moving from the modernization (1960s), basic human needs (1970s), and neoliberal (1980s) approaches to the sustainable human development approach (1990s). Japan has been pressured by the international aid regime to promote the sustainable human development paradigm and take a leadership role in improving international aid. Cooperation with NGOs is one of the key concepts of the sustainable human development paradigm. The incorporation of NGOs into the Japanese aid program can deflect international criticism and improve the image of the Japanese government abroad.

MOFA–NGO cooperation can also help the ministry strengthen its hand in domestic politics. Due to the fragmentation of the aid administrative structure and intense competition among ministries, MOFA needs domestic allies to pursue its own goals. By promoting grassroots aid with NGOs, MOFA may gain NGO support, which can give the ministry some additional leverage in ministerial infighting.

Cooperation with NGOs can also help MOFA gain public support for ODA. Japan has been going through a crisis of state authority and an increase of citizens' influence in politics. The state has become subject to public demands for accountability and can no longer ignore citizens' views of policies. Working with NGOs is advantageous for MOFA because NGOs are usually seen as less wasteful, corrupt, or bureaucratic than the state. The inclusion of NGOs in ODA can improve the image of ODA and MOFA and thus strengthen the ministry's domestic support.

At the same time, there are risks for MOFA in working with NGOs. MOFA could put interministerial relations at risk by accommodating NGO demands for radical reductions in infrastructure aid or adoption of complete untied aid policy for grant aid. If MOFA becomes overly accommodating, it could face backlash from the business sector, the Ministry of International Trade and Industry (MITI), or conservative politicians.

If MOFA chooses to work mainly with apolitical NGOs, it may be able to co-opt them and conduct ODA policy on its own terms. However, this will not help the ministry achieve aid reform.

In addition, there are questions of NGO accountability. It is possible that MOFA could pour public resources into organizations that the ministry knows very little about. MOFA may risk providing funds to organizations incapable of effectively implementing projects or to those not genuinely interested in providing quality services to recipients but merely motivated to expand their operations through public funding.

Furthermore, because NGOs often promote particular projects rather than overall developmental goals, their interests may clash with those of MOFA, which sees aid in a broader framework. NGOs often lack broad, cross-sectoral approaches to development, and their narrow focus can be biased against certain sectors or projects that may be beneficial to aid recipients.

For NGOs, cooperation with MOFA can mean a steady flow of financial assistance, desperately needed by the majority of Japanese NGOs. Many NGOs also hope to influence ODA policy by cooperating or collaborating with MOFA. They welcome opportunities to discuss development issues with MOFA officials whenever possible. In fact, many NGO–MOFA meetings were initiated by NGOs that wanted to see their views reflected in ODA policy.

At the same time, there are many potential dangers for NGOs in cooperating with MOFA. The central concern on the part of NGOs is the risk of co-optation. Many NGOs fear that they could be deprived of autonomy from the state and see their role as agents of social and political change weakened. Through cooperation with the state, they may be forced to tailor their activities to the priorities of MOFA rather than to those of the people they intend to represent (concerned citizens in Japan) or to serve (local communities in the developing world).

The risk of co-optation is high for Japanese NGOs. Japan lags behind Western countries in NGO development. MOFA thus tries to help Japanese NGOs strengthen their organizational capacity and catch up to their Western counterparts. In return for MOFA's financial support, NGOs may be expected to be loyal to the ministry. This can result in a patronage relationship between MOFA and NGOs, akin to what MITI has established with Japanese ODA business interests.

Related to autonomy is the concern that state funding can distort NGOs by enticing them to do things that may not reflect their goals and priorities. The fear of "vendorism" (Salamon, 1995, p. 103), or the distortion of organizational missions in pursuit of state funding, is strong among NGOs because MOFA is more comfortable with a service delivery role for NGOs rather than a broader role to empower people and promote democracy and human rights. The ministry's narrow interest in service delivery can severely limit NGOs and diminish their advocacy role.

In addition, NGOs have different goals from MOFA. MOFA officials consider aid as a diplomatic tool to promote Japan's security, economic growth, and status in the international community. To many NGOs, the primary objective of ODA should be assisting the poor in the developing world; whether or not the Japanese government achieves its foreign policy goals is irrelevant to these NGOs' concerns. MOFA's emphasis on the use of ODA to promote Japan's *kokueki,* or "national interest" (under the ministry's own definition), clashes with NGOs' efforts to make aid beneficial to the needy.

Many NGOs are also concerned that involvement with ODA programs tends to bureaucratize their organizations. State agencies must guarantee that program operations meet certain standards of accountability. These include effective financial management, accounting, and maintenance of minimum quality standards. To cope with the financial accountability standards of state programs, NGOs may have to develop internal management processes that reduce their flexibility and threaten their informal, voluntary nature. For example, a representative of Shanti Volunteer Association (SVA) reported that one of the most difficult things about dealing with MOFA was the ministry's financial management and accounting requirements. He complained that the staff in his organization spent so much time filing receipts for MOFA-funded projects that it detracted from the group's own activities.[1]

In short, although state–NGO cooperation can provide financial assistance and political opportunities to NGOs, it can also undermine their independence, divert them from their original organizational mission and goals, and result in excessive bureaucratization that can hamper their grassroots orientation.

Thus, one cannot simply say that MOFA–NGO cooperation is unambiguously good for either side. Both sides must take great care to manage the partnership effectively, balancing potential risks and opportunities.

Civil Society and Democracy

Can civil society organizations such as NGOs promote democracy in Japan? If so, how can they?

According to Tocqueville (1969), a virtuous and viable democracy depends on robust associational life. Democratic theorists generally agree that various associations such as issue networks, advocacy groups, labor unions, and even recreational associations and religious groups enhance democracy by cultivating citizenship, promoting public deliberation, and providing voice and representation.[2] For example, Putnam's (1993; 2000) studies of Italy and the United States indicate how associational life and successful democratic governance go hand in hand.

Japanese NGOs, based on networks of cooperation and trust, can strengthen democracy via collective actions. They provide alternative views and representation and contribute to develop the capacities of democratic citizenship. Through involvement in NGOs, citizens learn democratic values and become more fully aware of their political rights and liberties. As shown in chapters 4 and 5, many Japanese NGOs provide space and avenues for citizens to participate in political life and influence public policy.

What struck me during my observation of Japanese NGOs was the level of cooperation among like-minded NGO leaders, especially those who have regular contact with MOFA. These NGO representatives know each other very well, send e-mail to one another on a regular basis (especially to coordinate their stands on aid policy for their upcoming meetings with MOFA officials), organize protest rallies together, collaborate on specific aid projects, and copublish books and articles. Even though they work for different NGOs, they constitute a closeknit community based on trust and reciprocity.

At the same time, democracy requires not only trust but also conflict, albeit nonviolent. Trust can develop where interests converge, but in politics interests often lead to conflict (Warren, 1999). Democracy requires a healthy distrust of the interests of others, especially the powerful. Citizens should be able to oversee the bureaucracy, by scrutinizing its conduct of behavior with some degree of skepticism, and demand state accountability to the public. Japanese NGOs are suited to help play this role. As discussed in chapter 4 and 5, they can challenge aid policies promoted by the state–business alliance and pressure the state to address problems of social injustice in the developing world.[3] Japanese NGOs thus serve as a counterweight to the state, demanding state accountability and checking and limiting state power. This is one of the most important functions of NGOs.

Another important function of NGOs is to serve as a channel for articulation of interests outside party politics. NGOs can represent citizens' views of ODA and further promote democracy in Japan. As Chapters 4 and 5 show, Japanese NGOs offer a valuable means for citizens to participate in ODA decision making. NGOs now provide a legitimate channel for citizens' political participation that was not previously provided by the state.

NGOs have contributed to pluralism on the Japanese political scene. In the case of ODA, Japanese NGOs have diversified the profile of participants to aid decision making. Citizens without business connection to the state can have a say in ODA and demand policy change via NGOs. NGO participation is now institutionalized though regular NGO–MOFA meetings and JICA–NGO meetings, as discussed in Chapter 5. Thus, NGOs can strengthen democracy by building institutional pluralism.

While necessary for a democracy, civil society is not always "an unmitigated blessing" (Schmitter, 1997, p. 247). Civil society organizations can hamper democracy if they lack autonomy from the state, accountability, transparency, or internal democracy.

First, NGOs may concentrate their energy on the upward link with the state but neglect to forge a strong downward linkage with the public. The Association of Medical Doctors of Asia (AMDA; discussed in Chapter 5) is a case in point. Since AMDA is eager to get public funding and participate in state-sponsored projects, it may attempt to cater to the needs of state bureaucrats rather than those of civil society. AMDA does want to maintain good public relations, but the way the organization conducts aid operation (e.g., sending a few doctors and nurses to a developing country when the latest calamity is publicized in the news, then quickly withdrawing them after a couple of days) does not reflect the wishes of concerned citizens. In an attempt to establish a strong relationship with the state, AMDA and other Japanese NGOs can be co-opted by the state and reinforce a hierarchical relations between the state and civil society, rather than help create more horizontal, equal state–civil society relations. Such scenarios are conceivable in Japan, where the state traditionally exerted strong influence over civil society and where many NGOs have meager funding and try to get state money.

Second, accountability is a problem for Japanese NGOs. They are not elected officials or government employee who are required to be accountable to the general public. To whom are NGOs accountable? Obviously, NGOs should be accountable to their members and the people they represent. At present, though, the support base of Japanese NGOs is still limited. For example, even the Japan International Volunteer Center (JVC), one of the largest development NGOs in Japan, has only about 1,800 members (Japan International Volunteer Center, 2000). Even the membership of all Japanese NGOs combined represents a small segment of the population. Does this mean that NGOs should be accountable to only a small number of people? On the contrary, even if NGOs have a limited number of members, that does not mean that they should be detached from the larger population. Many people who do not belong to NGOs still support their goals and activities, either actively (e.g., by sending donations or participating in seminars and bazaars) or passively (i.e., having positive views of their activities). Although there are no statistics available as to how many people support NGOs, it is safe to say that millions of Japanese are in favor of an increased role of NGOs in ODA. This means that NGOs have to be accountable not only to their members but also to a much larger population.

Also, transparency is another problem that many Japanese NGOs face. Many NGOs are weary of sharing information and are skeptical of people unaffiliated with them. These NGOs are hesitant to make information available to the public that could cast an unfavorable light on their activities. However, most NGOs that I came in contact with, such as JVC and Shapla Neer, openly shared organizational information including funding sources. These open NGOs are well aware that to become legitimate and to contribute to a strong civil society, they have to provide transparent information to the public.

Finally, NGOs can be dominated by charismatic but autocratic leaders who undermine internal democracy. Fortunately, few Japanese NGOs seem to have this problem. Most have a horizontal organizational structure where members are in general treated as equal (except for part-time workers and volunteers who are usually not able to participate in the decision making process). In addition, Japanese NGOs have a relatively high level of cooperation among their members. United by shared values and goals and similar experiences (e.g., working in developing countries), they exhibit strong levels of internal democracy. However, there is a possibility that NGOs can become a victim of one-person rule. NGO members need to be vigilant, bearing in mind that undemocratic NGO leaders can hinder the development of NGOs and the democratic consolidation of society.[4]

NGOs can overcome the above mentioned obstacles and contribute to the strengthening of civil society and democracy. They need to be conscious of the risks that might hamper democracy. Can NGOs and civil society become a potent force in Japanese politics in the future? I believe so. Even though they are limited in finance and membership, they can effectively represent the public on important issues and serve as a watchdog of state behavior if they are vigilant in guarding their own autonomy, accountability, transparency, and democracy.

Japan and East Asia

What does the erosion of the developmental state model and the rise of civil society in Japan mean for the rest of the world, particularly East

Asia? For a long time, Japan's development was envied by many developing Asian countries that tried to move out of their developing world status. Does the erosion of the Japanese developmental state indicate that Japan's development model is unsustainable and thus unfit for the rest of Asia?

There is no doubt that the Japanese developmental state "worked" in the eyes of the admirers of this model, since the state, especially the bureaucracy, successfully initiated development policies, implemented them, and brought about rapid growth, making the country one of the world's wealthiest countries in just a few decades. At the same time, Japan failed to develop a vigorous civil society in the heyday of the developmental state in the 1950s–1970s. The state was intent on suppressing or ignoring civil society (through legal means and ignoring citizens' demands) than on supporting it. Few people were concerned about this because people desperately wanted to industrialize the nation and civic activism was of secondary importance. The public was fully united in support of the goal of the developmental state to bring about a rapid growth through mercantilist economic policies.

The paradox of the Japanese developmental state is that once Japan "caught up" with the West (in terms of GNP indicators), the *raison d'être* of the developmental state ended. Japanese people realized that they had paid a price for their rapid industrialization; they had not had many life options other than to climb the corporate ladder to generate growth for the nation, and they lacked meaning in their lives. Now that the Japanese have become affluent, they demand more freedom and do not want their society to be dominated by the state–corporate alliance. The need for the developmental state has further diminished due to the delegitimation of the state, deriving from the pervasive corruption among state and business leaders and from the chronic economic crises of seemingly never-ending recession and worsening budget deficits.

Is Japan's development model a viable option for other Asian developing countries? It still has an enormous appeal to some political leaders in the region who are convinced that civil society needs to be sacrificed for the greater goals of the society (i.e., bringing about economic growth and elevating the living standards of the people). Malaysia's Prime Minister Mahathir Mohamad, for example, openly expresses his admiration of the developmental state model, urging other Asian leaders to take a "look East" policy, rather than adopting Western liberalism. To Mahathir and others, having an active civil society is a luxury or detraction from addressing the issue of economic growth and improvement of people's economic welfare. Obviously, this way of thinking is based on the belief that growth and civil society activism (or more broadly democracy) are inherently incompatible and that an active civil society is detrimental to economic growth.

The erosion of the Japanese state raises questions about the applicability of the developmental model. Given the problems Japan faces today, it is apparent that the Japanese model is not a long-term solution. The Japanese developmental state now faces the monsters it has created, including pervasive corruption due to the closeknit power triangle of bureaucrats, politicians and business leaders; economic crises due to bureaucratic mismanagement; and the weakening of competitiveness of some Japanese industries that have been well protected by the state. In addition, the state now faces popular demands for more political space for citizens' activism.

The admirers of the developmental state model should be aware of these potential pitfalls. The model creates enormous problems that cannot be easily overcome, and these problems seriously hamper further development, as exemplified by today's economic recession in Japan. The Japanese economy, which earlier grew at rapid rates, has been essentially stagnant for an entire decade with no end in sight.

The chances of the developmental state model working are even poorer in today's era of globalization. As seen in Chapter 3, the Japanese state can no longer protect its companies as Japan becomes further integrated into the global market. For other countries, too, the chance of even medium-term, let alone long-term, benefits from such mercantilist policies is reduced. Similarly, it becomes more difficult to shut down citizens' rights when global media make people aware of democratic practices elsewhere, and help spread both the values and the tools that make these practices more likely.

One interesting example of this process is Malaysia, which viewed international investment in its "Multimedia Corridor" as a critical component of the country's economic development. However, many leading companies around the world cut back on their investments in the corridor after Mahathir cracked down on the Malaysian democratic movement.

The developing world needs another model, one that promotes short-term economic growth while also nurturing the conditions for sustainable economic, social, and human development. NGOs play a crucial role in this mix. The emergence of NGOs as a key political actor in Japan should be an important lesson for other political and economic leaders in the region who seek to "look East."

APPENDIX

Evolution of Japanese Aid

Japanese aid policy is currently experiencing important changes. A review of the historical context of Japanese foreign aid during the past several decades will help us understand Tokyo's recent official development aid (ODA) shift toward an increase in soft aid and the incorporation of nongovernmental organizations (NGOs) into aid implementation.

The evolution of Japanese aid policy can be divided into three phases, each of which reflects the relationship of aid to the international and domestic environments: (1) Japanese economy-first policy (from the mid-1950s to the mid-1970s); (2) promotion of broader foreign policy objectives (from the mid-1970s to the late 1980s); and (3) further politicization and diversification of aid (from the late 1980s to present). The first period was characterized by the single-minded pursuit of economic growth by both the Japanese government and the corporate sector. Aid was primarily used to promote Japan's postwar economic recovery and rapid growth and to secure natural resources. In the second period, politico-strategic objectives of aid emerged under a policy of "burden sharing" with Tokyo's Western allies. During this phase, Japan's ODA was used not only to bring economic benefits to Japanese firms but also to consolidate relations with the West. During the last period, ODA is being used to contribute to the maintenance of international stability in the post-Cold War era. Economic interests still exist, but political objectives are more pronounced, and the nature of aid has changed.

The nature of Japanese ODA has changed significantly since the 1950s. Initially very business-centered, over the decades Japanese aid has diversified to have multidimensional objectives (Koppel & Plummer, 1989; Koppel & Orr, 1993; Rix, 1989–1990; Rix, 1993; Yasutomo, 1986; Yasutomo, 1989–1990; Yasutomo, 1993) and a diverse array of programs. Contrary to the stereotype of ODA solely representing the economic interests of Japanese firms (Arase, 1993; Arase, 1994; Arase, 1995; Ensign, 1992; Söderberg, 1996; Taylor, 1998), Japanese aid is not monolithic but has complex, multifaceted dimensions see Table A.1).

Phase One: ODA and Japan's Economic Development

Japan's ODA policy from the 1950s to the 1970s was a response to changing international and domestic environments. The main feature of Tokyo's external relations in the yearly years after World War II was a high degree of dependence on the U.S. The U.S. provided not only a market for Japanese goods but also military protection against threats from the communist bloc. Washington encouraged Tokyo to foster good relations with U.S. allies in Asia by means of trade, investment, and

Table A.1   Evolution of Japanese foreign aid

Phase	Aid characteristics	International and domestic contexts	Objectives and types of aid
Phase I (1950s to Mid-1970s) *Japanese economy-first policy*	• War reparations • Aid to promote Japanese investment and trade in Asia • Resource diplomacy	• Japan's defeat in World War II • National efforts for "Income Doubling Plans" and U.S. support for Japan's economic policy in Asia • Oil crisis	• Predominantly economic objectives • Predominantly infrastructure-based project aid
Phase II (Mid-1970s to Late-1980s) *Beginning of aid diversification and politicization*	• Fukuda Doctrine and rapid increase of ODA • Strategic aid to countries of geopolitical importance • Aid recycling to debtor countries	• U.S. withdrawal from Indochina and emerging Japanese economic power • Heightened Cold War tensions around the world • Debt crisis in the developing world	• Predominantly economic but emerging importance of political objectives • Continued emphasis on infrastructure-based project aid but emergence of non-traditional aid
Phase III (Late-1980s to Present) *Further diversification and politicization of aid*	• Emphasis on democratization and marketization • Use of ODA for U.N. peace-keeping efforts • Increasing emphasis on soft aid • Emphasis on least less-developed countries • Miyazawa Plan • Japan's aid fatigue	• End of the Cold War and dissolution of the Soviet bloc • Increasing regional conflicts • Emergence of global issues and Japan's domestic movement for aid reform • Aggravating poverty in least less-developed countries • Asian economic crisis and Japan's own recession • Japan's fiscal problem	• Strong political objectives and weakened economic objectives • Reduced infrastructure-based aid and increasing grassroots aid

ODA to the region. In return, the Japanese government was attentive to geopolitical interests of the United States and followed its Cold War leadership in Asia.

Domestically, the Japanese government, represented by the Ministry of International Trade and Industry (MITI), attempted to respond to internal economic needs. Tokyo concentrated on its "economics above all" policy—a policy launched by Prime Minister Shigeru Yoshida in the 1950s to promote economic growth while under U.S. military protection[1]—by pursuing overseas markets for Japanese industrial products and acquiring raw materials vital to Japanese economic development. The Japanese government used the term *keizai kyōryoku* (economic cooperation) rather than ODA in reference to the transfer of a wide range of official and private capital flows from Japan to the developing world. This term blurred the distinction between ODA, other official flows, and private capital flows. ODA coupled economic cooperation with private capital transfer (Loutfi, 1973).

It is significant that during the first phase of Japanese aid, two key aid ministries, MITI and the Ministry of Foreign Affairs (MOFA), agreed to use ODA to promote domestic economic prosperity, even though they had slightly different interests. MITI's ultimate goal was the promotion of Japanese trade in Asia. From their perspective, aid was part of a new postwar trade policy in the region, designed to develop markets for the products of Japan's industry. In contrast, with the emergence of the Cold War and the Vietnam War, MOFA was concerned about Tokyo's role in supporting U.S. military efforts. The ministry tried to design Japanese aid programs in line with U.S. interests in Asia and support U.S. allies in the region. Yet, the different interests of MITI and MOFA did not affect the overall aid policies during the first phase, because MOFA agreed with MITI in principle that economic aid was necessary for Japan's own growth and openly acknowledged that Asia was important markets for Japanese exports, as well as sources of raw material (see Orr, 1990).

During this first phase of Japanese aid, three policies emerged as the core of Japanese foreign aid: (1) war reparations from the mid-1950s to the mid-1960s, (2) aid to promote the "Income Doubling Plan" by Prime Minister Hayato Ikeda in the 1960s, and (3) "resource diplomacy" in the 1970s. These policies, including war reparations, were designed to promote Japanese economic development in the post–World War II era.

War Reparations

Japan's bilateral aid started with war reparation programs.[2] The San Francisco Peace Treaty of 1952, which ended the occupation of Japan by Allied forces, stipulated that the Japanese government pay reparations to the Asian countries that Tokyo had occupied during World War II for the damages and suffering inflicted on them. Reparations were counted as grant aid and were intended to fulfill Japan's international obligations to wartime indemnities. At the same time, the reparations were designed to promote Japan's own economic recovery by means of distribution of Japanese goods and services to recipient countries. MOFA established an internal reparations divisions and became the primary agency to manage reparations programs.

In the latter half of the 1950s, the Japanese government settled reparations agreements with Southeast Asian countries, specifically, with Burma (1955), the Philippines (1956), Indonesia (1958), and South Vietnam (1960). Tokyo also concluded agreements for quasi-reparations (grants in lieu of formal reparations commitments) from the late 1950s and 1960s with Cambodia (1959), Laos (1959), Thailand (1962), South Korea (1965), Burma (1965), Singapore (1968), and Malaysia (1968) (Rix, 1980). Although the total amount of the reparations and quasi-reparations was relatively small (approximately US$1 billion for the reparations and US$490 million for the quasireparations) (Hasegawa, 1975), they benefited the Japanese economy significantly. Procurement of reparations was tied to Japanese industrial goods, thus helping Japanese firms expand manufactured production. Furthermore, the Japanese products under the reparations brought about further demands for Japanese goods in the recipient countries as local markets became dependent on them.

In the 1950s and early 1960s, Japanese private companies, especially consulting firms, expanded their business activities in Southeast Asia, undertaking infrastructure projects funded by the reparations. For example, Nippon Koei, a leading Japanese consulting firm that had undertaken development projects in Korea and Manchuria under the Japanese colonial occupation during World War II, conducted surveys and supervised construction of ODA-funded large-scale hydroelectric infrastructure projects in Southeast Asia; the Da Nhim Dam project in South Vietnam and the Brantas River project in Indonesia are specific instances (Rix, 1980; Nippon Koei, 1994; Nippon Koei, 1996).

During the period of reparations aid, the Japanese government consolidated its aid institutions. In the early years of Japanese ODA, the chief implementing agency for concessional loans was the Export–Import Bank of Japan (Ex–Im Bank). In 1961, the Overseas Economic Cooperation Fund (OECF) was established as a quasigovernmental lending institution to assume control of all official loan programs previously managed by the Ex–Im Bank. In the following year, the Overseas Technical Cooperation Agency (OTCA) was established as a technical assistance agency. In 1965, OTCA began to oversee the newly established Japanese Overseas Cooperation Volunteers (JOCV), the Japanese version of the Peace Corps (Caldwell, 1972).

Aid to Support the Income-Doubling Plan

By the 1960s, Japan had achieved postwar recovery and double-digit economic growth rates. By then, economic assistance to developing countries was not limited to the reparations programs. In 1958, Japan distributed its first bilateral loan aid as part of the World Bank Consortium for India. Subsequently, Japanese bilateral loans began in other countries, such as South Vietnam, Pakistan, and Brazil, in the late 1950s and the early 1960s (Yanagihara & Emig, 1991).

In the 1960s, Japan's ODA was closely linked to Prime Minister Ikeda's Income-Doubling Plan, a domestic economic policy that he announced in 1960 for doubling national income within ten years. This plan encouraged exports of Japanese heavy industrial products to Asia, envisaging a 10 percent annual increase in the total volume of Japanese exports and a 13 percent annual increase in the exports of heavy industrial products. The goal of the export-oriented policy was to redirect Japan's industrial structure from light to heavy industry (Little & Clifford, 1965). Led primarily by MITI, ODA became an important tool to assist Japanese heavy industry firms in finding large markets in Asia. Aid was vital in promoting Japan's export-based growth.

As a result of the government's strong support, Japanese aid increased rapidly in the 1960s. Japan's bilateral loans grew from US$48 million in 1960 to US$191.3 million in 1968. During the same period, Japan's bilateral grants and grantlike flows (including reparations) expanded from US$67 million to US$117 million, and multilateral aid increased from US$30 million to US$48 million (Rix, 1980).

Resource Diplomacy

The 1970s saw the emergence of Japanese ODA to secure a supply of natural resources. After the oil crisis of 1973, the use of Japanese aid for export promotion remained strong, but another economic objective emerged—securing resources in regions beyond Asia for Japan's own industrial development. After the Organization of Petroleum Exporting Countries (OPEC) imposed an embargo on industrialized states perceived as being pro-Israel, the Japanese government under Prime Minister Kakuei Tanaka immediately downgraded its ties with Israel and tried to appease the OPEC nations with economic aid. Tokyo supported Resolution 242 of the UN Security Council, which urged Israel to withdraw from the territories it occupied during the 1967 war. Tokyo then increased its aid contributions (from US$1 million in 1973 to US$5 million in 1974) to the United Nations to assist Palestinian refugees. In addition, Tokyo disbursed aid packages to Arab and Gulf countries, such as Egypt, Syria, and Iran (Hasegawa, 1975).

Economic aid was a necessary diplomatic tool because Japan lacked military means to pursue its foreign policy. Tokyo attempted to secure oil from OPEC members by resource diplomacy. The oil crisis triggered the globalization of Japanese aid, with expansion not only to the Middle East but also to Central America and Africa. As a result, Asia's share in Japanese aid rapidly dropped to about two thirds (Yasutomo, 1989–1990), although the actual amount of disbursement to the region continued to increase.

During the 1970s, institutionalization of ODA agencies was further accelerated. OTCA was abolished and replaced by the Japan International Cooperation Agency (JICA) in 1974. JICA began implementing grant aid, and the aforementioned OECF took charge of loan aid.

In summary, the Japanese reparations and other ODA programs from the 1950s to the mid-1970s (first phase) were primarily intended to benefit the domestic economy. Japanese firms became crucial actors in aid, initially undertaking reparations projects and subsequently contracting loan and grant aid projects. Most of these bilateral projects, both loans and grants, were tied to the procurement of Japanese goods and services, thus exclusively benefiting Japanese firms (Hasegawa, 1975). As Yanagihara and Emig (1991) observe, economic interests explicitly dictated Japanese aid programs:

> Early government statements of aid policy made no attempts to hide the high priority assigned to developing Japanese industry and fostering Japanese economic prosperity through aid. Tokyo justified this approach on the basis of the extensive needs and limited capability of the nation's economy. (p. 38)

Although Japanese aid during this phase was not confined to merely economic purposes,[3] political objectives were generally implicit and overshadowed by strong economic interests (Yasutomo, 1995).

During the first phase of ODA, several aid patterns emerged that had a significant impact on the course of future Japanese ODA. Because Japan's aid was largely business-oriented, it was offered primarily in the form of large-scale, infrastructure-based projects. Loans typically comprised more than 50 percent of Japanese aid, in sharp contrast with other donor countries in the Development Assistance Committee (DAC) of the Organization for Economic Cooperation and Development (OECD), of which Tokyo became a member in the early 1960s. Many of the DAC countries, such as Australia, France, and Sweden, began to allocate more than 70 percent of their ODA commitments for grants (Hasegawa, 1975). In addition, the terms of Japanese loans were hard, offering fewer grant elements than average DAC countries.[4]

Another distinct feature of Japanese aid during this time was its geographical concentration. In 1963, for example, Tokyo provided more than 98 percent of its ODA to Asian countries (Rix, 1980). Although Japanese aid globalized as a result of the oil crisis in the 1970s, by the end of the decade, Asia's share remained as high as two thirds of Japan's total aid. The early emphasis on Asia established the pattern of geographic concentration of Japanese aid.

Phase Two: Politicization of Japanese Aid Begins

The second period of Japanese ODA (from the mid-1970s to the late 1980s) witnessed rapid changes in aid orientation, reflecting the volatile climate of international politics. Three major developments affected the aid policy at that time. First, the withdrawal of U.S. forces from Indochina at the end of the Vietnam War left a power vacuum in the Southeast Asia region. Second, Cold War tensions heightened in the late 1970s, with a series of conflicts between the Communist and Western blocs. In particular, three incidents of 1979 were of critical importance to the Japanese government: (1) the establishment of the Vietnam-backed People's Republic of Kampuchea (PRK), (2) the Soviet invasion of Afghanistan, and (3) the Iranian hostage crisis. Third, debt crisis spread among developing countries in the mid-1980s, posing threats to the stability of the world economy.

These international incidents prompted Japanese policy makers to take action. By the mid-1970s, Japan was a wealthy country, and the international community expected Tokyo to take a larger role in world affairs. Japanese leaders were well aware that they needed to take measures to cope with the problems via "spending strategies" (Wan, 1995, p. 85), particularly ODA. Japanese policy makers saw ODA as an effective foreign policy tool because Japan lacked military means to conduct diplomacy.

Japan's ODA during this second phase consisted of three main policies corresponding to the aforementioned international contexts (i.e., the withdrawal of U.S. forces from Southeast Asia, heightened Cold War tensions, and debt crisis): (1) aid used to play a political role in Asia, as announced by Prime Minister Takeo Fukuda in his 1977 speech in Manila (the so-called Fukuda Doctrine); (2) the introduction of the concept of burden sharing through "strategic aid" to countries of critical importance to the Western world; and (3) further efforts in the burden sharing through capital recycling plans for debt-ridden developing countries (Sudo, 1986). During the second phase of Japanese ODA development, a clear political-strategic dimension of aid emerged as an explicit and integral component of

Japanese aid policy. The Japanese government decided to take part in burden sharing to maintain good diplomatic relations with the West by implementing strategic aid. The government also tried to strengthen its relations with Western governments by recycling its surplus capital to debtor countries. Although economic interests remained prominent, political purposes were explicitly pronounced and received priority (Sudo, 1988).

The Fukuda Doctrine

The first feature of this period deals with the so-called Fukuda Doctrine of 1977. Presented in a speech by Prime Minister Fukuda, the doctrine signaled a significant departure from Japan's traditional economy-first aid policy. It was a timely speech because by then the U.S. government had withdrawn its troops from Indochina, and the American presence in the region had declined. Fukuda presented three principles: (1) rejection of the role of a military power, (2) consolidation of the relationship of mutual confidence and trust based on "heart-to-heart" understanding, and (3) equal partnership with the Association of South East Asian Nations (ASEAN) for building peace and prosperity throughout Southeast Asia. The third principle was particularly significant in Japanese foreign policy, indicating that the Japanese government was willing to act as a political mediator between ASEAN and Indochina to bring about a peaceful coexistence between the two blocs. The Fukuda Doctrine was the first official statement in the post–World War II era that explicitly expressed Tokyo's political intentions as to its Asia policy.[5] The highlight of Fukuda's speech was the US$1 billion aid pledge for five ASEAN regional projects. Fukuda's declaration responded to Singapore Prime Minister Lee Kuan Yew's earlier call for Japan's aid for industrial projects in the ASEAN region. Although the US$1 billion pledge was not completely fulfilled due to the delay on the recipient side in determining and initiating the projects,[6] Fukuda's pledge demonstrated Japan's willingness to utilize economic aid for the purposes of playing larger political and economic roles in Southeast Asia (Sudo, 1992).

More important, the aid pledge signaled the beginning of Japan's aid policy with an emphasis on quantity. Fukuda's announcement was the first major pledge to support the "aid doubling plan" (the First Midterm Aid Expansion Plan), which he had announced earlier at the 1977 Bonn summit. Under Fukuda's leadership, Japanese ODA in the late 1970s grew rapidly. Although the original goal of the plan was to double the cumulative ODA in five years, the numerical target was easily achieved within three, from US$1.4 billion in 1977 to US$3.3 billion in 1980 (Rix, 1993; Yasutomo, 1989–1990). Bloch (1989) observes that Japanese aid has undergone a major transformation since Fukuda's aid doubling plan: "Japanese aid as a single-minded extension of 'Japan, Inc.' ended at about that time" (pp. 11–12). Succeeding prime ministers from the late 1970s to the early 1990s, such as Zenko Suzuki, Yasuhiro Nakasone, Noboru Takeshita, and Toshiki Kaifu, followed Fukuda's lead with similar slogans promising to double the amount of aid disbursement.

Strategic Aid

The second significant event from the mid-1970s to the late 1980s was the emergence of burden-sharing efforts through the adoption of strategic aid. Because Japan's constitution prohibits the use of force to promote its overseas interests, ODA was used for countries in regions strategically significant to the Western allies. By implementing strategic aid, the Japanese government (i.e., MOFA) hoped to bolster the Western security alliance. Worsening U.S.–Japan trade was another factor prompting the Japanese government to act. U.S.–Japan trade friction began in the 1960s involving textile industries, but bilateral trade relations rapidly deteriorated in the late 1970s and the 1980s. In the mid-1980s, Japan's trade surplus with the United States set a new record—more than US$50 billion (Schoppa, 1997).

During the 1980s, the Ohira government implemented strategic aid by developing two new concepts of aid: "countries bordering conflict" (*funsō shūhenkoku*) and "comprehensive national security" (*sōgō anzen hoshō*). Countries bordering conflict—that is, Western allies crucial to warding off Soviet influence, specifically Thailand, Pakistan, and Turkey—were designated as priorities for Japanese aid policy. Turkey had no conflict on its immediate border but was considered an important Western ally in the Middle East. Thailand and Pakistan were considered frontline states against the Vietnam-backed PRK and the Soviet invasion of Afghanistan, respectively. As a result, in 1980, Japan's ODA to Thailand increased by 1.3 times over the previous year, to Pakistan by 3.7 times, and to Turkey by about 10 times (Yasutomo, 1986; Tanaka, 1995).

In addition to the three countries bordering conflict, Egypt emerged as a strategically important country in the Middle East in the late 1970s and 1980s. After Egypt's 1977 Camp David peace agreement with Israel, Western donors increased their aid to Cairo. Following in the footsteps of its Western allies, Japanese ODA to Egypt went from ¥32 billion in 1980 to ¥50 billion in 1981 (Yasutomo, 1986). The Ohira administration also used ODA to sanction countries under Soviet influence. For example, it froze aid to Vietnam after Hanoi overthrew the infamous Pol Pot regime and helped establish the pro-Vietnam government in Cambodia in 1979. Japan's aid to Cambodia, which had stopped in the mid-1970s due to intensified civil war in the country, remained frozen because Tokyo decided to follow U.S. leadership in isolating the Phnom Penh government. Similarly, Japan stopped or reduced aid to Afghanistan, Cuba, Angola, and Ethiopia for political reasons (Yasutomo, 1986; Tomoda, 1997).

The other concept developed by the Ohira administration, comprehensive national security (*sōgō anzen hoshō*), recognized not only military but also nonmilitary threats to the national security of Japan and urged nonmilitary countermeasures against them. Nonmilitary measures included conservation and stockpiling of resources, ODA, development of high-technology industries, and other endeavors. ODA was considered a particularly useful tool to deter threats by contributing to the creation of a stable and favorable international environment for Japan.

Ohira's successor, Prime Minister Zenko Suzuki, continued the policy of strategic aid. Although Suzuki changed the rhetoric of "countries bordering conflict" to "areas that are important to the maintenance of peace and stability of the world," the underlying message carried the same intention: Japan would continue to utilize economic aid for countries of strategic significance.

Strategic aid was also extended to the Pacific Island region. In 1987, during a visit to Fiji, Foreign Minister Tadashi Kuranari of the Nakasone government announced a policy later termed the Kuranari Doctrine, outlining objectives of Japanese policy toward Pacific Islands. One of the key elements of Kuranari's speech was the use of Japanese aid to counter increased Soviet presence in the South Pacific, a presence that prompted U.S. officials to pressure the Japanese government to take measures for the maintenance of Western security in the Pacific. Tokyo complied with Washington's demands by increasing its aid volume in South Pacific from US$68 million in 1987 to US$93 million in 1988, and to US$114 million in 1990 (Takeda, 1993).

Capital Recycling

While Japan increased its aid to countries of strategic importance to take part in burden sharing with the West, the government also promoted another type of burden sharing—maintaining the international financial system and assisting debtor countries in the face of an economic crisis first triggered in Mexico in 1984. By the mid-1980s, Japan had accumulated trade surpluses of approximately US$100 billion (Yasutomo, 1995). The Japanese government decided to provide Tokyo's recycled surplus savings to debtor countries in the second half of the 1980s. Japan's use of recycled capital was to mitigate mounting pressure on Tokyo from Western countries, particularly the United States, to make a significant contribution to improving economic conditions in the developing world as the world's largest creditor. Aid packages helped meet the international expectation of Japan to take part in burden sharing for the debt crisis (see Wood, 1986). Given Japan's limited defense role, capital recycling was considered a suitable way to achieve such goals.

Between 1986 and 1989, the Japanese government devised three separate debt relief plans, which took place mainly through the coordination between Japanese public and private banks, multilateral development banks (MDBs), and other international financial institutions (IFIs). First, Finance Minister Miyazawa announced in 1986 that Japan would recycle US$10 billion in public and private capital to developing countries through multilateral development agencies for the next three years.[7] Second, Prime Minister Nakasone announced further efforts in capital recycling in 1987. Although the majority of these contributions were not ODA, the total amount extracted for ODA in this plan was still substantial (US$4 billion in total, with US$1 billion deriving from government contributions to the MDBs and US$3 billion from OECF as loans) (Yanagihara & Emig, 1991).[8] Third, at the Arche summit in 1989, Prime Minister Noboru Takeshita pledged to provide debtor countries with additional US$35 billion by 1992 (Yanagihara & Emig, 1991). The new pledge was to support the Brady plan, a plan previously proposed by US Treasury Secretary Nicholas Brady that had emphasized the role of IFIs in rescuing debtor countries.[9]

During the 1980s, Japanese aid became a multipurpose instrument for Tokyo's preventive diplomacy, being closely linked to U.S.–Japan relations in terms of trade and security issues and easing tensions with Tokyo's allies through burden sharing. ODA disbursement increased drastically during the second period due to the aid-doubling plans implemented by Prime Minister Fukuda and his successors, for example, jumping from US$3.3 billion in 1980 to about US$50 billion in 1986 (Yasutomo, 1995), so although the politicization of Japan's aid did not diminish, Japan's economic interest in ODA was occasionally overshadowed by the more urgent political needs of supporting Tokyo's Western allies.

Phase Three: Diversified Aid in the Post-Cold War Era

Japanese ODA in the late 1980s and the 1990s diversified to a complex mixture of purposes and a broad array of programs, reflecting changes in the international and domestic environment. On the international front, the Cold War ended and new issues of development emerged, such as the democratization and marketization of the former Soviet bloc. But since the end of the Cold War, regional conflicts have intensified, increasing the need for U.N.-mediated peacekeeping efforts. Following the collapse of the Soviet bloc, globalization has accelerated, creating international awareness of such global issues as environmental deterioration, the spread of AIDS, rapid population growth, and worsening poverty in the developing world (see World Commission on Environment and Development, 1987). Japan has been pressured by other donor countries to take a more constructive role in international aid and development, especially by increasing grassroots soft aid. Yet, at the same time, many donor countries have suffered aid budget cuts and have shown signs of aid fatigue, thus raising expectations that Japan, the world's largest aid donor, will take a more proactive role in poverty-stricken least less-developed country (LLDCs), such as certain African countries. Meanwhile, the Asian economic crisis of 1997 has made many East Asian countries seek assistance from Japan (Castellano, 1999a).

On the domestic front, several significant changes have occurred. As Japan became the world's largest donor, government officials and the Japanese public have become more aware of their country's responsibility as a world power. This awareness has been intensifying since the Gulf War in 1990–1991, during which the Japanese government earned sharp international criticism for its tardy response to the Iraqi aggression in Kuwait. The Japanese government failed to find appropriate means to participate actively and swiftly in the war effort and reacted defensively to U.S. pressure without taking any clear stance on the crisis. Despite Tokyo's financial contribution totaling US$13 billion in the end, approximately 20 percent of the total cost of the Desert Storm campaign, Tokyo failed to earn international recognition.[10] The Gulf crisis taught the Japanese public and officials the lesson that Japan can no longer continue its passive, reactive foreign policy, but must become actively involved in world affairs and take a role of political leadership commensurate with its economic strength. The blunder of the Japanese government in the Gulf War was a humiliating experience for many Japanese people, making them yearn for international prestige and respect.

One of the criticisms of Japan's policy during the Gulf War was its unwillingness to provide *jinteki kōken* (human contributions). The Japanese government simply paid large checks for the forces involved and several countries bordering the conflict region (e.g., Egypt, Jordan, Syria), but sent neither its Self-Defense Forces nor large-scale official humanitarian rescue teams to the Gulf region. The war experience led to intense domestic debate on how Japan should make *kokusai kōken* (international contributions) without merely resorting to "checkbook diplomacy." The Japanese came to realize that human involvement would be necessary in future foreign policy. Some felt this need strongly in the realm of military cooperation. Others felt that Japan should not send its military abroad but should make contributions peacefully through humanitarian aid involving a large number of Japanese people.

Meanwhile, other serious problems have been emerging. Exposed to endless corruption scandals of government officials and politicians, Japan has also suffered a prolonged economic recession, the worst in the post–World War II era, and worsening fiscal deficits that threaten the rapidly aging Japanese society. Japan can no longer spend massive amounts of ODA without fiscal consideration.[11] The silver lining of these domestic crises, however, is that these problems create new opportunities for Tokyo to reform the existing political-economic system, including how ODA is spent. Aid reform has drawn public support in the face of fiscal problems, with a new emphasis placed on the effectiveness and efficiency of aid. With less money budgeted for foreign aid, people have started demanding that the government enact reform to optimize its assistance to the developing world (see Kusano, 1998; *Nikkei Weekly*, 1998a). More people in civil society have begun to participate in debate on aid and demand that Japan's ODA be used in the social sector, rather than in the economic sector, and that the aid be spent on the basic human needs (BHNs) of the poor in the developing world.

As in all the phases, Japanese ODA in the 1990s has been shaped by the international and domestic contexts. Aid is used to address emerging global issues and to promote Japan's *kokusai kōken* (international contributions). Japanese aid has become more politically oriented. The aim of the aid is to strengthen relations with other countries, increase influence in global politics, and gain the respect of the international community. For the first time, aid has been linked to issues of democracy, human rights, and U.N.-sponsored peacekeeping operations.

In short, since the late 1980s, at least six new directions of ODA have emerged: (1) the incorporation of the concepts of democratization, human rights, and market economy; (2) the use of aid in association with U.N.-related peace-keeping efforts; (3) a new emphasis on soft aid to address global issues and respond to Japan's aid reform movement; (4) a new emphasis on LLDCs, especially countries in Indochina and Africa; (5) the use of aid in response to the Asian economic crisis; and (6) a reduction of ODA growth (Japan's own aid fatigue). These directions are distinct from the features of the second period of Japanese aid. The main difference in aid programs between the 1990s and the mid-1970s to late 1980s is that the aid in the 1990s is far more diverse and globalized. Aid is now used to promote the political and economic stability of the entire world (not just that of the Western bloc) and to cope with emerging global issues. In addition, ODA has reduced in quantity, a sharp contrast to the rapid aid growth in the second phase. These six directions are Tokyo's strategies for dealing with the new situations in the post–Cold War era.

Democratization, Human Rights, and Market Economy

The first policy change—that is, the incorporation of the concept of democracy, human rights, and market economy—was verbalized immediately after the dissolution of the Soviet Union. The collapse of the Soviet bloc triggered a political and economic transformation of Eastern Europe, the Central Asian republics of former Soviet Union, and other Asian countries formerly under the Soviet orbit. The "victory" of the West over the Soviet bloc had a significant impact on Japan's ODA policy, leading Tokyo to incorporate concepts of democracy, human rights, and the market economy into its own ODA policy for the first time. In Eastern Europe, Prime Minister Toshiki Kaifu announced in 1990 that Japan would play a political role as a member of the industrialized democracies and that Tokyo would readily support the democratization of Eastern Europe (Hisani, 1990). When Japan became a member of the European Bank for Reconstruction and Development (EBRD), the Japanese government accepted the EBRD's political and economic mandates, that is, that recipients of the EBRD must "(1) adhere to the rule of law, (2) respect human rights, (3) introduce a multiparty political system, (4) hold free and fair elections, and (5) develop market-oriented economies" (Yasutomo, 1995, p. 103). This was the first time the Japanese government accepted political conditions for giving aid.

About the same time, Japan took the lead in getting the former Soviet republics of Central Asia—Kazakhstan, Uzbekistan, Tajikistan, Kyrgyzstan, and Turkmenistan—on the DAC list of developing countries, thereby justifying Japan's disbursement of ODA to the region. Although small in scale, Japan began humanitarian assistance and technical assistance to the Central Asian countries in the early 1990s. Japan also began to assist other former Soviet allies, such as Mongolia, which signed agreements to receive Japanese loan aid (commodity loans) in 1991. In Southeast Asia, Japan resumed its ODA to Cambodia and Vietnam following Hanoi's withdrawal of troops from Cambodia in 1989. Japan resumed its ODA to Cambodia (grant aid for emergency relief) in 1991 for the first time in 16 years and to Vietnam (commodity loans) in 1992 for the first time in 13 years (Ministry of Foreign Affairs, 1995b). In all these cases, Japan's aid to the former Soviet republics and allies can be seen as a contribution to the international community's effort to support democratization, human rights, and the market economy, as well as an effort to increase Japanese influence in newly opened markets.

The concepts of human rights, democracy, and market-led development were officially integrated into Japanese aid policy in 1992, when the Japanese government adopted an official ODA charter. The fourth principle of the charter proclaims, "Full attention should be paid to efforts for promoting democratization and the introduction of a market-oriented economy, and the situation regarding the securing of basic human rights and freedoms in the recipient country" (Ministry of Foreign Affairs, 1997). In creating the ODA Charter, Japan sought to demonstrate to the United States and Europe its commitment to international support of Western aims.

Although the ODA Charter was supported in Japan, some scholars and human rights organizations criticized its application. They pointed out that the charter was mainly applied to countries of minor economic and political interest to Japan, such as Sudan, Nigeria, and Gambia, whereas it was applied only minimally to countries of major economic and political significance, such as China (Arase, 1993; Hook & Zhang, 1998). This same criticism has certainly been leveled against other Western countries, for example, the United States. But in the case of China at least, it was Japan that pushed most strongly for resumption of international aid, which had been cut after the June 1989 events at Tiananmen Square. Thus, Japan's new ODA charter is incomplete in its application. But this does not diminish the fact that the acceptance of the charter represented an important step in setting new standards to which the government could be held accountable.

ODA for UN Peace-Keeping Efforts

The second characteristic of Japanese ODA in the 1990s is the linkage of aid with U.N.-related peacekeeping efforts. After receiving strong international criticism of Japan's initial lukewarm support for the U.S.-led UN effort in the Gulf War in 1990, Tokyo committed a total of US$13 billion to Operation Desert Storm and to Middle Eastern countries affected by the conflict, as discussed above. Furthermore, the aforementioned aid resumption to Cambodia in 1991 also took place within the framework of U.N.-led peacekeeping efforts, namely, the United Nations Transitional Authority of Cambodia (UNTAC). Tokyo participated in UNTAC by dispatching Japanese Self-Defense Forces, the first deployment of Japanese forces to the Asian mainland since the end of World War II. To support UNTAC's efforts, the Japanese government took the major international initiative in promoting reconstruction and development in Cambodia, as discussed below. Again, Japan's participation in U.N. efforts was politically motivated, as Tokyo sought to earn trust and respect from the United States and other countries as part of its ongoing effort to gain a permanent seat on the U.N. Security Council.

Emphasis on Soft Aid to Address Global Issues

In the 1990s, the Japanese government has begun to emphasize soft aid to address global issues, such as environmental protection, population growth, AIDS, poverty alleviation, and women in development (WID). This has involved (1) a shift in target sector of aid (e.g., from economic institutions to health care); (2) a shift in emphasis within particular target sectors (e.g., from building hospitals to training community health practitioners as well); (3) an expansion of groups to carry out aid projects (e.g., NGOs have been added to Japanese business firms); and (4) a new emphasis on LLDCs, including Indochina and Africa. This shift from hard to soft aid is still in its relatively early stages (i.e., Japan still devotes large amounts of funding for infrastructure projects carried out by Japanese construction firms); nevertheless, it is a significant step toward following the path of other industrialized donor countries.

The emphasis on soft aid is politically motivated. Soft aid—usually small-scale grants—does not bring as much profit to contracting firms as does hard aid, usually through large-scale loans. Increasing soft aid is to show a gesture of *kokusai kōken* and is intended to improve Tokyo's international standing.

In addition, soft aid is the most feasible solution to mounting domestic criticisms of Japanese aid. In the face of increasing fiscal problems and media revelation of corrupt practices among aid officials and business contractors (see Chapter 3), demands for efficient and effective use of aid have arisen. In particular, NGOs have criticized wasteful capital projects, pointing out that Japan should shift its emphasis from hard to soft aid. The media and academicians have echoed NGOs, claiming that Japan should increase grassroots-based soft aid as it is less expensive than infrastructure-based hard aid.

Aid to LLDCs

The recognition of the need to address issues of poverty in LLDCs has led to a reprioritization of aid recipient countries and regions. MOFA has begun to give priority to certain regions of importance while cutting funds for others. Of particular importance are LLDCs in Indochina and Africa that previously did not receive large flows of Japanese aid. As mentioned above, aid to Indochina resumed in the early 1990s after the withdrawal of the Vietnamese forces from Cambodia, when Japan became the largest bilateral aid donor in Cambodia and Vietnam. The Japanese government under MOFA's leadership took several initiatives for the development of Indochina. In 1992, the government hosted a Ministerial Conference on the Rehabilitation and Reconstruction of Cambodia to coordinate international economic assistance to Cambodia. The next year, MOFA established an aid-coordinating body called the Forum for Comprehensive Development of Indochina (known as the Indochina Forum). Aid to Indochina has both economic and political objectives. ODA to Vietnam, in particular, is primarily economic, with the high level of participation of Japanese firms in many large-scale capital projects. In contrast, aid to Cambodia is highly political. Cambodia, still suffering the aftereffects of its devastating civil war, does not have much economic potential for most Japanese firms. In fact, until 1999, Cambodia received no Japanese loans for large-scale infrastructure projects. Yet, Tokyo emphasizes ODA to Phnom Penh because its stability is crucial to the integration of Indochina into the rest of Southeast Asia.

Africa has also emerged as an important region for Japan, attracting MOFA officials interested in expanding Japan's political role by increasing allies in the region. Japan's economic relationship with Africa is of minor importance to Tokyo's own economic prosperity. Rather, MOFA hopes to strengthen Japan's relations with African countries and gain support for Japan's international political agendas from them (e.g., Japan's application to be a permanent member on the UN Security Council). In 1985, Japan's aid spending in Africa was US$253 million. In 1990, it grew to US$792 million and in 1995 reached US$1.333 billion primarily in grants (Ministry of Foreign Affairs, 1997). Africa has become the second largest recipient region of Japanese aid after Asia (Castellano, 1999c; Castellano, 1999d).[12]

Asian Economic Crisis

The fifth aspect of Japanese aid during the third phase is to help the countries affected by the Asian financial crisis. The international community, frustrated by Japan's initial inability to take initiatives to lead neighboring countries to overcome their economic crisis, pressed Tokyo to take bold action. In 1998, Tokyo responded to the criticism by announcing the Miyazawa Plan, an aid package of US$30 billion over and above its regular ODA budget (*Japan Times Online*, 1999). The two main political purposes of the package were to quell international criticism that Japan was not doing enough to relieve the stress associated with the economic crisis and to create goodwill between Tokyo and its neighbors. Japan's bilateral relations with many Asian countries are still delicate due to Japan's aggression in the region during the World War II. The Miyazawa Plan was intended to help smooth these relations. Although the bulk of the fund did not qualify as ODA and thus was handled by the Export–Import Bank, some funding was considered ODA and handled by OECF as concessional loans (Castellano, 1999a; see *International Development Journal,* 1999b; *Asahi Shimbun Online,* 1998).[13]

At the same time, Tokyo's aid commitment under the Miyazawa Plan had economic motives. Strong East Asian economies help Japanese firms, promote the internationalization of the Japanese yen, and strengthen the viability of the yen in the face of increased competition from the euro and dollar. Japanese firms normally conduct a substantial amount of business in East Asian countries via trade and investment, and they were seriously hurt by the Asian crisis. The region's recovery from the crisis would be crucial for the survival of these firms. Also, the provision of large sums in the form of loans could contribute to the efforts of the Japanese government to circulate the yen in East Asia and strengthen the currency.

Declining ODA Growth

Another important direction in Japanese aid is the decline in aid budgets due to Japan's fiscal problems. The 1996 aid budget dropped nearly 35 percent from the 1995 level in U.S. dollar terms, partly due to a weakened yen (*Asahi Shimbun,* 1997a). In 1997, the fifth aid-doubling plan was abandoned because of the difficulty of acquiring funds. In the same year, the government decided to slash the 1998 aid budget by 10.4 percent. This decision was significant because the cutback was not just for 1998 but for three consecutive years. Although the 10 percent slash was temporarily stalled in 1998 because of the economic crisis (*International Development Journal,* 1999d), the cutback is expected for FY2002 (*Asahi Shimbun,* 2001c).

In the face of mounting fiscal problems, Japan has gradually shifting its focus from quantity to quality of aid. But it is important to point out that the budget for grassroots-based technical aid and humanitarian aid actually increased. Budgets to assist NGOs were spared severe cuts (see *International Development Journal,* 1999e). Japan's rapid aid expansion is over, but Tokyo is expected to provide more funds to soft aid in the coming years.

In summary, since the end of the Cold War, Japanese aid has become increasingly more complex, with multiple motives and diverse programs. ODA is used to contribute to the international community for the creation of a stable and peaceful world, to strengthen Japan's relations with other countries, to increase Japan's influence in global politics to alleviate problems the world face today, and to help Japanese firms recover from the economic crisis in Asia.

Also, as political purposes of aid have been established, the content of aid has begun to change. Prior to the 1990s, the majority of Japanese aid funded capital projects, or hard aid. In the 1990s, the Japanese government began to stress the importance of and shifting its emphasis to humanitarian, or soft aid. Soft aid[14] is an effective tool to advance the political interests of the Japanese government. The government can earn trust and respect from the international community by giving soft aid because it is more humanitarian in orientation and brings less economic gain to Japanese firms. Furthermore, as ODA has become more politically oriented with an emphasis on soft aid, new countries have drawn attention from Japanese officials, such as LLDCs in Indochina and Sub-Saharan Africa. This does not mean that Japan's traditional aid recipients in Asia are neglected or that Japan's economic motives have disappeared. The Japanese government does continue to attend to its traditional recipients and to the needs of Japanese firms. For example, the economic interest of Japanese aid was exemplified during the Asian financial crisis in the late 1990s, when the Japanese government provided substantial aid to other countries to stabilize the Asian market for Japanese firms. At the same time, however, the Asian financial crisis aid was also seen as an example of *kokusai kōken* (international contribution) to help bring about stability in Asia.

Conclusion

From the mid-1950s to the mid-1970s, Japanese ODA policy served as an extension of Japan's own postwar reconstruction, export promotion, and resource acquisition efforts. Since that time, the needs of Japan and the world have changed tremendously, and Japanese aid has changed accordingly. Today, Japanese ODA reflects less a priority on economic objectives than on strategic political objectives. The former continue to play a role, but they are balanced or even overshadowed by the latter. At the same time, Japanese policy makers are paying closer attention to the humanitarian needs of people in LLDCs and to global issues, such as population growth and the spread of AIDS. These new concerns motivated the Japanese government, particularly MOFA, to shift its emphasis from hard aid to incorporate soft aid.

The politicization of aid has created new challenges and demands for the Japanese government. Although Japan started some new aid policies in the 1990s, critics complain that implementation has been inconsistent. To meet international and domestic expectations, Tokyo must now broaden its commitment to new aid policies based on clear political objectives. But planning and implementing new policies is difficult given the structure and traditions of the Japanese aid administration. One of the most challenging tasks is finding effective ways to disburse politically oriented aid, particularly soft aid. The Japanese government is experienced in channeling hard aid in the developing world, but not soft aid. In many ways, channeling the latter through various small-scale, grassroots projects is far more difficult than implementing the former through capital projects. Soft aid is labor intensive and requires extensive knowledge about the political, economic, cultural, and social conditions of local communities. Hard aid requires no such knowledge; indeed, hard-aid programs allow the transference of large amounts of aid money with relatively few human resources or investigation. Is the Japanese government capable of implementing many soft aid programs? At present, the answer is no. The Japanese aid administration lacks enough qualified personnel to take part in grassroots aid projects. The lack of a strong development staff with expertise in grassroots aid seriously impedes Japan's efforts to reform aid.

In this context, the incorporation of NGOs into Japanese ODA becomes clear: NGOs can help the government implement soft aid programs. Because government agencies or traditional aid contractors for hard aid (such as construction or trading firms) lack expertise in grassroots development, the bureaucracy increasingly relies on NGOs to meet these new challenges.

In summary, throughout the history of Japan's ODA, aid policies have been shaped according to the international and domestic contexts. Incorporation of soft aid and NGOs into Japan's ODA program represents a continuation of the historical influence of external and internal factors. The response of the Japanese government (i.e., MOFA) has been to tailor Japanese aid to meet the changing needs of the international and domestic circumstances.

NOTES

Introduction

1. My differences with Johnson's use of the term are explained in Chapter 1.
2. Exceptions to this are edited collections by Yamamoto (1998) and Yamamoto (1999). These books provide general description of Japan's nonprofit sector rather than a political analysis. A third edited collection has recently been published (Pharr & Schwartz, 2002); it was not available for review at the time of this writing.

Chapter One   Civil Society and NGOs in Japan

1. Personal communication with a researcher at the Japan Center for International Exchange, Tokyo, July 12, 2001.
2. When religious groups are engaged in public ends, such as efforts to fight poverty or crime or to improve educational institutions in the community, they are participating in civil society. Thus, this type of organizations is simultaneously involved in both parochial and civil society.
3. The exclusion of parochial society, particularly recreational and entertainment groups, from civil society differs from Putnam's (2000) treatment of civic community. In his examination of American civic community, Putnam focuses on horizontal networks of apolitical civil associations (e.g., choral societies, bird watching clubs, bowling leagues) that are generating norms of reciprocity, interpersonal trust, and voluntary cooperation—essential ingredients of social capital necessary for community development. Putnam does not consider policy-oriented social movements and nonprofit organizations in the United States (e.g., the Sierra Club, the National Organization for Women or NOW) as critical segments of civic community, on the grounds that most of them are membership organizations merely collecting checks from their members without promoting civic engagement.
4. Since renamed the Ministry of Economy, Trade, and Industry (METI), but referred to by its original name throughout this book.
5. An exception to this is the Japan Red Cross Society (JRCS). In legal terms, JRCS is a special public corporation (*tokushu hōjin*). However, JRCS can be considered an NGO, since it is a membership organization with a large number of volunteer groups and works relatively independently of the state (Amenomori & Yamamoto, 1998). JRCS is treated as a Japanese NGO by the UN High Commissioners for Refugees (UNHCR) and became an active member the Partnership in Action (PARinAC), a scheme designed to promote UNHCR–NGO cooperation.

6. Perhaps the first important social movement in postwar Japan was the anti–U.S. Security Treaty movement in the late 1950s and early 1960s, which involved massive demonstrations among left-wing college students. This movement, however, was hardly peaceful, and violent protest led to many injuries. Thus, this study does not consider it a civil society movement.

7. While the term *shimin undo* has a political connotation of the expansion of citizens' rights, *jumin undo* has a narrower, less political connotation of community movement.

8. The Meiji government began a campaign, largely through education, to promote familism (*kokutai*), by which it meant the importance of obedience and loyalty to authority, in particular, the emperor. The idea was that as citizens, the Japanese people should respect and follow the leadership of the Emperor as father of the nation.

9. This does not necessarily mean that the bureaucracy enjoyed unchecked power during the developmental state era. As Pempel (1989) notes, the bureaucracy was "technically and practically subject to the policy-making controls of parliament and the LDP" (p. 31). When the bureaucracy was powerful, for example in ODA policy making, its power and policy were approved or supported by the political world.

10. In my view, Japan's goal of surpassing the Western industrialized countries was achieved only in terms of GNP rates. Living conditions, symbolized by the "rabbit hutch" phenomenon, lag far behind those of other industrialized countries, largely because of scarcity of land in large cities and the exclusion of foreign firms to compete in Japanese real estate market—the legacy of the developmental policies.

11. JSRC renamed itself Sotoshu Volunteer Association in 1981 and then Shanti Volunteer Association (SVA) in 1999.

12. For example, Japanese government agencies prevented European body-searching dogs from entering the Kobe region for rescue efforts because the dogs had not undergone quarantine for six months. The bureaucracy also denied an offer of free mobile telephones for use in rescue work by a corporation because the phones lacked appropriate certification labels for the Kobe area. Furthermore, the bureaucracy kept the emergency Self-Defense Forces officers outside Kobe because of real or imagined antimilitary sentiments by local people (Pempel, 1998). In the first ten days following the earthquake, the government received offers of assistance from 57 countries but accepted only 15 (Ministry of Foreign Affairs, 1995a).

13. These numbers refers only to NGOs specializing in international aid and development. It excludes those engaged in international cultural exchanges.

14. Fujisaki et al. (1996–1997) actually use the term *software aid* and *hardware aid*. They define it as assistance to promote "human resource development and institutional building in economic and social development" (p. 519).

15. However, NGO meetings with MOF representatives usually involve Japan's multilateral aid, rather than its bilateral aid, via the Asian Development Bank (ADB) and the World Bank.

16. Most NGOs are membership organizations.

17. These figures are based on the US$1 = ¥120 conversion.

18. The figure is based on the US$1 = ¥120 conversion.

19. The figure is based on the US$1 = £0.61 conversion.

20. Based on the US$1 = ¥120 conversion.

21. Interview with Secretary General of AMDA, on March 3, 1997, in Tokyo.

22. AMDA also disapproves a "Western" approach to development and democracy. The General Director of AMDA claims that the concept of human rights is based on Christian thought and lacks a universal appeal (Suganami, 1995).

23. In one case, a Japanese refugee organization received state funding for a nonexistent project it created on the paper. According to a representative of this group, a lack of personnel to carry out the project for which the group received funds accounted for this mismanagement (*International Development Journal*, 2000).

Chapter Two   Globalization and Pluralism

1. ECFA is under the jurisdiction of MITI and receives subsidies from it.

2. A JICA-posted official in Phnom Penh who oversaw proposals submitted to the Japanese government by Cambodian ministries acknowledged the critical role of Japanese firms in identifying and formulating projects. According to him, many of the proposals submitted to him were written by Japanese firms. He could clearly tell which proposal was written by a Japanese firm because of the writing style in the proposal, which was fairly distinct from Cambodian officials' writing style. He remarked that some proposal forms for Japanese grant aid were quite complex, even requiring the applicant to specify what type of machinery they would need for the project they were proposing—an impossible task for Cambodian officials without assistance from a Japanese firm. Interview, JICA employee working at the Cambodian Rehabilitation and Development Board on May 28, 1997, in Phnom Penh.

3. However, a few Japanese firms have been trying to adapt to the changing aid environment by exploring new fields. For example, some engineering firms (e.g., Nisshin Support Engineering, Caterpillar Mitsubishi, and Yamanashi Hitachi Construction Machinery) have been conducting research to invent effective demining machines. At present, demining, primarily conducted by governments and NGOs, is time consuming due to a lack of appropriate technology. These Japanese firms have begun to work with JICA and aid recipient governments and *agencies* (*International Development Journal*, 1998d,h).

4. As seen in the case of Myanmar, many Japanese firms attempt to promote their views through Keidanren, the largest and most powerful chamber of commerce in Japan. Through public relations campaigns, Keidanren has voiced its members' concerns that Japanese corporations are increasingly distancing themselves from ODA as they cannot win international bids. As a step to solve this problem, Keidanren has demanded a greater role of the private sector in aid decision making: "There is a limit on what the government can achieve within its own jurisdiction. ... The private sector is ready to share or replace some of the government functions" (Keidanren, 1997). Keidanren also argues that ODA should be used to support private-sector investments and corporate assistance for developing countries (Keidanren, 1994). At the same time, Keidanren claims that its ODA policy is based on a win–win approach, in which both the corporate sector and NGOs can gain by collaborating with the government. Keidanren does not oppose NGO participation in ODA. What it objects to is the reduction of infrastructure aid that prevents Japanese firms from participating in ODA. In fact, Keidanren has attempted to promote NGO participation in aid. In 1994, Keidanren urged the government to (1) simplify the legal procedure for NGOs applying for corporate status, (2) provide tax exemptions to NGOs, (3) train NGO staff so that they can gain specialized knowledge necessary to conduct international cooperation and aid, and (4) provide financial assistance for education on NGO activities at public schools (Keidanren, 1994). Keidanren publicly acknowledges that NGO activities can complement governmental aid due to the effective grassroots organizing of NGOs in developing countries (Keidanren, 1994). Keidanren's stance on NGOs is understandable. The federation is concerned with its image as the leader of Japanese businesses, and it is considered politically incorrect in Japan to say that Japanese NGOs should not participate in ODA. Many observers of aid, however, are skeptical that a win-win situation is really possible for Japanese firms and NGOs, because they have dramatically different views of aid and compete in influencing aid policy.

5. Interview with general manager at Nippon Kōei, on May 8, 1997, in Hanoi.

6. I adopt Kuhn's (1970) definition of a paradigm: "Universally recognized scientific achievements that for a time provide model problems and solutions to a community of practitioners" (p. viii).

7. This study borrows a definition of epistemic community by P. Haas (1992): "An epistemic community is a network of professionals with recognized expertise and competence in a particular domain and an authoritative claim to policy-relevant knowledge within that domain or issue area" (p. 3).

8. I adopt Krasner's (1982) definition of international regimes: sets of "implicit or explicit principles, norms, rules, and decision-making procedures around which actors' expectations converge in a given area of international relations. Principles are beliefs of fact, causation, and rectitude. Norms are standards of behavior defined in terms of rights and obligations. Rules are specific prescriptions or proscriptions for action. Decision-making procedures are prevailing practices for making and implementing collective choice" (p. 186). Although this study deals with regime theory, it does not focus on the international aid regime itself. Rather, I examine how the Japanese government has responded to restrictions imposed by the aid regime.

9. Inada (1990) argues that individual recipient countries can exert pressure on the Japanese government. However, this study claims that individually pressed *gaiatsu* from recipient countries usually influences specific project-level decisions, but that it does not determine the overall framework for Japanese aid policy.

10. The irony, however, is that, on the one hand, the U.S. government has encouraged the Japanese government to reduce the level of loans in ODA, but, on the other hand, Washington has demanded that Tokyo open its bilateral loan bidding system so that American firms can fully take part in Japanese loan projects. These demands have coincided with U.S. efforts to open the Japanese market for U.S. construction firms to take part in Japanese public works (Armacost, 1996). USAID, for example, sponsored two conferences in 1989 for American business representatives on how to get involved in Japanese ODA projects. In 1992, President George Bush pressed Prime Minister Miyazawa on opening the Japanese ODA market, and they agreed that the two countries should organize and support a program to introduce American firms to Japan's ODA. Following that commitment, the U.S. Department of Commerce held a Tokyo ODA conference in 1992, representing more than seventy U.S. firms (Johns, 1993). These events illustrate that a strong motive of the U.S. government for pressing the Japanese government on aid policy was to further their own economic interests. Interestingly, though, some members of Congress, American business leaders, and other American policy makers wanted to emulate Japanese aid. For example, members of Congress introduced several legislative initiatives to increase opportunities for American firms under American aid. The "Aid for Trade Bill," introduced by several senators in 1991, intended to shift aid spending from program assistance to infrastructure projects. Congress adopted some portions of the bill to established a Capital Projects Bureau within USAID (Hankes, 1993).

11. Most NGO representatives I met in 1999 who have regular contact with MOFA officials through meetings support the view that MOFA's perspectives of aid have been gradually changing. They noted that MOFA's views of aid were becoming closer to those of many NGOs promoting grassroots aid. For example, personal communication with a representative of the Japanese NGO Center for International Cooperation (JANIC) on August 3, 1999, in Tokyo; interview with secretary general of Shapla Neer on August 4, 1999, in Tokyo.

12. In 1993, for example, MOFA, together with the Dutch government and UNDP, sponsored a project to discuss implementing a new development paradigm. With the participation from governments and NGOs, this project resulted in a working paper that explores a new development paradigm (Griesgraber & Gunter, 1996).

13. By a broad definition by the Japanese government, technical assistance is considered part of grant aid.

14. In the 1990s, the state came to take a more relaxed, laissez-faire stance to NGO activities. For example, in the 1980s, NGO assistance to Cambodia was frowned on by Japanese government officials because Cambodia was seen as a Soviet/Vietnam satellite state. Today, NGO assistance to Cambodia is welcomed, and NGOs are even invited to support Japanese ODA programs in Cambodia.

15. See, for example, Ministry of Foreign Affairs (1996c). The report emphasizes that Japan lacks natural resources and foodstuffs at home and depends on a supply of fuels, foodstuffs, and other materials. The report concludes that Japan has to maintain good relations with resource-rich countries and contribute to the maintenance of a healthy world trade system to ensure continued access to raw materials.

Chapter Three   Domestic Crises and Pluralism

1. From 1946 to 1952, an American NGO consortium, the Licensed Agencies for Relief in Asia (LARA), gave Japanese people about ¥40 billion, more than one-third of Tokyo's 1946 General Account Budget (GAB). During the same period, another U.S. NGO, the Cooperative for Assistance and Relief Everywhere (CARE), gave the Japanese approximately ¥18 billion (Saotome, 1999).

Chapter Four   NGO Advocacy

1. Meanwhile, some professional organizations also began to conduct investigations. For example, in 1989 the Federation of Japanese Bar Associations (Nihon Bengoshi Rengō-kai), a federation actively involved in Japan's domestic pollution cases, began an investigation of Japan's ODA in Asia and the impact of aid on the environment in the region. Their 1991 report on the investigation claims that Japanese firms "export" pollution in Asia, promote environmental degradation by cutting native rain forests, and violate the rights of indigenous peoples (Nihon Bengoshi Rengō-kai, 1991, p. i).

2. Also based on an interview with Kazuo Sumi, Professor of Law, Niigata University, April 25, 1997, Tokyo.

3. For example, in November 1989, six House members led by James Scheuer wrote a letter to President Conable to reconsider the Bank's decision to proceed with the construction (Udall, 1995).

4. Interview with Kazuo Sumi, Professor of Law, Niigata University, April 25, 1997, Tokyo.

5. In the World Bank's case, the main immediate cause for halting the dam project was an internal study conducted by Bradford Morse, former administrator of the United Nations Development Program (UNDP), which pointed out serious environmental problems with the project (Udall, 1995).

6. They also allegedly told Cambodian officials to make a request to FAO for pesticide aid, thereby making a precedent of UN pesticide assistance to Phnom Penh. FAO rejected this request by the Cambodian officials (Japan International Volunteer Center, 1995).

7. Interview with a member of JVC on March 13, 1997 in Tokyo.

8. The ICBL was established by Handicap International, Human Rights Watch, Medico International, Mine Advisory Group, Physicians for Human Rights, and Vietnam Veterans of America Foundation.

9. Interview with a member of JCBL on December 26, 2000 in Tokyo.

10. For instance, the Association to Aid Refugees (AAA), one of the reading NGOs involved in demining issues, held a parallel NGO landmine conference at the time of the government conference on demining technology in Tokyo in March 1997. The NGO conference, the first of its type in Japan, emphasized the suffering of mine victims and appealed to the public the need to eradicate landmines.

11. As early as February 1997, an NGO representative (Shimizu, 1997) noticed a difference in position between officials in MOFA and those in the Defense Agency. In his view, MOFA was already becoming aware of the growing international and domestic public support for a ban treaty "to the extent that the government would need to show its willingness to reduce the number of preexisting mines and newly manufactured mines (within Japan)" (p. 2). In contrast, the Defense Agency tried to defend the status quo.

12. Interestingly, the bureaucrats at the agency (*sebiro-gumi,* "suite group") opposed the treaty more adamantly than the members of the Self Defense Forces (*seifuku-gumi,* "uniform group"), which the agency oversees (Osa, 1997).

13. Internal JCBL letter to its members (dated September 11, 1998); interview with a JCBL member on October 11, 2000.

14. Interview with a JCBL member on December 26, 2000, in Tokyo.
15. Japanese UN Ambassador Hisashi Otwada took advantage of the 13-hour time difference between Tokyo and New York and submitted Japan's ratification document to the United Nations in time, on September 30, 1998 (Mekata, 1998).

Chapter Five   NGO–MOFA Cooperation and
Contention in Aid

1. Strictly speaking, the Volunteer Postal Savings International Aid is not considered part of ODA funds, but is included here because it is a major source of revenue for NGOs.
2. Until recently, Japanese NGOs did not have access to many official ODA documents. In 1999, information freedom law was passed in the Diet, enabling NGOs to request information to relevant ministries (*Nikkei Weekly*, 1999b,c).
3. The author visited JVC offices on many occasions in early 1997. JVC officials were jubilant at the results of the conference and highlighted it in their internal and external publicity.
4. Interview with Director of the International Development Research Institute at FASID, on March 18, 1997 in Tokyo.
5. Interview with a member of JVC, on March 14, 1997, in Tokyo.
6. Interview with Secretary General of Shapla Neer, on August 4, 1999, in Tokyo.
7. Interview with Secretary General of Shapla Neer, on August 4, 1999, in Tokyo.
8. Interview with Chief Program Officer at the International Program and Research Division in SVC, on August 4, 1999, in Tokyo.
9. Parallel to the establishment of the parliamentarian group for NGOs, another parliamentarian group was established to support NPOs in 1999. Diet members launched the Parliamentary League to Support NPOs with the aim of strengthening the legal environment for NPOs, especially in regard to tax measures for donations made to unincorporated NPOs. The LDP's Koichi Kato, former secretary general of the party, is the president (Japan Center for International Exchange, 1999).
10. Also, personal communication with a member of JANIC, on August 3, 1999, in Tokyo.
11. While conducting emergency relief work on the Thai–Cambodian border camps in the early 1980s, JVC first sent irrigation materials to people inside Cambodia through Western NGOs. Then, in 1982, JVC sent its representative to Phnom Penh for the first time to monitor the distribution of the materials it was sending. Next, it sent an engineer to take part in Oxfam's irrigation project in late 1982. After this preliminary work, JVC established its office in Phnom Penh in 1986 (Kumaoka, 1993).
12. Interview with a member of JVC, on March 13, 1997, in Tokyo.
13. In 1992, Domoto established an NGO named the Japan Women's Global Environmental Network International (GENKI). It promotes women's involvement in environmental decision making (United Nations Environmental Program International Environmental Technology Center, 1997).
14. Interview with a representative of the International Relief Division at Japanese Red Cross Society, on February 28, 1999, in Tokyo.
15. AMDA. "AMDA International: Better Quality of Life for a Better Future," undated pamphlet.
16. Ibid.
17. Ibid.
18. Unlike the majority of Japanese unincorporated NGOs, AMDA has close working relations with the private sector. With its headquarters in Okayama City, a provincial city between Osaka and Hiroshima, it has established special arrangements with local businesses. For example, it made an agreement with Toyota car dealers in Okayama in which AMDA receives a donation of ¥6,000 per Toyota car sale. In addition, AMDA collaborates with local banks such as All Japan Trust and Banking Co. and Chugoku Bank, through special AL AMDA (All Japan + AMDA)

credit card and AMDA Volunteer CD systems. For example, 0.05 percent of a customer's charge for the ALAMDA credit card goes to AMDA and 20 percent of the interest earned in the AMDA Volunteer Certified Deposit at Chugoku Bank, after tax deductions, goes to AMDA. AMDA's director general, Kondo, claims that it is advantageous for the group to be located in a small town away from Tokyo as the people and business establishment there are "more cooperative." Interview with Secretary General of AMDA, on March 3, 1997, in Tokyo.

19. Interview with Secretary General of AMDA, March 3, 1997, in Tokyo.
20. Ibid.
21. Ibid.
22. NGOs may be able to establish a working relationship with the United Nations by attaining consultative status with ECOSOC. NGOs of Special Category "have a special competence in, and are concerned specifically with, only a few of the fields of activity covered by the ECOSOC" (United Nations Economic and Social Council, 2001). These NGOs tend to be small in scale and recently established. In contrast, NGOs of General Category are "concerned with most of the activities of the ECOSOC and its subsidiary bodies" (United Nations Economic and Social Council, 2001). They tend to be larger and older.
23. Interview with a representative of the International Relief Division, the International Department, the Japanese Red Cross Society, on February 28, 1997, in Tokyo.
24. Interview with General Director of Shapla Neer, on August 4, 2000, in Tokyo.
25. In any case, the chances for cooperation between Amnesty International Japan and MOFA are limited right now, since MOFA refuses to fund aid and development projects that focus on human rights. Interview with Public Relations Director of Amnesty International Japan, on August 5, 1999, in Tokyo; personal communication with Second Secretary at the Embassy of Japan in Egypt, on July 28 and September 14, 1999, in Cairo.

Chapter Six   Conclusion

1. Interview with chief program officer in the International Program and Research Division of SVA, on August 4, 1999, in Tokyo.
2. As discussed in Chapter 1, my definition of civil society does not include recreational and entertainment organizations as they are mainly concerned with inward-looking, private activities.
3. In this study civil society is not equivalent to the so-called associational life. I exclude certain types of associations that Putnam (1993; 2000) examined in his studies on Italy and the United States, such as those primarily focused on inward-looking activities (i.e., recreational and religious groups), as part of civil society. As discussed in Chapter 1, civil society organizations are concerned with public ends, not private ends.
4. See for example, Brysk's (2000) discussion of autocratic NGO leaders in Latin America.

Appendix: Evolution of Japanese Aid

1. Yoshida insisted that attaining high economic recovery, rather than rearmament to fight the communist bloc, was Japan's high priority. In 1950, he rejected the request by U.S. Secretary of State John Dulles that Japan rearm against communist expansion in Asia (Sudo, 1986).
2. Multilateral aid also began through the Colombo Plan in 1954. The plan, which originated in the 1950 Common Wealth Foreign Ministers' meeting in Colombo, Ceylon (now Sri Lanka), was a scheme for providing assistance to the countries of South and Southeast Asia.
3. The Japanese government did take several important multilateral aid initiatives in the 1960s to promote regional cooperation and strengthen Japan's international stance, including its contribution to the establishment of the Asian Productivity Organization, the Asian Development Bank (ADB), and the Ministerial Conference for the Economic Development of Southeast Asia (M. Haas, 1989).

4. Grant element is an index of financial terms of assistance that takes account of interest rate, grace period, and maturity.

5. The first and second principles were designed to reduce anti-Japanese feelings, which had arisen in Southeast Asia due to the rapid penetration of Japanese goods into the region since the end of World War II. The anti-Japanese sentiment was demonstrated by local riots occasioned by Prime Minister Kakuei Tanaka's trips to Jakarta and Bangkok in 1974. Japanese leaders realized that they would urgently need to articulate Japan's policy stance toward the region to soften the local opposition to the Japanese presence in the region (Sudo, 1992).

6. Japan ultimately financed three projects in Thailand, Indonesia, and Malaysia, but could not implement the remaining projects in the Philippines and Singapore (Sudo, 1986).

7. The Miyazawa plan of 1986 contained four key elements: (1) a US$2 billion contribution to the World Bank, including the establishment of a Japan Fund; (2) a US$2.6 billion contribution to the World Bank's soft loan facility, the International Development Association (IDA); (3) a US$1.3 billion contribution to the soft loan facility (the Asian Development Fund) of the Asian Development Bank; and (4) a US$3.6 billion government loan to the International Monetary Fund (IMF) (Yanagihara & Emig, 1991).

8. During his visit to Washington, DC, Nakasone pledged US$20 billion worth of contributions that consisted of three components: (1) untied loans through the Ex-Im Bank and Japanese commercial banks (US$3 billion); (2) official contributions and private capital lending to establish special funds at MDBs, such as ADB and the Inter-American Development Bank (US$8 billion); and (3) nonproject, policy-based loans through OECF, the Ex–Im Bank, and Japanese commercial banks, in coordination with the World Bank and the IMF (US$9 billion) (Arase, 1995).

9. The Takeshita plan contained Ex-Im Bank loans to support structural adjustment in debtor countries (US$13.5 billion), OECF loans to the targeted countries in the Brady plan (US$7 billion), and contributions to the World Bank and other international financial institutions (US$14.5 billion) (Yanagihara & Emig, 1991).

10. Failing to recognize how serious the crisis was, Japan was initially unwilling to make even financial contributions for the forces in Iraq. In August 1990, Tokyo pledged merely US$1 billion. In the following month, Japan reluctantly announced that it would provide an additional US$3 billion as a result of U.S. pressure. It was only in March 1992, well after the war ended, that Japan decided to make an additional US$9 billion contribution to the Desert Storm operations (Lincoln, 1993).

11. However, Japan remains the world's largest aid donor (Castellano, 1999b).

12. For example, in 1996, the share of aid to Africa in Japan's total ODA spending was 12.8 percent, as opposed to Latin America (11.8 percent), Middle East (6.7 percent), and Oceania (2.4 percent) (Ministry of Foreign Affairs, 1997).

13. For example, under the Miyazawa Plan, Japan has promised to lend about US$250 million for Thailand's economic recovery and social programs through OECF and that the agency would also co-finance a US$250 million loan for an agricultural program with ADB. Also, Tokyo has announced that the OECF would provide nearly US$975 million in loans to Malaysia, the largest loan package ever earmarked for the country (Castellano, 1999b).

14. Fujisaki et al. (1996–1997) actually uses the terms *software aid* and *hardware aid* (p. 519).

REFERENCES

Alexander, A. J. (1998). Japan's fiscal deficit projected to soar. *Japan Economic Institute Report,* 46(December 11).

Amenomori, T., & Yamamoto, T. (1998). Introduction. In T. Yamamoto (Ed.), *The nonprofit sector in Japan,* (pp. 1–18). Manchester: Manchester University Press.

Anchordoguy, M. (2001). Whatever happened to the Japanese miracle? *Japan Policy Research Institute* (Working Paper, no. 80).

Araki, M. (1998a). Kao no mieru enjo o ayaukusuru senmonka haken seido. *International Development Journal,* 496, 12–13.

Araki, M. (1998b). Mushō shikin kyōryoku no seidoteki mōten o kangaeru. *International Development Journal,* 502, 6–7.

Araki, M. (1999). Totsuzen taido enjo to iwaretemo ki ni naru anken hakkutsu no jinzai busoku. *International Development Journal,* February, 6–7.

Arase, D. (1993). Japanese policy toward democracy and human rights in Asia. *Asian Survey,* 33(10 October), 935–952.

Arase, D. (1994). Public-private sector interest coordination in Japan's ODA. *Pacific Affairs,* 67(2 Summer), 171–199.

Arase, D. (1995). *Buying power: The political economy of Japan's foreign aid.* Boulder, CO, and London: Lynne Rienner.

Arato, A. (1990). *Civil society, constitution, and legitimacy.* Lanham, MD: Roman & Littlefield.

Armacost, M. H. (1996). *Friends or rivals?: The insider's account of U.S.–Japan relations.* New York: Columbia University Press.

Asahi Shimbun (1990a, April 22). Nihon enjo no damu no zehi: Indo kōshi mo shussekishi shinpo, p. 30.

Asahi Shimbun (1990b, June 20). Jumin hantai no Indo damu kensetsu tsuika shakkan miokuru, p. 3.

Asahi Shimun (1990c, April 20). ODA damu chuushi sasete, p. 30.

Asahi Shimbun. (1996, December 15). Hatsu no NGO sanka PKO, p. 3.

Asahi Shimbun. (1997a, April 8). ODA jisseki 35 persent gen, p. 1.

Asahi Shimbun. (1997b, February 2). ODA nyūsatsu rūto minaoshi, p. 1.

Asahi Shimbun. (1998a, June 7). Būtan de konsarutanto gaisha mukyoka de keikaku henkō, p. 1.

Asahi Shimbun. (1998b, June 26). Būtan e no ODA jigyō de akarumi ni, enjo taikoku fusei nobanashi, p. 4.

Asahi Shimbun. (1998d, March 1). Myanmā en shakkan saikai: Taibei kankei kenen zairyō ni mo, p. 2.

Asahi Shimbun. (1998e, June 7). Nen 1000-ken ni shokuin 50-nin kyogi houkoku minukezu, p. 30.

Asahi Shimbun. (1998g, April 28). ōkura shokuin no shobun risto, p. 3.

Asahi Shimbun. (2001a, August 31). Sōgō-shōsha no kanban dō nokosu, p. 9.

Asahi Shimbun. (2001b, September 11). Gaimusho, yaku-30-ka ni uragane, p. 1.

Asahi Shimbun. (2001c, December 15). ODA yosan 10% chō-sakugen, p. 9.

Asahi Shimbun Enjo Shuzai-han. (1985). *Enjo tojōkoku Nippon.* Tokyo: Asahi Shimbun-sha.

Asahi Shimbun Online. (1998, December 13). Tokubetsu en-shakkan 600-oku-en tai ASEAN. Available: http://www.asahi.com/paper/front.html [December 13, 1998].

Asahi Shimbun Online. (1999, February 22). Kaisetsu. Available: http://www.asahi.com/paper/editorial.html [February 22, 1999].

Asahi Shimbun Weekly AERA. (1994, September 19). ODA no nyūsatsu dangō wa motto ne ga fukai, 30.

Association of Medical Doctors of Asia. (1998). *Kokumin sanka-gata ODA.* Available: http://www.amda.or.jp/contents/journal/journal5/15.html [1998, September 3].

Bank of Japan. (1999). *Kokusai hikaku tokei.* Tokyo: Bank of Japan.

Baron, B. F. (1997). *Funding civil society in Asia: Philanthropy and public–private partnerships* (The Asia Foundation Working Paper, No. 3).

Blaker, M. (1993). Evaluating Japan's diplomatic performance. In G. L. Curtis (Ed.), *Japan's foreign policy after the Cold War: Coping with change* (pp. 1–42). Armonk, NY: M.E. Sharpe.

Bloch, J. C. (1989). A U.S.–Japan aid alliance: Prospects for cooperation in a era of conflict (USJP Occasional Paper, vol. 89-07). Program on U.S. Japan Relations, Harvard University, Cambridge, MA.

Brysk, A. (2000). Democratizing civil society in Latin America, *Journal of Democracy,* 11(3), 151–165.

Caldwell, J. A. (1972). The evolution of Japanese economic cooperation: 1950–1970. In H. B. Malmgren (Ed.), *Pacific basin development: The American interests.* Lexington, MA: Lexington Books.

Callon, S. (1997). *Divided sun: MITI and the breakdown of high tech industrial policy, 1975–1995.* Stanford, CA: Stanford University Press.

Canadian Department of Foreign Affairs and International Trade. (1996). *Towards a global ban on anti-personnel mines: Declaration of the Ottawa conference.* Ottawa: Department of Foreign Affairs and International Trade.

CARE International. (1999). *CARE 1998 annual report: 1998 CARE USA overview.* Available: http://www.care.org/publications/annualreport98/care_usa_overview.html [1999, November 2].

Carlile, L. E. & Tilton, M. C. (1998). *Is Japan really changing its ways?: Regulatory reform and the Japanese economy.* Washington, DC: Brookings Institution Press.

Castellano, M. (1999a). Japanese foreign aid: A lifesaver for East Asia? *Economic Institute Report,* 6A.

Castellano, M. (1999b). Japan remains world's largest aid donor. *Japan Economic Institute Report,* 23B(June 18), 8–10.

Castellano, M. (1999c). G-7 agrees to debt-relief plan for poorest nations. *Japan Economic Institute,* 24B(June 25), 4–5.

Castellano, M. (1999d). Industrialized world backs debt relief for poor countries. *Japan Economic Institute Report,* 37B(October 1), 6–7.

Castells, M. (1997). *The rise of the network society.* Oxford, UK: Blackwell Publishers.

Castells, M. (1997). *The power of identity.* Oxford, UK: Blackwell Publishers.

Castells, M. (1998). *End of millennium.* Oxford, UK: Blackwell Publishers.

Chang, Y. (1999, December 28). Japan fears cults thriving despite crackdowns, *Reuters.* Available: http://www.rickross.com/reference/aum/aum176.html [September 5, 2001]

Citizen-NGO Liaison Council for ODA Reform. (1997). *ODA kaikaku ni mukete no teigen*. Tokyo: Citizen-NGO Liaison Council for ODA Reform.

Clarke, G. (1998). *The politics of NGOs in South-East Asia: Participation and protest in the Philippines*. London: Routledge.

Coalition for Legislation to Support Citizens' Organizations. (1998). *Kaisetsu NPO hōan: Sono kei'i to sōten*. Tokyo: Coalition for Legislation to Support Citizens' Organizations.

Cohen J., & Arato, A. (1992). *Civil society and political theory*. Cambridge, MA: MIT Press.

Cooperation Committee for Cambodia. (1994). *Directory of humanitarian assistance in Cambodia*. Phnom Penh: Cooperation Committee for Cambodia.

Covey, J. G. (1998). Is critical cooperation possible? Influencing the World Bank through operational collaboration and policy dialogue. In J. A. Fox & L. D. Brown (Eds.), *The struggle for accountability: The World Bank, NGOs, and grassroots movements* (pp. 81–119). Cambridge, MA: MIT Press.

Cumings, B. (1999). The Asian crisis, democracy, and the end of "late" development, in T. J. Pempel (Ed.), *The politics of the Asian economic crisis* (pp. 17–44). Ithaca, NY: Cornell University Press.

Curtis, G. L. (1999a). *Japan at the crossroads: Asia Pacific Issues Analysis*. Honolulu: East–West Center.

Curtis, G. L. (1999b). *The logic of Japanese politics: Leaders, institutions, and the limits of change*. New York: Columbia University Press.

Diamond, L. (1994). Rethinking civil society: Toward democratic consolidation. *Journal of Democracy*, 5(3), 5–17.

Diamond, L. (1999). *Developing democracy: Toward consolidation*. Baltimore, MD: Johns Hopkins University Press.

Development Assistant Committee of the Organization for Economic Cooperation and Development. (1999). *Development co-operation review of Japan: Summary and conclusions*. Available: http://www.oecd.org/dac/htm/ar-jpana.htm [1999, July 25].

De Vos, G. A. (1973). *Socialization for achievement: Essays on the cultural psychology of the Japanese*. Berkeley: University of California Press.

Economic Planning Agency. (1999). *Keizai hakusho*. Tokyo: Economic Planning Agency.

Economist. (1997, January 25). *Failing to bite the bullet train*, pp. 33–34.

Economist. (2001, April 21). *Poor little rich kids*, pp. 34–35.

Eldridge, P. J. (1995). *Non-government organizations and democratic participation in Indonesia*. Oxford: Oxford University Press.

Engineering Consulting Firms Association. (1996/1997). *Engineering consulting firms association report*. Tokyo: Engineering Consulting Firms Association.

English, J. (1998). The Ottawa process: Paths followed, paths ahead, *Australian Journal of International Affairs*, 52(2), 121–132.

Ensign, M. M. (1992). *Doing good or doing well?* New York: Columbia University Press.

Farrell, W. R. (1999). *Crisis and opportunity in a changing Japan*. Westport, CT: Quorum Books.

Forbes Global. (1998). *Phony medicine*. Available: http://www.global.forbes.com/forbes/98/0706/0107091a.htm [1999, September 22].

Friedman, T. L. (1999, April 30). *Japan's nutcracker suite*, The *New York Times*. Available: http://www.nytimes.com/library/opinion/friedman/043099frie.html [1999, June 14].

Fujisaki, T., Briscoe, F., Maxwell, J., Kishi, M., & Suzuki, T. (1996–1997). Japan as top donor: The challenge of implementing software aid policy. *Pacific Affairs*, 69(4), 519–539.

Fuke, Y., & Fujibayashi, Y. (Eds.). (1999). *Nihonjin no kurashi no tame datta ODA*. Tokyo: Komonzu.

Fukiura, T., Yanase, F., & Osa, Y. (2000). *Jirai o nakusō: "Jirai de wa naku hana o kudasai" 50-man dokusha kara no shitsumon*. Tokyo: Jiyu Kokumin-sha.

George, A. (1988). Japanese interest group behaviour: An institutional approach, in J. A. A. Stockwin (Ed.), *Dynamic and immobilist politics in Japan* (pp. 106–140). Honolulu: University of Hawai'i Press.

Griesgraber, J. M., & Gunter, B. G. (1996). *Development: New paradigms and principles for the twenty-first century*. London: Pluto Press.

Gordenker, L., & Weiss, T. G. (1995). Pluralizing global governance: Analytical approaches and dimensions, *Third World Quarterly*, 16(3), 357–387.

Haas, E. B. (1990). *When knowledge is power: Three models of change in international organizations*. Berkeley and Los Angeles: University of California Press.

Haas, M. (1989). *The Asian Way to Peace*. New York: Praeger.

Haas, P. M. (1990). *Save the Mediterranean*. New York: Columbia University Press.

Haas, P. M. (1992). Introduction: Epistemic communities and international policy coordination. *International Organization*, 46, 1(Winter), 1–35.

Hadfield, P. (1993). Japanese aid may upset Cambodia's harvests, *New Scientist Magazine*, 137(March 13), p. 5.

Hankes, N. J. (1993). *Japan's foreign aid*. Available: http://www.gwjapan.com/ftp/pub/policy/crs/1993/93-494f.txt [1999, July 26].

Hasegawa, S. (1975). *Japanese foreign aid: Policy and practice*. New York: Praeger.

Havens, T. R. (1987). *Fire across the sea: The Vietnam War and Japan 1865–1975*. Princeton, NJ: Princeton University Press.

Heyzer, N. (1995). Toward new government–NGO relations for sustainable and people-centered development. In N. Heyzer, J.V. Riker, & A. B. Quizon (Eds.), *Government–NGO relations in Asia: Prospects for people-centered development*, 1–13. London: MacMillan Press.

Hisani, M. (1990, January 10). Kaifu expresses support for East Europe reforms. *The Asahi Shimbun*, pp. 1, 3.

Honnoki USA. (1992). *Japanese working for a better world: Grassroots voices and access guide to citizens' groups in Japan*. San Francisco: Honnoki USA.

Hook, S.W., & Zhang, G. (1998). Japan's aid policy since the Cold War: Rhetoric and reality. *Asian Survey*, 38(11), 1051–1066.

Hosmer, E. (1988). Aid, incorporated: The real beneficiaries of Japanese foreign assistance, *Multinational Monitor*, 9(11). Available: http://www.essential.org/monitor/hyper/issues/1988/11/mm1188 06.html.

House of Representatives, National Security Affairs Committee. (1998). *National Security Affairs Committee minute*, No. 5, 143rd Diet Meeting, September 28.

Huntington, S. (1993). *The clash of civilizations and the rethinking of world order*. New York: Simon & Schuster.

Ikegami, K. (1996). Jizoku kanōna kaihatsu to NGO katsudō. *Kokusai Mondai*, 441(December), 29–50.

Inada, J. (1990). Kokusai sistemu ni okeru nihon no ODA no ichizuke. *Kokusai Seiji*, 93(March), 115–130.

Inglehart, R. (1990). *Culture shift in advanced industrial society*. Princeton, NJ: Princeton University Press.

Inglehart, R. (1997). *Modernization and postmodernization: Cultural, economic, and political change in 43 societies*. Princeton, NJ: Princeton University Press.

Inman, J. L. (1998). *Japan's official development assistance challenged by a changing world* (The Asia Foundation Working Paper, 7).

Inoguchi, T. (1997). Japanese bureaucracy: Coping with new challenges. In P. Jain & T. Inoguchi (Eds.), *Japanese politics today: Beyond karaoke democracy?* (pp. 92–107). New York: St. Martin's Press.

Institute for the Development of Agricultural Cooperation in Asia. (1995). *What's IDACA?* Available: http://www2.rim.or.jp/ci/ja/idaca/ [January 17, 2000].

International Campaign to Ban Landmines. (1999). Asia-Pacific states parties. Available: http://www.igc.org/hrw/reports/1999/landmine/WEBAS1.html [October 1, 2000].

International Development Journal. (1998a). 11-nen-do ODA yosan wa zaikaku-hō tōketsu no taishō-gai, 502, 55.

International Development Journal. (1998b). Būtan jiken no teiryū ni yokotawaru mushō shikin kyōryoku no seidoteki hirō, 502, 17–19.

International Development Journal. (1998c). Gijyutsu o kanzen ni jūshi shita tsū-enverōpu hōshiki no genkaku na jisshi o, 502, 24–25.

International Development Journal. (1998d). Kakkiteki na jirai jyokyo kizai "rōtarī katta" kaihatsu, pp. 24–25.

International Development Journal. (1998e). Kokkai giin ni kiku: Yosan sakugen o keiki ni enjo no muda mo kezuru doryoku o, 502, 12–13.

International Development Journal. (1998f). Kuzureru ka, "mushō wa taido" no enjo shinwa, 505, 8–10.

International Development Journal. (1998g). NGO news, 504, 81.

International Development Journal. (1998h). Nihon seifu kongo gonen-kan ni 100-oku-en no jirai kanren shishutsu, 501, 8–10.

International Development Journal. (1998i). ODA kihon-hō seitei de kitai sareru kokumin-teki giron no kassei-ka, 500, 10–11.

International Development Journal. (1998j). Segin Japan fando wa ōkurashō shukkōsha ni nigi-rareteiru, 505, 14–15.

International Development Journal. (1998k). Zenekon kakusha ga chūmoku suru mushū no panchiryoku, 505, 64–66.

International Development Journal. (1999a). "Dai-ni no Marukosu" ni naru no ka Indonesia daitōryō senkyo kaunto daun, 507, 11.

International Development Journal. (1999b). Enshakkan dai-1-gō wa betonamu no kyryō to kōwan seibi, 510, 8–9.

International Development Journal. (1999c). Gaimushō, NGO hontai no kyōka shien ni sho-seido shinsetsu, 514(September), 10–11.

International Development Journal. (1999d). Heisei 11-nendo ODA yosan tettei shōhō, 508, 20–39.

International Development Journal. (1999e). Kakkitekina shinkijiku o morikonda yosan hensei, 508, 20–21.

International Development Journal. (1999f). Kokkai giin ni kiku: ODA to kaku haizetsu wa Nihon gaikō no rippa na kao ni naru, 509, 12–13.

International Development Journal. (1999g). Kokkai giin ni kiku: Seido hirō o okoshiteiru gaikō o bijon o shimeshinagara kasseika suru, 517, 18–19.

International Development Journal. (1999h). Kokkai giin ni kiku: Seishin-ron dake no ODA kihon-hō wa hitsuyō nai, 510, 14–15.

International Development Journal. (1999i). Kokusai kyōryoku jigyōdan no soshiki kaikaku no gaiyō to kinō no kyōka, 507, 10.

International Development Journal. (1999j). ODA no tekisei shiyō jōkō no kokusai hikaku, 511, 14–15.

International Development Journal. (1999k). "ODA ryūgaku ni kanryō tokubetsu-waku" to iu houdou to dou yomeba yoi no ka, 510, 12–13.

International Development Journal. (1999l). Chūmoku sareru enjo jisshi taisei no henyō, 514, 74–75.

International Development Journal. (1999m). Dai-l-kkai "Kokusai Kyōryoku NGO-Kokkai Giin Fōramu" kaisai, 510, 92.

International Development Journal (2000). NGO no hojokin henkan hōdō ni omou, 521, p. 70.

International Herald Tribune. (1998, December 17). Answering Asian critics, Japan unveils new loans. *International Herald Tribune*, pp. 1, 7.

Islam, S. (1991). Beyond burden-sharing: Economics and politics of Japanese foreign aid. In S. Islam (Ed.), *Yen for development: Japanese foreign aid and the Politics of burden-sharing* (pp. 191–230). New York: Council on Foreign Relations Press.

Japan Campaign to Ban Landmines (1998, September 27). Personal letter sent by JBCL to Toshihisa Fujita of the League.

Japan Center for International Exchange. (1996). The recent debate on the role of NPOs in Japan and private-sector responses. *Civil Society Monitor* (Fall). Available: http://www.jcie.or.jp/civilnet/civil_soc_monitor/fall_96.html [April 3, 2000].

Japan Center for International Exchange. (1999). The NPO law and civil society's new phase of development. *Civil Society Monitor* (September). Available: http://www.jcie.or.jp/civilnet/civil_soc_monitor/fall_99.html [April 3, 2000].

Japan Economic Institute. (1999). Land-mine meeting. *Japan Economic Institute Report*, 19B(May 14), 8–9.

Japan International Cooperation Agency, and Japanese NGO Center for International Cooperation. (1999). *NGO–JICA sōgō kenshū*. Tokyo: Japan International Cooperation Agency.

Japan International Cooperation Agency. (1996). *JICA sateraito*. Available: http://www.jica.go.jp/jicanews/jcns9606/jcns9606-h01.html [1999, November 1].

Japan International Volunteer Center. (1993). *Sutoppu! Kiken na noyaku enjo: Kanbojia shakai ni, ima, nani ga hitsuyoo ka*. Tokyo: Japan International Volunteer Center.

Japan International Volunteer Center. (1995). NGO kara mita ODA: Seidojō, risōjō no mondaiten. In K. Hashimoto (Ed.), *Senryaku enjo: Chuto wahei shien to ODA no shoraizo*, 183–210. Tokyo: PHP Research Institute.

Japan International Volunteer Center. (1997a). *Emergency relief activities*. Available: http://www.jca.ax.apc.org/jvc/english/emergency.html [1998, September 4].

Japan International Volunteer Center. (1997b). *JVC no gaiyō*. Available: http://www.jca.ax.apc.org/jvc/whatis/gaiyo_jp.htm [1998, September 4].

Japan International Volunteer Center. (2000). *Soshiki no ayumi/zaigen*. Available: http://www.jca.ax.apc.org/jvc/stp.html [October 14, 2001].

Japan Productivity Center for Socioeconomic Development. (1997). *Homepage gaiyō*. Available: http://shinto.jpc-sed.or.jp/sed/toc.html [January 17, 2000].

Japan Times (1998, June 16). Tokyo urged to sign land mine treaty, p. 2.

Japan Times Online. (1999, September 7). Crisis triggers 71% rise in ODA to Asia. Available: http://www.japantimes.co.jp/news/news9-99/news9-7.html [September 7, 1999].

Japan Times Online (2001a, January 26). Fired foreign ministry official facing embezzlement charges. Available: http://www.japantimes.co.jp/cgi-bin/getarticle.pl5?nn20010126a1.htm [September 8, 2001].

Japan Times Online (2001b, July 17). Bureaucrats held for padding G-8 limo bills by 13 Million Yen. Available: http://www.japantimes.co.jp/cgibin/getarticle.p15?nn20010717a1.htm [September 8, 2001].

Japan Times Online (2001c, September 8). Official says he padded bills for 20 years. Available: http://www.japantimes.co.jp/cgi-bin/getarticle.p15?nn20010908a5.htm [September 8, 2001]

Japan Times Weekly International. (1996, December 30). Fiscal council sounds alarm over Japan's debt, p. 14.

Japan Times Weekly International. (1998a, March 23–29). Tokyo resumes Myanmar loans, pp. 1, 6.

Japan Times Weekly International. (1998b, October 26–November 1). MITI to Promote tied yen loans to developing nations, p. 14.

Japan Times Weekly International. (1999, August 11). ODA to be guided by national interest, with eye for efficacy, p. 1.

Japanese NGO Center for International Cooperation. (1994). *NGO data book: Sūji de miru Nihon no NGO*. Tokyo: Japanese NGO Center for International Cooperation.

Japanese NGO Center for International Cooperation. (1997a). *JANIC board of trustees*. Available: http://www.geocities.co.jp/WallStreet/3294/board.html [1998, November 3].

Japanese NGO Center for International Cooperation. (1997b). *What is JANIC?* Available: http://www.geocities.co.jp/WallStreet/3294/whatjanic.html [1998, November 3].

Japanese NGO Center for International Cooperation. (1998a). *NGO dēta bukku 1998: Sūji de miru Nihon no NGO.* Tokyo: Japanese NGO Center for International Cooperation.

Japanese NGO Center for International Cooperation. (1998b). *NGO direkutori 1998: Kokusai kyōryoku ni tazusawaru Nihon no shimin soshiki yōran.* Tokyo: Japanese NGO Center for International Cooperation.

Johns, E. (1993). The Tokyo official development assistance conference: Fulfilling a U.S. and Japanese government commitment to assist U.S. firms to work on Japanese foreign aid projects. *Business America,* 114(1), 2–6.

Johnson, C. (1982). *MITI and the Japanese miracle: The growth of industrial policy, 1925–1975.* Stanford: Stanford University Press.

Johnson, D. T. (2001). Bureaucratic corruption in Japan, *Japan Policy Research Institute Working Paper,* No. 76.

Kanda, H. (1999a). ODA kaikau ni wa NGO no rikiryō ga kakatte Iru. *Gaiko Forum,* 131(July), 54–59.

Kanda, H. (1999b, September). Tamesareru NGO no seisaku teigen nōryoku. *Kansai NGO Council Newsletter.*

Kansai NGO Council. (1999). *1999-nen-do kihon hōshin to jigyō keikaku.* Available: http://www.sun-inet.or.jp/%7Eknc/99housin.htm [1999, October 28].

Katz, R. (1998). *Japan the system that soured: The rise and fall of the Japanese economic miracle.* Armonk, NY: M.E. Sharpe.

Katz, R. (1999, September 14). Obuchi succumbs to budget-cutters of the MOF. *Asahi Evening News,* p. 6.

Keck, M. E., & Sikkink, K. (1998). *Activists beyond borders: Advocacy networks in international politics.* Ithaca, New York & London: Cornell University Press.

Keidanren. (1994). *Japan's international contributions and the role of its economic cooperation in the post-Cold War era: Developing new economic cooperation for sustainable global economic growth.* Available: http://www.keidanren.or.jp/english/policy/pol013.html [1998, December 11].

Keidanren. (1997). *Reforming official development assistance in Japan: Four basic principles towards fundamental reform of the ODA administration.* Available: http://www.keidanren.or.jp/english/policy/pol059/principles.html [1998, December 11].

Kidder, S. H. (1998). *ODA handbook.* U.S. Embassy in Tokyo. Available: http://www.ita.doc.gov/industry/sif/sifuai/uhandbk.html [1998, December 14].

Koiso, A. (1991). *Fuji ginko koin no kiroku.* Tokyo: Bansei-sha.

Koppel, B. M., & Plummer, M. (1989). Japan's ascendancy as a foreign-aid power. *Asian Survey,* 29(11), 1043–1056.

Koppel, M. B., & Orr, R. M. J. (Eds.). (1993). *Japan's foreign aid: Power and policy in a new era.* Boulder, CO: Westview Press.

Krasner, S. D. (1982). Structural causes and regime consequences: Regimes as intervening variables. *International Organization,* 36(2), 185–205.

Kuhn, T. (1970). *The structure of scientific revolutions.* Chicago: University of Chicago Press.

Kumaoka, M. (1993). *Kanbojia saizensen.* Tokyo: Iwanami Shoten.

Kuroda, Y. (1972). Protest movements in Japan: A new Politics. *Asian Survey,* 12(11), 947–952.

Kuroda, Y. (1993). Challenging Japanese pesticide aid, *Global Pesticide Campaigner,* 3, 11–13.

Kusano, A. (1993). *ODA itchō-nisen-oku-en no yukue.* Tokyo: Toyo Keizai Shimpō-sha.

Kusano, A. (1998, April 13–18). Making ODA work for Japan. *Japan Times Weekly International,* p. 8.

Kyodo News International. (1998, January 29). Japan to bar U.S., European firms from overseas bidding, p. 6.

Larimer, T. (1999, May 3). From we to me. Available at: http://www.time.com/time/asia/asia/magazine/1999/990503/cover1.html [May 7, 2000].

Lincoln, E. J. (1993). *Japan's new global role.* Washington, DC: Brookings Institution.

Lincoln, E. J. (1998). Japan's financial mess. *Foreign Affairs, 77*(3), 57–66.

Little, L. M. D., & Clifford, J. M. (1965). *International aid.* Chicago: Aldine.

Loring, D. (1995). Struggling to keep Cambodia off the pesticide treadmill. Available: http://www.igc.org/panna/resources/pestis/PESTIS.1995.117.html [August 13, 2001].

Loutfi, M. F. (1973). *The net cost of Japanese foreign aid.* New York: Praeger.

Mainichi Daily News. (1994, July 28). JICA admits sending agro-chemicals to Cambodia was mistake, pp. 1, 14.

Mainichi Daily News. (2001a, July 30). *Ambassador to US quits over Denver scandal.* Available: http://www12. mainichi.co.jp/news/mdn/search-news/833368/denver20consul-0-4.html [September 7, 2001].

Mainichi Daily News. (2001b, September 4). Foreign ministry embezzler loved living the high life. Available: http://www12.mainichi.co.jp/news/mdn/search-news/833368/diplomatic20fund-0-1.html [September 7, 2001].

Mainichi Interactive. (1999, November 22). Itai hōchi no hoteru sōsa miira-ka jiken de Chiba-ken-kei. Available: http://www.mainichi.co.jp/eye/feature/article/lifespace/199911/22-2.html [September 5, 2001].

Mainichi Interactive. (2001, September 10). "Hōno-hana" sagi-jiken moto-kanbu ni yuzai Tokyo-chisai hanketsu, evening issue. Available: http://www.mainichi.co.jp/eye/feature/article/hounohana/2001/0710.html [September 5, 2001].

Mainichi Shimbun. (1997, October 23). *Nihon no gijutsu, jirai jokyo ni,* p. 4.

Mainichi Shimbun. (1998, June 3). Otemori segin shōgakukin 6-wari ga ōkura kanryō kenshū, p. 1.

Mainichi Shimbun Shakai-bu ODA Shuzai-han. (1990). *Kokusai enjo bijiness: ODA wa dou tsukawarete iru ka.* Tokyo: Aki Shobō.

Mallet, V. (1993, March 24). Poisoned chalice—A Japanese gift of 35,000 liters of pesticide to Cambodia has caused uproar. *The Financial Times,* p. 17.

Maruyama, M. (1997a, October 23). Nihon no gijutsu jirai jokyo ni, *Mainichi Shimbun,* p. 4.

Maruyama, M. (1997b, November 18). Gaiso ni jirai kinshi jyoyaku shomei-shite. *Mainichi Shimbun,* p. 11.

Matsui, Y. (1990). *Shimin to enjo: Ima nani ga dekiru ka.* Tokyo: Iwanami Shoten.

McKean, M. A. (1976). Pollution and policymaking. In T. J. Pempel (Ed.), *Policymaking in contemporary Japan* (pp. 201–238). Ithaca, New York: Cornell University Press.

McKean, M. A. (1981). *Environmental protest and citizen politics in Japan.* Berkeley: University of California Press.

McMichael, P. (1996). *Development and social change: A global perspective.* Thousand Oaks, CA: Pine Forge Press.

Mekata, M. (1998). *Jirai naki chikyu e: Yume o genjitsu ni shita hito-bito.* Tokyo: Iwanami Shoten.

Mekata, M. (2000). Building partnerships toward a common goal: Experiences of the International Campaign to Ban Landmines, in A. M. Florini (Ed.), *The third force: The rise of transnational civil society* (pp. 143–176). Tokyo: Japan Center for International Exchange; and Washington, DC: Carnegie Endowment for International Peace.

Menju, T., & Aoki, T. (1995). The evolution of Japanese NGOs in the Asia Pacific context. In T. Yamamoto (Ed.), *Emerging civil society in the Asia Pacific Community: Nongovernmental underpinnings of the emerging Asia Pacific regional community* (pp. 143–160). Singapore: Japan Center for International Exchange, Institute of Southeast Asian Studies.

Metraux, D. A. (1999). *Aum Shinrikyo and Japanese youth.* Lanham, MD: University Press of America.

Ministry of Finance. (2001). *The Japanese budget in brief, 2001*. Available: http://www.mof.go.jp/ english/budget/brief/2001/brief13.htm [February 8, 2002].

Ministry of Foreign Affairs. (1994). *Japan's ODA annual report 1993*. Tokyo: Association for Promotion of International Cooperation.

Ministry of Foreign Affairs. (1995a). *January 27, 1995 press conference by press secretary*. Available: http://www.mofa.go.jp/annonce/press/1995/1/127.html#2 [1999, September 30].

Ministry of Foreign Affairs. (1995b). *Japan's ODA annual report 1994*. Tokyo: Association for Promotion of International Cooperation.

Ministry of Foreign Affairs. (1996a). *Japan's ODA annual report 1995*. Tokyo: Association for the Promotion of International Cooperation.

Ministry of Foreign Affairs. (1996b). *Waga-kuni no seifu-kaihatsu-enjo: ODA hakusho*. (Vol. 2). Tokyo: Association for Promotion of International Cooperation.

Ministry of Foreign Affairs. (1997). *Japan's ODA annual report 1996*. Tokyo: Association for Promotion of International Cooperation.

Ministry of Foreign Affairs. (1998a). *Third NGO Tokyo conference on antipersonnel landmines* (Conference proceedings, November 28, p. 38).

Ministry of Foreign Affairs. (1998b). *Japan's ODA annual report 1997*. Tokyo: Association for Promotion of International Cooperation.

Ministry of Foreign Affairs. (1999a). *Japan's medium-term policy on official development assistance*. Ministry of Foreign Affairs. Available: http://www.mofa.go.jp/policy/oda/mid-term/1999/ index.html [1999, September 24].

Ministry of Foreign Affairs. (1999b). *Japan's ODA annual report 1998*. Tokyo: Association for Promotion of International Cooperation.

Ministry of Foreign Affairs. (2000a). Waga-kuni no seifu kaihatsu enjo no jyogyo ni kansuru nenji hokoku. Available: http://www.mofa.go.jp/mofaj/gaiko/oda/seisaku/seisaku_4.shien/jirai.html [June, 2001].

Ministry of Foreign Affairs. (2000b). *Heisei 11-nendo ODA minkan monitā hōkoku*. Available: http://www.mofa.go.jp/mofaj/gaiko/oda/monitor99/m_index.html [2000, February 21].

Ministry of Foreign Affairs. (2000c). *FY2000 general account budget*. Available: http://www.mofa. go.jp/policy/oda/budget/2000_g.html [February 8, 2002].

Ministry of Posts and Telecommunications. (1999). *Kokusai borantia chokin*. Available: http://www.volunteer-post.mpt.go.jp/kokusai/a2.html [1999, October 28].

Mulgan, A. G. (2000). A setting sun? *Foreign Affairs, 79*(4), 40–52.

Murai, Y. (Ed.). (1991). *Musekinin enjo taikoku Nippon*. Tokyo: JICC Shuppankyoku.

Murai, Y. (Ed.). (1992). *Kenshō nippon no ODA*. Tokyo: Gakuyo Shobo.

Nakabori, M. (1997, November 18). Nooberu heiwa-sho jushoo-shiki ni shusseki-suru jirai kinshi kokusai kyanpeen no menbaa, Tun Channaretto-san, *Mainichi Shimbun*, p. 5.

Nakane, C. (1970). *Japanese society*. Berkeley: University of California Press.

Nakano, K. (1998). The Politics of Administrative Reform in Japan, 1993–1998: Toward a More Accountable Government? *Asian Survey, 38*, 3(March), 291–309.

Nakauchi, I. (1996, February 8). ODA o sofuto jūshi ni tenkan shiyō. *Asashi Shimbun*, p. 4.

Nihon Bengoshi Rengō-kai. (1991). *Nihon no kōgai yushutsu to kankyō hakai: Tōnan Ajia ni okeru kigyō shinshutsu to ODA*. Tokyo: Nihon Hyōron-sha.

Nihon Keizai Shimbun. (1994, September 7). ODA de dangō giwaku, p. 1.

Nikkan Kogyo Shimbun Tokubetsu Shuzaihan (1989). *Kenshō Maekawa report: Yutakasa, Nihon no kōzō*. Tokyo: Nikkan Shobo.

Nikkei Weekly. (1996, October 7). Foreign ministry bemoans aid slump, p. 2.

Nikkei Weekly. (1997a, December 15). Japan lays out leaner, greener aid plan, p. 1, 21.

Nikkei Weekly. (1997b, June 19). MITI panel to urge ODA to tie to purchases, p. 3.

Nikkei Weekly. (1997c, June 9). New breed seeks quality in foreign aid, not quantity, p. 2.

Nikkei Weekly. (1998a, December 7). Foreign-aid backers seek transparency, p. 2.

Nikkei Weekly. (1998b, October 19). The healing power of cooperation, p. 20.

Nikkei Weekly. (1998c, February 9). Japan sees effectiveness of foreign aid fall with yen, p. 4.

Nikkei Weekly. (1998e, April 27). Resumption of Myanmar aid puts new strategy to test, pp. 1–23.

Nikkei Weekly. (1998f, April 4). Scandals drain finance ministry's power, p. 2.

Nikkei Weekly. (1999a, March 1). Grassroots approach to aid needed in Africa, diplomat says, p. 17.

Nikkei Weekly. (1999b, May 17). Information law lifts long-closed curtain, p. 2.

Nikkei Weekly. (1999c, May 17). Information-freedom law points to open government, p. 14.

Nikkei Weekly. (1999d, March 19). New law enhances volunteer groups, p. 17.

Nikkei Weekly. (1999e, July 19). Japan to write off $6.1 billion in ODA, p. 14.

Nikkei Weekly. (1999f, August 2). No relief in sight for record jobless rate, p. 2.

Nippon Koei. (1994). *Niji o kakeru otoko-tachi.* (Vol. 1). Tokyo: International Development Journal, Co.

Nippon Koei. (1996). *Niji o kakeru otoko-tachi.* (Vol. 2). Tokyo: International Development Journal, Co.

Nishikawa, J. (Ed.). (1991). *Enjo to jiritsu: Negrosu-tō no keiken kara.* Tokyo: Dobunkan.

Nongovernmental Organization—Ministry of Foreign Affairs Regular Council Meeting. (1998, June 23). *Minutes.*

Nongovernmental Organization—Ministry of Foreign Affairs Regular Council Meeting. (1999a, January 30). *Minutes.*

Nongovernmental Organization—Ministry of Foreign Affairs Regular Council Meeting. (1999b, May 12). *Minutes.*

Nongovernmental Organization—Ministry of Foreign Affairs Regular Council Meeting. (1999c). *NGO-gaimushō sōgo gakushū to kyōdō hyōka hōkoku-sho.* Tokyo: JANIC and the Ministry of Foreign Affairs.

O'Brien, R., Goetz, A. M., Scholte, J. A., & Williams, M. (2000). *Contesting global governance: Multilateral economic institutions and global social movements.* Cambridge, UK: Cambridge University Press.

Oda, M. (Ed.) (1968). *Shimin undō to wa nani ka: Beheiren no shisō.* Tokyo: Tokuma Shoten.

Ohmae, K. (1995). *The end of the nation state: The rise of regional economies.* New York: Free Press Paperbacks.

One World. (1998). Disarmament-Japan: Approval of landmine pact earns praise, *Inter Press Service.* Available: http://www.oneworld.org/ips2/oct98/09_20_014.html [August 4, 2001].

Organization for Economic Cooperation and Development. (1992). *DAC and OECD public policy statements on participatory development/good governance.* Paris: Organization for Economic Cooperation and Development.

Orr, R. M. J. (1990). *The emergence of Japan's foreign aid power.* New York: Columbia University Press.

Osa, Y. (1997). *Jirai Mondai Handobukku.* Tokyo: Jiyu Kokumin-sha.

Osawa, M. (1995). Aum wa naze sarin ni hashittaka. *Gendai,* October.

Ostrom, D. (2000). New decade, Old problems: Japan struggles to achieve sustainable growth in 2000, *Japan Economic Institute Report,* February 25.

Oxfam. (1997). *The Financial Year 1996–97.* Available: http://carryon.oneworld.org/textver/ocfam/atwork/anrev97/ar12.htm [1999, June 6].

Pekkanen, R. (2000). Japan's new politics: The case of the NPO law, *The Journal of Japanese Studies,* 26(1), 111–143.

Pempel, T. J. (1982). *Policy and politics in Japan: Creative conservatism.* Philadelphia: Temple University Press.

Pempel, T. J. (1989). Prerequisites for democracy: Political and social institutions, in T. Ishida and E. S. Krauss (Eds.), *Democracy in Japan* (pp. 12–37). Pittsburgh: University of Pittsburgh Press.

Pempel, T. J. (1998). *Regime shift.* Ithaca, New York: Cornell University Press.

Pesticide Action Network North America. (1992). *Japan pesticides to Cambodia: Japanese NGOs speak on agro-toxic aid to Cambodia,* January 22. Available: http://www.panna.org/resources/pestis/PESTIS.burst.4.html [August 13, 2001].

Pharr, S. J. (2000). Officials' misconduct and public distrust: Japan and the trilateral democracies, in Susan J. Pharr and Robert D. Putnam (Eds.), *Disaffected democracies: What's troubling the trilateral countries?* (pp. 173–201). Princeton, NJ: Princeton University Press.

Pharr, S. J., & Schwartz, F. (Ed.) (2002). *Restating the state perspective on civil society in Japan.* Oxford: Oxford University Press.

Potter, D. (Ed.). (1996). *NGOs and environmental policies: Asia and Africa.* London & Portland, OR: Frank Cass.

Putnam, R. (1993). *Making democracy work: Civic transitions in modern Italy.* Princeton, NJ: Princeton University Press.

Putnam, R. (2000). *Bowling alone: The collapse and revival of American community.* New York: Simon & Schuster.

Pyle, K. B. (1989). The burden of Japanese history and the politics of burden sharing. In J. H. Makin & D. C. Hellmann (Eds.), *Sharing world leadership: A new era for America and Japan* (pp. 41–77). Washington, DC: American Enterprise Institute for Public Policy Research.

Rix, A. (1980). *Japan's economic aid: Policy-making and politics.* New York: St. Martin's Press.

Rix, A. (1989–1990). Japan's foreign aid policy: A capacity for leadership? *Pacific Affairs, 62*(4), 461–475.

Rix, A. (1993). *Japan's foreign aid challenge: Policy reform and aid leadership.* London and New York: Routledge.

Rosenau, J. N. (1990). *Turbulence in world politics: A theory of change and continuity.* Princeton, NJ: Princeton University Press.

Rosenau, J. N. (1997). *Along the domestic-foreign frontier: Exploring governance in a turbulent world.* Cambridge: Cambridge University Press.

Rosenau, J. N., & Fagen, W. M. (1997). A new dynamism in world politics: Increasing skillful individuals? *International Studies Quarterly, 41*(4), 655–686.

Salamon, L. M. (1994). The rise of the nonprofit sector. *Foreign Affairs, 73*(4), 109–122.

Salamon, L. M. (1995). *Partners in public service: Government—nonprofit relations in the modern welfare state.* Baltimore, MD & London: Johns Hopkins University Press.

Salamon, L. M., & Anheier, H. K. (1996). *The emerging nonprofit sector: An overview.* Manchester, UK: Manchester University Press.

Sankei Shimbun. (1996a, August 29). Okayama-shi de dai-ikkai AMDA kokusai fōramu. *Sankei Shimbun.*

Sankei Shimbun. (1996b, August 21). Senryaku-teki ODA, p. 8.

Sanyō Shimbun. (1996, November 16). Takokuseki ishidan kessei e, p. 10.

Saotome, M. (1999). Imakoso motomerareru ōru Japan no kokusai kyōryoku, *Gaiko Forum,* 127(March), 34–40.

Schmitter, P. C. (1997). Civil society: East and West, in L. Diamond, M. F. Plattner, Y. H. Chu, and H. M. Tien (Eds.), *Consolidating the third wave democracies* (pp. 239–262). Baltimore, MD & London: Johns Hopkins University Press.

Schoppa, L. J. (1997). *Bargaining with Japan: What American pressure can and cannot do.* New York: Columbia University Press.

Schoppa, L. J. (2001). Japan, the reluctant reformer, *Foreign Affairs, 80*(5), 76–90.

Schreurs, M. A. (1996). *International environmental negotiations, the state, and environmental NGOs in Japan,* Occasional Paper 14, Harrison Program on the Future Global Agenda. Available: http://www.bsos.umd.edu/harrison/papers/paper14.htm [2000, January 12].

Schumpeter, J. (1976). *Capitalism, socialism and democracy.* London: Allen & Unwin. Reprint of 1942.

Shimizu, T. (1997, February 28). *Taijin jirai o kangaeru kai hokokusho.* Tokyo: Japan Campaign to Ban Landmines.

Söderberg, M. (Ed.). (1996). *The Business of Japanese foreign aid: Five case studies from Asia.* London: Routledge.

Sogge, D. (Ed.), with Biekart, K., & Saxby, J. (1996). *Compassion and calculation: The business of private foreign aid.* London: Pluto Press.

Steinhoff, P. G. (1989). Protest and democracy. In T. Ishihara & E. S. Krauss (Eds.), *Democracy in Japan* (pp. 171–198). Pittsburgh: University of Pittsburgh Press.

Stockwin, J. A. A. (1999). *Governing Japan*, 3rd ed. Oxford, UK: Blackwell Publishers.

Strange, S. (1996). *The retreat of the state: The diffusion of power in the world economy.* Cambridge: Cambridge University Press.

Sudo, S. (1986). Nanshin, superdomino, and the Fukuda doctrine: Stages in Japan–Southeast Asian relations. *Journal of Northeast Asian Studies,* 5(3), 35–51.

Sudo, S. (1988). Japan–ASEAN relations: New dimensions in Japanese foreign policy. *Asian Survey,* 18(5), 509–525.

Sudo, S. (1992). *The Fukuda doctrine and ASEAN: New dimensions in Japanese foreign policy.* Singapore: Institute of Southeast Asian Studies.

Suganami, S. (1995). Sōgo fuyō shisō koso kaihatsu enjo no rinen, *Gaiko Forum,* 77, 38–39.

Sugishita, T. (1998a). NGO saizensen: No. 14. *Gaiko Forum,* 116(February), 82–83.

Sugishita, T. (1998b). NGO saizensen: No. 17. *Gaiko Forum,* 118(May), 88–89.

Sugishita, T. (1998c). NGO saizensen: No. 18. *Gaiko Forum,* 119(June), 88–89.

Sugishita, T. (1998d). NGO saizensen: No. 21. *Gaiko Forum,* 123(October), 88–89.

Sumi, K. (1989). *ODA enjo no genjitsu.* Tokyo: Iwanami Shinsho.

Sumi, K. (Ed.). (1990). *Kirawareru enjo: Segin, nihon no enjo to Narumada Damu.* Tokyo: Tsukiji Shoten.

Takeda, I. (1993). Japan's aid to the Pacific Island states. In B. M. Koppel & R. M. J. Orr (Eds.), *Japan's foreign aid: Power and policy in a new era* (pp. 229–251). Boulder, CO: Westview Press.

Tanaka, Y. (1995). *Enjo to iu gaikō senryaku.* Tokyo: Asahi Sensho.

Taylor, B. (1998). Clarifying the foreign aid puzzle: A comparison of American, Japanese, French, and Swedish aid flows. *World Politics,* 50(2), 294–323.

Tilton, M. C. (1996). *Restrained trade: Cartels in Japan's basic materials industries.* Ithaca, NY: Cornell University Press.

Tobin, R. J. (1996). Bilateral donor agencies and the environment: Pest and pesticide management, *U.S. Agency for International Development Technical Paper* (Office of Sustainable Development Bureau for Africa), No. 2, December.

Tocqueville, A. de (1969). *Democracy in America.* New York: Harper & Row.

Tokyo Shimbun. (1994, September 10). Shōsha nado tantōsha ga heiseikai, p. 1.

Tokyo Shimbun (1997a, April 10). *Taijin jirai zenpai e, choto-ha de "kessoku,"* p. 8.

Tokyo Shimbun (1997b, December 4). *Jirai haizetsu e "kinyu" teisho,* evening edition, p. 1.

Tomoda, S. (1997). *Resumption of Japan's ODA to Vietnam: Watershed of Nippo-Vietnamese relations* (Project Report). Tokyo: Asia Research Institute at Asia University.

Udall, L. (1995). The international Narmada Campaign: A case study of sustained advocacy, in W. F. Fisher (Ed.), *Toward sustainable development? Struggling over India's Narmada River* (pp. 201–227). Armonk, New York: M.E. Sharpe.

Udall, L. (1998). The World Bank and public accountability: Has anything changed? In J. A. Fox & L. D. Brown (Eds.), *The struggle for accountability: The World Bank, NGOs, and grassroots movements* (pp. 391–436). Cambridge, MA: MIT Press.

Umemori, N., with Rempel, M. (1997). The new political culture in Japan, in T. N. Clark & M. Rempel (Eds.), *Citizen politics in post-industrial societies* (pp. 85-109). Boulder, CO: Westview Press.

United Nations Environmental Program International Environmental Technology Center. (1997, August 7). *IETC's insight.* Available: http://www.unep.or.jp/ietc/Publications/INSIGHT/ Aug_97/6.html [1998, September 3].

United Nations Development Program. (1995). *Human development annual report 1994: Overview.* Available: http://www.192.124.42.15/undp/publications/anrep95/overvie.htm [1998, November 15].

United Nations Economic and Social Council. (2001). NGO related frequently asked questions. Available: http://www.un.org/esa/coordination/ngo/faq.htm [October 21, 2001].

United States Department of Commerce. (1995). *ODA/OOF: Report on interviews with Japan's ODA/OOF parties*. Available: http://www.ita.doc.gov/industry/sif/sifuai/0134000.uai [1999, February 16].

United States Department of Commerce. (1998). *ODA handbook*. United States Department of Commerce. Available: http://www.ita.doc.gov/industry/sif/sifoai/uhandbk.html [1998, December 14].

United States General Accounting Office. (1990). *Economic assistance: Integration of Japanese aid and trade policies* (Report to the Chairman, Subcommittee on Economic Resources and Competitiveness, Joint Economic Committee, U.S. Congress). Washington, DC: United States General accounting Office.

Wan, M. (1995). Spending strategies in world politics: How Japan has used its economic power in the past decade. *International Studies Quarterly*, 39(1), 85–108.

Wanner, B. (1998). Japan's growing nonprofit sector: Responses to government shortfalls. *The Japan Economic Institute Report*, 21(June 5). Available: http://www.jei.org/Archive/JEIR98/9821f.html#Heading2 [June 20, 2000].

Wanner, B. (2000). Economic problems, political changes challenge Japan's cozy business-government ties, *Japan Economic Institute Report*, 22A(June 9). Available: http://www.jei.org/Archive/JEIR00/0022f.html#Heading2 [June 20, 2000].

Wapner, P. (1994). Green politics: Environmental activism and global civil society, *Dissent*, 41(3), 389–393.

Wapner, P. (1996). *Environmental activism and world civic politics*. Albany: State University of New York Press.

Warren, M. E. (Ed.) (1999). *Democracy and trust*. Lincoln, NE: Foundation Books.

Weiss, T. G., & Gordenker, L. (Ed.). (1996). *NGOs, the UN, and global governance*. Boulder, CO & London: Lynne Rienner Publishers.

Wood, R. (1986). *From Marshall Plan to debt crisis: Foreign aid and development choices in the world economy*. Berkeley: University of California Press.

World Bank. (1981). *The McNamara years at the World Bank: Major policy addresses of Robert S. McNamara 1968–1981*. Baltimore, MD: Johns Hopkins University Press.

World Bank. (1992). *World development report 1992: Development and the environment*. Oxford, UK: Oxford University Press.

World Bank. (1993). *The East Asian miracle: Economic growth and public policy*. New York: Oxford University Press.

World Commission on Environment and Development. (1987). *Our common future*. Oxford, UK: Oxford University Press.

Yamamoto, T. (1998). *The nonprofit sector in Japan*. Manchester, UK: Manchester University Press.

Yamamoto, T. (Ed.) (1999). *Deciding the public good: Governance and civil society in Japan*. Tokyo: Japan Center for International Exchange.

Yamaoka, Y. (1998). On the history of the nonprofit sector in Japan. In T. Yamamoto (Ed.), *The nonprofit sector in Japan* (pp. 19–58). Manchester, UK: Manchester University Press.

Yanagihara, T., & Emig, A. (1991). An Overview of Japan's Foreign Aid. In S. Islam (Ed.), *Yen for Development: Japanese foreign aid and the politics of burden sharing* (pp. 37–69). New York: Council on Foreign Relations Press.

Yasutomo, D. T. (1986). *The manner of giving: Strategic aid and Japanese foreign policy*. Lexington, MA/Toronto: D.C. Health and Company.

Yasutomo, D. T. (1989–1990). Why aid? Japan as an "aid great power". *Pacific Affairs*, 62(4), 490–503.

Yasutomo, D. T. (1993). The politicization of Japan's "post-Cold War" multilateral diplomacy. In G. L. Curtis (Ed.), *Japan's foreign policy after the Cold War: Coping with change* (pp. 323–346). Armonk, New York: M.E. Sharpe.

Yasutomo, D. T. (1995). *The new multilateralism in Japan's foreign policy*. New York: St. Martin's Press.
Yokoyama, M. (1994). *Firipin enjo to jiritsu kōsei-ron*. Tokyo: Akashi Shoten.
Yomiuri Shimbun. (1999a, April 1). Chūkai-yaku "rakusatsu, kin no chikara da yo," p. 39.
Yomiuri Shimbun. (1999b, April 2). "Fuhai atta ga …" nigai chinmoku, p. 39.
Yomiuri Shimbun. (1999c, April 1). ODA ribēto tsuichō kazei, p. 1.
Yomiuri Shimbun. (1999d, April 2). Tōkai kōgyō mo 1000–man–en, p. 1.

INDEX